A Spy's Guide to the Kennedy Assassination

With Walking Tours of Washington, New Orleans, and Dallas

E.B. Held

ISBN: 1482684160
ISBN-13: 978-1482684162

To Dave Cohen, Al Romig, and Marion Scott in appreciation of their friendship and encouragement.

Contents

Prologue

In the highly emotional period following the tragic 1963 assassination of President John F. Kennedy, speculation that the Soviet KGB and/or the Cuban DGI intelligence services had, at one time or another, clandestine operational relationships with the assassin Lee Harvey Oswald was suppressed by Soviet and Cuban as well as American authorities.

Had the authorities not done so, the situation could have spun out of control and a nuclear holocaust might well have resulted. As more and more information has been revealed, especially since the end of the Cold War, the existence of separate KGB and DGI operational relationships with Oswald is obvious to those who care to see with clear eyes.[1]

The purpose of this book *Spy's Guide to the Kennedy Assassination* is to provide non-intelligence professionals a straightforward and objective explanation of what probably happened between Oswald, the Soviet KGB, and the Cuban DGI. My objective is to capture the interest of a wide range of readers, from students born after the fall of the Berlin Wall to

[1] See the historical chronology below in the first appendix.

retirees like myself, from Cold War history buffs to tourists on short walking tours of Washington, New Orleans, or Dallas.

For those inspired to delve deeper into what is arguably the most genuine tragedy in American political history, I have included at the end of most chapters a "Suggestions for Further Reading" section. To bring the history to life, I have also included walking guides, as well as photos of where key events actually occurred and important characters actually lived.

***

Having spent a career as a professional conspirator, I can tell you that real life conspiracies tend to be simple. They should not be obvious at a glance, but once you view them from the proper angle, they are not hard to see. Regarding the Kennedy assassination tragedy, undisputed historical facts[2] would lead an experienced clandestine intelligence officer to conclude that:

1. The Soviet KGB intelligence service had a clandestine operational relationship with Oswald from late 1957 or early 1958 until April 1963.

---

[2] Vincent Bugliosi's *Reclaiming History: The Assassination of President John F. Kennedy*, (2007) is the essential reference for anyone interested in a factual understanding of the Kennedy assassination tragedy.

2. The Cuban DGI intelligence service had a clandestine operational relationship with Oswald from August 1963 through mid-November 1963.

3. The Soviet KGB had no role in Oswald's assassination of President Kennedy on 22 November 1963.

4. The Cuban DGI had both an opportunity to encourage Oswald to assassinate the President and a compelling motive to do so.

5. Oswald was the lone gunman involved in the assassination itself.

The key unanswered historical question is whether the Cuban DGI tacitly encouraged Oswald in his self-initiated assassination attempt or whether the Cubans gave Oswald an explicit green light to proceed. The answer to that question depends on whether Oswald and the Cubans communicated with each other between 19 November, when Oswald learned that the President would pass right into his crosshairs, and 22 November, when Oswald murdered the President and Dallas police officer J.D. Tippit. Only the Cuban government can answer that question.

To the Cubans' credit, on two occasions, 7 September and 10 October 1963, they attempted to warn Washington that they were prepared to retaliate in kind for persistent American plotting to assassinate Cuban President Fidel Castro. Unfortunately for everyone, neither my own CIA nor the FBI recognized these warnings. Had we done so, history might have turned out better.

***

Truth in advertising: I am a retired CIA operations officer, not a trained historian. As will be evident in the following pages, the way in which the personal histories of individuals intersect, overlap, and combine to become the history of nations is my great fascination as a tactical field intelligence officer.

Needless to say, there is a rather complex history between the CIA and Fidel Castro, including the historical fact that we conspired to kill him several times. In my early 20s as an economic analyst, I did some work on the Cuban economy for about a year, but I have never done any clandestine operational work related to Cuba. My cultural, educational, moral, and political background is quite different from that of Fidel Castro. I would never vote for him for any office, and I think he has left a mixed legacy for the Cuban people.

All that said, as a professional intelligence officer, I am obliged to give Fidel a bow of respect. He is a historical figure of complexity and consequence. I sincerely believe it would reflect great credit on Castro at this point in history before he himself passes from the scene to direct that the files on the relationship between Cuban intelligence and Lee Harvey Oswald be opened to examination by historians.

***

As is required for all current and retired CIA officers, I have submitted the manuscript for this book to the CIA's Publications Review Board for review. I appreciate the assistance the board has provided me. All statements of fact, opinion, or analysis are those of the author and do not reflect the official positions or views of the CIA or any other US Government agency. Nothing in the contents should be construed as asserting or implying US Government authentication of information or Agency endorsement of the author's views. This material has been reviewed by the CIA to prevent disclosure of classified information.

As director of intelligence and counterintelligence for the Department of Energy at the time of this writing, I have also submitted the manuscript for review and approval by DOE, as required again for the purpose of preventing any inadvertent disclosure of classified information. I would like to thank Mr. Andy Weston-Dawkes and his colleagues in the DOE Classification Office for their kind assistance.

***

Finally, I would like to pay special respect to the memory of Jacqueline Kennedy. A more gracious First Lady is hard to imagine.

Chapter 1
Murder on the Towpath

In 1964, Mary Pinchot Meyer was a stylish, 43-year-old divorcee and socialite. Well-born and well-mannered, comfortable with her sexuality, intelligent and fiercely independent, Mary exerted a primal attraction on men of power working in Washington, DC. Her former husband was the CIA's chief of propaganda, Cord Meyer. Her former lover was the late President of the United States, John F. Kennedy.

Following her 1957 divorce from Meyer, Mary lived in a quaint house located at 1523 34th Street in the chic Georgetown section of Washington. A carriage house was attached to Mary's home, and the two buildings wrapped around a small yard protected from the sidewalk by a short white picket fence. Tracy Barnes, who was the mastermind of the CIA's successful coup d'etat in Guatemala in 1954 and subsequently humiliated as a leader of the 1961 disaster at Cuba's Bay of Pigs, lived with his family just around the corner from Mary at 3410 Volta Place. Mary's sister, Tony, lived three blocks away in a stately town home at 3321 N Street with her second husband, Ben Bradlee.

At the time, Bradlee was the Washington editor of Newsweek; a decade later, he divorced Tony and became famous as the managing editor of the Washington Post who helped expose President Richard Nixon's role in the Watergate break-in. An aspiring painter, Mary used a space in the Bradlees' alley garage as her art studio and a secret rendezvous location. A few doors east of the Bradlee home was another stately town home at 3307 N Street where Senator and Mrs. John F. Kennedy lived from late 1957 until they moved into the White House on 20 January 1961.

On Sunday evening, 11 October 1964, Mary hosted a dinner party in her Georgetown home for the English theater director Peter Brook, who was in town directing the hit play Marat/Sade. After breakfast the next morning, 12 October, Mary walked over to her art studio and worked for a few hours on one of her paintings. As was her daily routine, Mary predictably left her studio at noon for a walk on the towpath of the C&O Canal that runs along the Potomac River at the bottom of Georgetown. She walked down the 34th Street hill to the busy intersection on M Street, Georgetown's main east-west thoroughfare. While waiting for the traffic light to change, another Georgetown neighbor Polly Wisner waved from a chauffeur-driven car that was taking her to National Airport to catch a flight to London. Polly was one of the grand ladies of Georgetown. Her husband, Frank, before his nervous breakdown, had been the CIA deputy director in charge of all clandestine operations and, thus, had been Cord Meyer's direct boss.

When the light changed, Mary crossed M Street and walked over a small footbridge and down some steps to the southern side of the towpath. It was a beautiful, brisk fall day. Mary walked west, away from the town. Passing the Potomac Boat Club on the left, Mary continued to a point below the merge of Canal Road and Foxhall Road where someone ambushed her and, at close range, shot one pistol bullet into her head and then another through her back into her heart. Mary died at the scene.

Amongst professionals, two bullets to the head are called "a hit," but one to the head and one to the heart are called "a message." A professional who had pre-cased the murder scene could easily have scurried down the slope and out of sight in five seconds, through a tunnel under the canal, back to the opposite side, and up onto Canal Street in ninety seconds, and then back in the vicinity of Georgetown University enjoying a cool drink well before the police could have sealed off the murder scene. The telltale signs of a professional hit and subsequent investigation would have made anybody privy to Mary's intimate relations with the former President, and the CIA very uncomfortable and hesitant to turn over too many rocks. A half-hearted attempt was made to pin the murder on a hapless black man found near the murder scene. But, in the end, the gun was never found, the murder never solved.

Mary was carrying nothing of value, neither a purse nor identification, so it took the Washington police several hours to determine that the unidentified victim might have a link to Ben and Tony Bradlee. Circa 9 PM on the evening of the 12th, Ben Bradlee arrived at the DC morgue and identified the body as, indeed, that of his sister-in-law Mary. Bradlee dutifully alerted the CIA which, in turn, informed Cord Meyer, who had traveled secretly to New York City on clandestine business.

Mary's murder on the towpath was the banner headline of the Washington Post on Tuesday, 13 October. The article noted that Mary had been a "close friend" of John Kennedy and his family and had often walked the same towpath with Jackie Kennedy before she had become America's First Lady. Reading the Post that morning, Ben and Tony Bradlee remembered that Mary had kept a revealing diary of her White House love affair with President Kennedy. Concerned that the diary might fall into the hands of the police, create a scandal, and damage the reputation of the recently assassinated President, they rushed over to Mary's house. When they came through the door, they were at first shocked but then quite relieved to find James Jesus Angleton already there.

Jim Angleton was Cord Meyer's best friend and the CIA's chief of counterintelligence. As such, Angleton was secretly one of the most powerful men in Washington at that time. Not wanting a scandal to damage anybody's reputation, Angleton asserted his clandestine authority and discreetly assumed official custody of Mary's revealing diary. Angleton eventually returned the diary to Tony Bradlee who burned it.[3]

***

Mary Pinchot was born in Eastern Maryland on 14 October 1920, the daughter of wealthy, left wing political figures, Amos and Ruth Pinchot. Her father was a noted pacifist and a founder of the influential isolationist group the America First Committee, who slit his wrists in 1942 out of despair that America had been drawn into World War II. Her

---

[3] The main facts included in each chapter are drawn from the books referenced at the end of the chapter, in this case Nina Burleigh's *A Very Private Woman* and Cord Meyer's *Facing Reality*. The home addresses of important characters were found in the Washington D.C. telephone books from the period.

independent and strong-willed mother was a journalist for *The Nation* and *The New Republic.*

Mary grew up on the National Historic Landmark of Grey Towers, the Pinchot family estate in Milford, Pennsylvania, 65 miles northwest of Manhattan. She was educated at the Brearley Girls' School on East 83rd Street in Manhattan, one of the most academically rigorous private schools in the country, where years later Caroline Kennedy would matriculate. In 1942, Mary graduated from Vassar College in Poughkeepsie, New York, where she befriended Cicely d'Autremont, Jim Angleton's future wife. Jacqueline Kennedy also studied at Vassar as a freshman and sophomore years later in 1947-49.

After graduation, Mary worked in Manhattan as a freelance journalist for United Press International and *Mademoiselle* magazine. She made her first splash in the gossip columns when she had a fling with Walter Pidgeon, the famous movie star who was twice her age but at the peak of his career. Mary was also active during this period in the left wing American Labor Party. In late 1944, Mary began dating a severely wounded young war hero Marine Corps Lieutenant Cord Meyer Jr.

Cord was the first of fraternal twins born in New York on 10 November 1920. His father, Cord Sr., had been a World War I fighter pilot and briefly a diplomat before returning to New York and making a considerable fortune in Long Island real estate. Cord and his twin brother, Quentin, were educated at St Paul's, the strict Episcopalian boarding school in Concord, New Hampshire, and spent their summers at the Meyer summer home on the New Hampshire coast. In 1939, Cord entered Yale University where he became acquainted with but not close to Jim Angleton, who had entered Yale two years earlier in 1937. Both Cord and Angleton were active in poetry and literary circles at Yale.

Following the 7 December 1941 attack on Pearl Harbor by the Japanese, Cord accelerated his studies in order to graduate nine months early in September 1942. Immediately after graduation, he enlisted in the Marine Corps, was sent to officer candidate school, and became a machine gun platoon commander. In February 1944, he participated in two separate amphibious assaults on the Eniwetok chain of atolls. On 20 July 1944, he went with the second wave of the amphibious assault on Guam where his platoon took heavy casualties. Cord himself was reported killed in action as a result of a grenade attack in the early morning hours of 21 July. In fact, he just barely survived, losing his left eye.

In September 1944, following two months of convalescence in Hawaii, Cord was sent back to Manhattan to live with his parents. He commuted to the Brooklyn Naval Hospital for further care, including plastic surgery and a glass eye. He briefly tried Yale Law School but found his wounds left him unable to focus sufficiently for such intense studies. So, he returned to Manhattan and worked to get his wartime letters to his parents published in *The Atlantic* magazine. The letters attracted favorable public attention, including that of Mary Pinchot.

Mary and Cord had been briefly acquainted before the war, when he was at Yale and she at Vassar. Both Ivy Leaguers from wealthy East Coast families, both writers, and both young and beautiful, Mary and Cord quickly hit it off. In April 1945, with Mary in early pregnancy, they were married at her mother's apartment in Manhattan in a quiet family ceremony presided over by the noted religious philosopher Reinhold Niebuhr. A few days later, they were off to San Francisco, Cord to attend the founding conference of the United Nations as an aide to US Delegate Harold Stassen, Mary to cover the conference as a wire service journalist.

It was at the UN Conference that Mary introduced Cord to another young wounded war hero John F. Kennedy. Mary had become acquainted and flirted with Kennedy a decade earlier while they were both in prep school. Cord and Kennedy disliked each other at first glance.

***

In mid-May 1945, during the UN conference, Cord received news that his twin brother, also a Marine lieutenant, had been killed in action on Okinawa. It was another heavy psychological blow on top of his own war trauma. Cord retreated to the couple's hotel room for a time, reading poetry and contemplating, while Mary tried to help him come to terms with his loss. Like her father, Mary had long been a pacifist and now helped direct Cord's grief into an idealistic determination to promote a federalized world government in order that the men of his platoon and his own twin brother would not have died in vain.

In autumn 1945, Cord entered Harvard's graduate school of government (now named The John F. Kennedy School), and the couple moved to Cambridge. In September, *The Atlantic* published Cord's article, "A Service Man Looks at the Peace," which conceded that the just-agreed-upon UN

Charter was probably the best that could be accomplished at the time but warned that further progress away from nationalism and towards a federalized world government would be required in order to contain the new menace of atomic weapons. In 1946, Cord won the O'Henry Prize for his short story, "Waves of Darkness," which used his combat experience in Guam as another vehicle to promote world peace and federalized world government. In 1947, Cord's book, *Peace or Anarchy,* was published with a dust cover endorsement from Albert Einstein.

At a February 1947 conference in Asheville, North Carolina, Cord was a founding member of the United World Federalists (UWF) and shortly thereafter, at age 26, was elected president of the organization. The idealistic goal of the UWF was to lead the fight for supranational and legally enforceable control of atomic power, including atomic weapons. The young Meyer family moved back to Manhattan, and for the next two years, Cord threw himself into his responsibilities as the UWF's principal organizer, fundraiser, lobbyist, and speechmaker, resulting in dues-paying membership growing to fifty thousand in two years. The American Communist Party viewed the growth of the UWF as an ideological threat and so attacked it as a group of cranks and idealists who naively served as a front for American imperialism.

Parallel to his work as UWF President, Cord was also active as a leader of the American Veterans Committee (AVC), an organization committed to keeping America engaged in world affairs and to avoid the isolationist mistake America made following World War I. In contrast to its view of the UWF, the American Communist Party saw the AVC as an organization with considerable potential for fomenting class struggle in America and, thus, actively sought to infiltrate it, bring it under communist control, and focus it on internal economic issues like veterans' bonuses. This led to an intense internal struggle between the AVC's moderate faction, including Cord, and the more radical, communist-backed faction.

Meanwhile, Mary tried to content herself with the joys of young motherhood. Their first son had been born in December 1945 and was named Quentin, in honor of Cord's deceased twin brother. A second son, Michael, was born in 1947 just as Cord became absorbed in UWF and AVC political affairs. There is no question that Mary was a loving and caring mother at this time, but Cord's frequent travel and intense focus on his political responsibilities clearly took a toll on their marital communication and on their relationship as a whole.

In the fall of 1949, the stresses inside his marriage coupled with abrupt changes in the international political environment led Cord to resign as President of the United World Federalists. It was a sad period for people like Cord Meyer, Albert Einstein, and J. Robert Oppenheimer who had supported peaceful international control of atomic power and atomic weapons. All in a matter of weeks, the Soviet Union tested its first atomic bomb years ahead of expectations, Soviet espionage against its American "war ally" became publicly known, and Chinese communists led by Mao Zedong marched victoriously into Beijing. Disillusioned politically and under stress personally, Cord retreated to Harvard to undertake PhD studies in economics. He was succeeded as UWF president by Alan Cranston, the future democratic senator from California.

Cord and Mary were just 29 years old when they returned to Harvard; Quentin was nearly 4 and Michael, 2. The family rented a small house on the outskirts of Cambridge and pursued an enjoyable, quiet life. Cord had more time to spend with the boys, and Mary had time to take painting lessons at the Cambridge School of Design. Soon, Mary was pregnant with their third son, Mark.

***

In the spring of 1951, re-energized and increasingly restless with academic life, Cord abandoned his pursuit of a Harvard PhD and visited Washington, DC to explore career opportunities with the government. Friends at the State Department were astonished when Cord asked them about his prospects for a diplomatic career. Since February 1950, right wing Senator Joseph McCarthy had been publicly accusing the State of harboring nests of communist spies. In that atmosphere, the State Department officers were quite blunt in advising that Cord's prominent association with left wing political causes disqualified him from consideration for America's diplomatic service.

Cord's reception at the CIA was just the opposite. Allen Dulles, the future director of CIA who was then serving as the deputy director in charge of clandestine operations, met personally with Cord for over an hour. Dulles impressed Meyer as having a sophisticated, cosmopolitan understanding of the world as well as a non-dogmatic view of America's role in that world. According to Cord's memoir, Dulles made "a firm offer of a job at a middle level of executive responsibility" on the spot, even though their acquaintanceship was supposedly limited to having played tennis together a few times at the Long Island homes of mutual friends.

Admittedly, CIA hiring practices were quite different in 1951 than they are today. Nonetheless, it is highly unlikely that Cord's tennis abilities were all that earned him an hour of the busy Deputy Director's time and an on-the-spot job offer. Given the McCarthyite tenor of the era, it is more likely that Cord had already been in clandestine contact with CIA and that Allen Dulles was fully aware of all the details.

Indeed, Cord's memoir hints at such previous contact. He coyly states that in 1950, there was an American student who helped organize non-communist student groups in Europe and the United States to ideologically contest the Soviet-dominated International Union of Students. Subsequently, that student joined the CIA and was able to use his official position to expand CIA covert financial assistance to the non-communist student groups, including America's own National Student Association.

Cord goes on to write that his first official responsibility after joining the CIA in 1951 was, coincidently, to expand covert financial assistance to non-communist student groups including America's National Student Association. Cord's nemesis in this ideological struggle for the hearts and minds of students worldwide was the vice president of the International Union of Students, Alexander Nikolayevich Shelepin, who in December 1958 became chairman of the Soviet KGB. One of Cord's allies was a young American student named Gloria Steinem, future leader of the women's liberation movement.[4]

Cord blithely asserts in his memoir that Mary was delighted with the prospect of moving to Washington because her sister, Tony, and other friends lived there. Cord most likely really believed that. Nonetheless, it is hard to imagine that his signing up for the CIA was not something of a shock for her. Mary's dream was to become famous as consort to an international statesman and peacemaker, not to remain in the shadows as housewife to a secret cold warrior. Whatever her misgivings, her options in that era were quite limited; she was nearly 31 years old with three young children.

The Meyer family bought an old white farmhouse in McLean, Virginia on Merchant Lane, just off Chain Bridge Road. The modest house, known grandly as Langley Commons, was 200 yards from the main entrance to present day CIA headquarters. Mary's sister and her first husband lived nearby. Less than a mile east was the truly opulent estate, Merrywood on the Potomac, where the eligible 22 year old, Miss Jacqueline Bouvier, lived along with her mother, Janet, and her stepfather, Hugh Dudley Auchincloss Jr. Although physical neighbors, Jackie was preoccupied with finding an appropriate husband and did not have any reason to socialize with the Meyers and their young children.

In October 1951, after passing a detailed CIA security screening, Cord started work in the temporary Agency buildings then located in downtown Washington, just northeast of the Lincoln Memorial alongside the Reflecting Pool. He started at the very moment that President Truman

---

[4] [4] "It Changed My Life," New York Times Book Review, July 4, 1976

approved an aggressive CIA covert action program to counter an equally aggressive KGB political and propaganda offensive worldwide. This made for a heady work environment that included ample budgets, expanding authorities, and high level, bipartisan political support. Cord, like many before and after him, found it all exhilarating.

Mary was less thrilled. She confronted the same reality with which generations of CIA spouses have had to cope. A CIA family arrives together at some new post, and the clandestine officer is immediately immersed in long hours of important work, while the spouse is left to cope with the mundane but pesky details of normal life. At night, the officer is frequently away from home, operating in an unknown alias at some unknown location and, thus, in times of family emergency, totally out of communication with the spouse. The children do not know what their parent does nor can the officer tell the spouse anything about the exciting aspects of the work. But when things go wrong, the whole family feels the consequences. Surprisingly, most CIA families thrive under these challenging circumstances, but it was not at all what Mary had expected.

***

In the summer of 1953, the first of many things went wrong. Towards close of business on Monday, 31 August, Cord was summoned to the office of Richard Helms, another future director who was then the second in command of clandestine operations. With evident regret, Helms advised Cord that the FBI claimed to have uncovered serious security issues related to his well-known left wing political activities and Mary's 1944 membership in the American Labor Party. Helms said the CIA had no choice but to suspend Cord without pay effective immediately. As was standard operating procedure then and remains today, Cord was relieved of his employee identification badge and escorted out of the building.

Cord and Mary were stunned. It was Kafka realized. At risk were not only Cord's current job but also their personal reputations and future prospects. Although both Mary and Cord came from wealthy families, they lived and fed their three boys on Cord's modest government income. Vindication would require expensive legal advice and take months, during which the family would have no income. But, Cord had lost an eye, a twin brother, and many friends defending American values; he most certainly was not about to submit passively to this type of un-American behavior.

On Friday, 4 September, Cord received a letter with a list of the formal charges, which he includes verbatim in his memoir:

> Charge one: "You are reported to have been in agreement with the concept that the international situation in 1947 was based upon a struggle between American Fascism and Russian Democracy."
>
> Charge two: "An individual in contact with you in 1948 is reported to have said that he had concluded, on the basis of that contact, that you must be in the Communist Party."
>
> Charge three: "You are reported to have stated that in 1947 the United States was attempting to press the

USSR into an incident in order to take advantage of the atom bomb and destroy Russia."

For an American today, reading the anonymous charges provides a disturbing glimpse into our country's political atmosphere in 1953. It is unsettling that such anonymous, unverifiable charges would be sufficient to suspend any person despite the CIA's own security background check and a distinguished war record.

In the face of such allegations, Cord recognized that his future depended on whether or not influential friends would stand by him and defend his character. In that, Cord was lucky that he worked for Allen Dulles at CIA and not Allen's brother, John Foster Dulles, at the State Department. After the controversy regarding Alger Hiss, the American diplomat who really was a Soviet spy, John Foster Dulles and the State Department leadership of the era had consistently demonstrated an unwillingness to defend even the most distinguished State Department diplomats against unsubstantiated McCarthyite accusations. Morale in the department had plummeted.

In contrast, Allen Dulles was defiant. When McCarthy and his cronies had gone after CIA analyst William Bundy a few months earlier, Dulles had refused to let them even interview Bundy, who was the son-in-law of President Truman's Secretary of State Dean Acheson and brother of the future national security advisor to President Kennedy, McGeorge Bundy. Surprised by Dulles's defiance, McCarthy had backed down over Bundy but had returned with a vengeance in targeting Cord.

After seeing the charges himself, Dulles personally called Cord to encourage him to respond and to assure him that he would be given a fair hearing based on the facts. At the same time, Dulles set about checking the facts himself and, in so doing, almost certainly relied heavily on James Jesus Angleton. Dulles considered Angleton the most gifted intelligence officer of his generation and would soon name Angleton the first chief of CIA's counterintelligence staff.

On 20 October, Cord submitted a "foot-thick" written response to the allegations, according to his memoir. Declining to convene a formal and time-consuming hearing board, Director Dulles made the decision personally, based on a month-long review and recommendation of his key aides. As a result, Dulles was able to call Cord on Thanksgiving Day to advise that he had been reinstated, that his back salary would be paid in full, and that Cord could be confident of a future career at CIA. Cord emerged from this ordeal knowing whom he could trust as a true friend and whom he could not. He idealized Dulles. It is also telling that ever after, Jim Angleton was both Cord's best friend and guardian to his children.

The attack on the CIA was the beginning of the end for Joe McCarthy. Journalists like Edward R. Murrow, Walter Lippmann, and Joseph Alsop, who knew and respected Dulles as well as Cord's immediate boss, Tom Braden, started to take on McCarthy more openly. From March to June 1954, the US Army challenged McCarthy's behavior in a series of senate hearings known as the Army-McCarthy Hearings. These hearings were the first ever covered live on TV, and the public-opinion impact of the broadcasts was amplified by daily summaries in all the major newspapers. McCarthy was revealed to the American public for the reckless demagogue that he was, and thus, his standing in public opinion plummeted. Many believe that Dulles and Braden at a minimum encouraged the press counterattack on McCarthy; some believe they actually orchestrated it.

Whether they did or not, it is clear that Dulles took advantage of McCarthy's decline in order to honor his word to Cord. In September 1954, Dulles promoted Cord to the senior rank of division chief. Today, division chiefs within the CIA's clandestine service are typically in their late forties or early fifties with at least twenty years of overseas clandestine operations experience. Cord made it two months shy of his 34th birthday with less than three years of CIA experience, none of which was on overseas assignment.

***

Cord's career recovered during 1954, but his marriage began to disintegrate. That summer, Mary, 33, and her younger sister, Tony, 30, escaped their husbands and seven young children, crossed the Atlantic on a cruise ship, and set off through France and Italy as if they were young college girls. Their mother, Ruth, had arranged and paid for this European adventure, evidently in hope that it would result in the breakup of her daughters' disappointing marriages, which it did.

In Paris, Tony called *Newsweek* magazine's European bureau chief, Ben Bradlee. Bradlee was an acquaintance who as press attaché at the American Embassy during 1951-53 had worked closely with the same CIA division that Cord worked in and would soon lead. Bradlee succeeded in seducing Tony but only after Tony had asked for and received permission from her big sister, Mary. Upon return to Washington a few months later, Tony promptly confessed to her husband, the well-known Washington lawyer Steuart Pittman, that she had fallen in love with another man. They soon divorced, allowing Tony to move to Paris in 1955 to marry Bradlee.

Mary's own European affair was with an Italian noble who anchored his yacht at Positano on the Amalfi coast, where he passed the time picking up American women on vacation. Mary likewise admitted her affair to Cord, describing it as sexually satisfying, nothing more. But she returned to Positano to visit the Italian again in 1955 and again in 1956. Finally, on her 36th birthday, 14 October 1956, Mary told Cord that she wanted a divorce so that she could marry the Italian with whom she had fallen deeply in love. This seems to have surprised the Italian at least as much as it surprised Cord. A good Catholic with no intention of ever divorcing his own wife, the Italian cut off the affair with Mary in short order.

Cord had been too busy with momentous world events during 1956 to pay much attention to Mary's emotional state of being. That February, in a secret speech to the 20th Congress of the Soviet Communist Party, Soviet Premier Nikita Sergeyevich Khrushchev had denounced his predecessor, Joseph Stalin, for crimes against humanity. Cord's best friend at the CIA, Jim Angleton, succeeded in obtaining a copy of Khrushchev's secret speech via his longtime friends in Israeli intelligence.

On 2 June, CIA Director Dulles leaked the full text of Khrushchev's speech to his own friends at the *New York Times*. Dulles then ordered Cord to take the details as published by the *Times* and rebroadcast them into Eastern Europe via the CIA-backed radio stations that Cord managed.

As Dulles expected, the explosive details provided by Khrushchev sparked a wave of political unrest in Eastern Europe, starting in Poland and tragically culminating in Hungary. For three weeks following Mary's 36th birthday, Hungary was in open revolt against Soviet control, incited at least in part by Cord's broadcasts of Khrushchev's secret speech. On 4 November, however, Soviet tanks rolled into Budapest and brutally crushed the Hungarian revolt, resulting in thousands of deaths.

Meantime, Cord didn't want a divorce any more than the Italian, even though Cord, too, had pursued many extramarital affairs. Through November and early December 1956, while the Hungarian revolt wound down, Cord and Mary tried to maintain an appearance of normalcy at home for the sake of their three boys. Then, personal heartbreak struck. A week before Christmas at dusk on 18 December, Cord and Mary's nine-year-old son , Michael, was hit by a car as he ran across Chain Bridge Road on his way home for dinner. He died at the scene in his mother's arms.

Michael's death pushed Mary to a state of near clinical depression and was the final blow to her marriage with Cord. In the spring of 1957, they sold the house in McLean with all of its sad memories and purchased a house in Georgetown on 34th Street. Mary and the two boys moved into that house in September. To be near the boys, Cord rented a room in the vicinity of Georgetown University at 3615 Prospect Place. Cord and Mary's relationship was acrimonious, so, at Cord's behest, Jim and Cicely Angleton stayed on friendly terms with Mary so that Jim could help keep an eye on the boys' upbringing as well as on Mary's social life.

There were two other new arrivals to the same Georgetown neighborhood during that fall of 1957. As Mary was moving into her quaint house on 34th Street, her sister, Tony, returned from Paris with Ben Bradlee and bought the stately townhouse three blocks away at 3321 N Street. At the same time, Senator and Mrs. John F. Kennedy were moving into their own stately townhouse at 3307 N Street, a few doors down from the Bradlees.

***

Suggestions for further reading:

1. *A Very Private Woman: The Life and Unsolved Murder of Presidential Mistress Mary Meyer,* Nina Burleigh, Bantam Books, 1998.

The basic facts regarding the life and death of Mary Meyer. Burleigh never quite finds her main theme, however.

2. *Facing Reality: From World Federalism to the CIA,* Cord Meyer, University Press of America, 1980.

The professional autobiography of a decorated patriot and legendary CIA officer. It says little directly about his emotional sentiments towards his first wife or the 35th President but, between the lines, the book's pedantic and superior tone speaks volumes.

Chapter 2
The Kennedys of Georgetown, 1953-1960

John F. Kennedy was beautiful, intelligent, rich, powerful, and by all accounts very funny. People sincerely liked to be around him and enjoyed his company even before he was President of the United States. The basic humanity of his character is revealed by his love of teasing friends and being teased back. He took his responsibilities seriously, but apart from some vanity regarding his personal appearance, he did not take himself particularly seriously.

As a man, Kennedy loved beautiful women. Jacqueline Bouvier, the young woman he selected carefully to be his consort and the mother of his children, matured into America's unofficial Queen and served in that capacity until the day she died, 19 May 1994, over thirty years after she had ceased being our official First Lady. His many mistresses counted amongst the most beautiful women of the era, including the iconic Marilyn Monroe as well as the mysterious Mary Meyer.

As a politician and statesman, Kennedy had an insatiable appetite for timely and accurate information. For this, he sought out sincere but mutually beneficial friendships with America's best journalists, including Ben Bradlee, Charlie Bartlett, the brothers Joe and Stewart Alsop, and Phil Graham. He sought out similar relationships with America's best spies, including Allen Dulles, Richard Bissell, John Bross, and Des Fitzgerald. An information-intelligence advantage over an adversary then was as much a source of real power as it remains today.

His love for women and for spies made Kennedy a natural fan of the new James Bond spy novels written by the former British naval intelligence officer Ian Fleming. The first Bond novel, Casino Royale, *was published in 1953. Kennedy read it in 1955 while recuperating from back surgery at the Kennedy family's summer mansion at 1095 North Ocean Boulevard in Palm Beach, Florida. Fleming's friend, the noted Georgetown hostess Oatsie Leiter for whom Fleming had named Bond's fictional CIA friend and colleague Felix Leiter to honor his friendship with her and her husband, Thomas, had given a paperback copy of* Casino Royale *to Kennedy as a recuperation gift. Two years later in 1957, Jackie Kennedy made a point to give a copy of* From Russia with Love *to CIA Director Allen Dulles who was vacationing next door at the Palm Beach mansion of oil baron Charles Wrightsman and had stopped by to say hello to Joe Kennedy and the promising young senator.*

Ian Fleming's March 1960 visit to the Leiters' home at 3259 R Street in Georgetown coincided with a lull in the Presidential primaries. So, on 13 March, the Kennedys invited them over to their 3307 N Street townhouse for Sunday dinner, along with the Alsop brothers and senior CIA official John Bross. Over brandy, Kennedy asked Fleming how James Bond would deal with Cuba's revolutionary leader, Fidel Castro. Fleming quipped that Bond would make Castro the subject of ridicule in the eyes of the Cuban people by doing something to make the hair of his beard fall out. Evidently, Bross reported all this back to CIA Director Dulles because bright and early the next morning, Dulles called the Leiter home hoping to discuss the idea in greater depth. Fleming had already departed. Nonetheless, the CIA did initiate a plot at this time to make Castro's hair fall out by sprinkling a depilatory, thallium powder, into his shoes.[5]

After winning the Presidential election in November 1960, Kennedy listed From Russia with Love *as one of his ten favorite books. Up until then, the Bond series had enjoyed only moderate success with the American public. After endorsement by the popular new President, the book sales took off and the legendary movie series began. The first two Bond movies came out during Kennedy's abbreviated presidency,* Dr. No *in 1962, followed by* From Russia with Love *in 1963.*

***

Although quite different in character, Jack Kennedy and Cord Meyer had remarkably similar backgrounds and experiences. Both were well-to-do Easterners, both were educated at Ivy League schools, both were wounded Pacific war heroes, both lost brothers in the war, both were authors, and both pursued political careers after the war. Kennedy was a far more pragmatic and empathetic character, however, which contributed greatly to his political success.

[5] *The Very Best Men* by Evan Thomas, p. 207-208

When Mary Meyer introduced the two during the 1945 UN Conference in San Francisco, Kennedy, as a journalist for the Hearst Syndicate, was the supplicant hoping for an interview from Meyer as a well-placed US government official. Meyer haughtily rebuffed the interview request, much to his subsequent regret after Kennedy had become President.

Kennedy's future wife, Jacqueline Bouvier, was born in the Hamptons of Long Island on 28 July 1929. Her mother, Janet, was a beautiful and aggressively ambitious socialite. Her father, "Black Jack" Bouvier III, was scion of a wealthy family, handsome but personally reckless. Black Jack was a womanizer whose drinking waxed as his financial fortune waned. After a stormy marriage and seeing greater opportunity elsewhere, Janet divorced Black Jack in 1941 and promptly married the sober and somber billionaire Hugh Auchincloss in 1942.

From adolescence, Jackie grew up at Merrywood on the Potomac, the opulent Auchincloss estate off Chain Bridge Road in McLean, Virginia. She was educated at the Holton-Arms School in Washington and later at Miss Porter's boarding school in Farmington, Connecticut. After two years at Vassar University, she did her junior year abroad at the Sorbonne in Paris and returned to graduate in 1951 from the George Washington University in DC.

While studying at George Washington, Jackie became acquainted with the Washington correspondent for the *Chattanooga Times*, Charlie Bartlett. In May 1951, Bartlett and his wife Martha invited the college senior to dinner at their home at 2237 48th Street in the Foxhall neighborhood, intent on promoting a match for her with Charlie's friend, the third-term congressman from Massachusetts, Jack Kennedy. Jackie was immediately attracted to the well-known man-about-town, but she was already considering marriage to another man who her mother considered a much safer match akin to her own husband, Auchincloss. In any case, Jackie soon departed on an extended European vacation with her younger sister, Lee.

However, the Bartletts refused to give up. After hearing that Jackie had broken off her engagement with her fiancé, the Bartletts arranged another matchmaking dinner with Jack in May 1952, a year after the first encounter. At this point, Jack was campaigning for the senate against the redoubtable republican Henry Cabot Lodge and had reluctantly come to accept his father's counsel that he would have to forsake bachelorhood and find a politically attractive wife if he hoped to advance further in his political career. Dinner at the Bartletts' proved a success this time, and within days, the 35-year-old Congressman invited the 23-year-old Miss Bouvier to a dinner dance and subsequently to the movies, along with his brother Bobby and Bobby's wife Ethel. Introducing Jackie to the Kennedy family was a certain indicator that Jack looked at her differently than the many other young, sexually attractive women in his life.

A big test came when Jack invited Jackie to spend the long Fourth of July weekend of 1952 with the boisterous Kennedy clan on their family compound in Hyannis Port, Massachusetts. Father Joe Kennedy instantly sized up Jackie as a perfect political match for Jack. Mother Rose Kennedy, who understood what lay in store for Jackie should she marry Jack, was protective. The siblings, except for Bobby, thought her too delicate and shy. But, she held her own and even made some cameo appearances in Quincy and Fall River where Jack squeezed in campaign speeches during the holiday weekend. From a long-standing Republican family, Jackie declared herself a converted Democrat after hearing Jack speak.

After he won an upset victory in the November Senate election, Jack's relationship with Jackie moved forward apace. In January 1953, they were the most eye- catching young couple at the Inaugural Ball for President Eisenhower. In February, she introduced Jack to her father, Black Jack. In May, Jack proposed marriage over a light meal at Martin's Tavern on Wisconsin Avenue just before Jackie departed for London on assignment for the *Washington Times Herald* to cover the coronation of Queen Elizabeth.

She accepted his proposal only upon her return from London when he met her at the airport more properly with a two-carat diamond and emerald engagement ring. They were married on 12 September 1953, during which time Cord and Mary Meyer were fighting for their reputations in face of the McCarthyite allegations and innuendos. Eight hundred people attended the wedding itself; twelve hundred attended the reception.

***

After a fairytale courtship, the first three years of the Kennedy marriage were traumatic for Jackie. In the fall of 1953, they rented a narrow little Georgetown house located at 3321 Dent Place, which may have been smaller than her bedroom suite at Merrywood. Jack was frequently absent, either working in the senate, pursuing his unabated nightlife, or back in Massachusetts on weekends to meet constituents. When he did visit the little house on Dent Place, he was generally accompanied by political colleagues who left empty beer bottles, whiskey glasses, and cigarette butts strewn about the home. Soon, the radiant young bride was a lonely, chain-smoking wraith. Perhaps as a result, she suffered a miscarriage in 1954.

Jack's own health problems became so severe in 1954 that he almost died. During that spring and summer, as the Army-McCarthy hearings were broadcast across the nation and Mary Meyer and her sister Tony pursued their European affairs, Jack's doctors told him that he would be wheelchair bound for the rest of his life if he did not undergo complicated surgery for the back problems that had afflicted him since youth and been made worse as a result of his war wounds. The surgery was potentially life threatening, however, due to his Addison's disease. Despite the risks, Jack agreed to the surgery in October at New York Hospital in Manhattan.

For two months, he was confined to the hospital at death's door. During this period, Jack, at 6'1", dropped from a slim 170 pounds to a skeletal 115, resulting in a body mass index of a mere 15. Constantly at his side, Jackie resided in Manhattan hotels or with friends until just prior to Christmas, when she had Jack medically evacuated to the more cheerful surroundings of the Kennedy winter mansion in Palm Beach. In February 1955, Jack underwent a second back surgery and spent several more months in recuperation. By May of 1955, he had finally recuperated sufficiently that he was able, with help from regular injections of painkillers, to make token appearances back in the senate.

Jackie approached this crisis as an opportunity to enhance Jack's political prospects and to attempt to build a firmer emotional bond with her husband. To these ends, Jackie had the idea to use this time to have a book written in Jack's name about other American senators who overcame adversity in order to rise to greatness. With Jackie serving as executive assistant and Ted Sorensen serving as principal scribe and wordsmith, Jack directed creation of the book that would be published in early 1956 as *Profiles in Courage.* The book immediately became a best seller and won a Pulitzer Prize, thanks in part to the ethically dubious lobbying of the Pulitzer Committee by Joe Kennedy's friend at the *New York Times,* Arthur Krock.

Despite Jackie's loyal efforts, Jack's infidelities resumed the minute he was physically able. In August 1955, he and a Massachusetts congressional colleague took a junket ostensibly to consult with NATO allies in Europe. On the side, Kennedy took pains to have one final fling with a Swedish blonde named Gunilla von Post, with whom he had been smitten several years previously. Jackie was crushed when she became aware of it and, in December, confided to her father-in-law that she was not sanguine the marriage could survive. Knowing that a divorce would doom Jack's chances of ever becoming President, Joe offered Jackie a payment of one million dollars not to divorce his son.[6]

As the historically momentous year of 1956 began, Jackie learned that she was pregnant again and so rededicated herself to making the marriage work. She and

---

[6] *Jacqueline Bouvier Kennedy Onassis: A Life* by Donald Spoto, p. 131

Jack moved back to Merrywood with her mother and stepfather while renovations were being made on Hickory Hill, an expansive hilltop mansion at 1147 Chain Bridge Road, just 1.5 miles west of Merrywood, which she and Jack had purchased for $125,000 the previous October. While Jack rode the wave of good publicity from *Profiles in Courage,* Jackie focused on transforming Hickory Hill into her future dream home with custom designed elements to ease her husband's physical pain as well as a warm and cozy nursery for her much anticipated first child.

Profiles in Courage had exactly the political impact that Jackie had intended; it gave Senator John F. Kennedy name recognition across America during the presidential election year of 1956. The 38-year-old senator briefly flirted with the idea of challenging Adlai Stevenson for the presidential nomination of the Democratic Party. Father Joe, however, was convinced that incumbent President Eisenhower was sure to win a second term and so counseled his son to show patience. Jack agreed and fell in line behind Stevenson as the Democratic standard bearer but did insist on making a stab at the vice presidential nomination.

Jack's chances for that nomination were lost when former First Lady Eleanor Roosevelt pointedly criticized those who admired courage but had failed to actually demonstrate it by speaking out against Joe McCarthy and his ilk. Indeed, Jack and the entire Kennedy clan had considered it politically pragmatic to stay on personally good terms with the rabidly anti-communist McCarthy, a fellow Irish Catholic who was popular in Massachusetts. One of Jack's sisters had even briefly dated McCarthy.

After the August 1956 Democratic convention, Jack went

off on a sailing vacation in the Mediterranean with his brother Teddy and his friend Florida Senator George Smathers, leaving his dismayed wife eight months pregnant and on her own. Consequently, Jack was out of contact on 23 August when Jackie was rushed to the hospital in agony. It fell to brother Bobby to tell Jackie that her baby daughter, Arabella, was stillborn. Jack did not learn the sad news until the sailing group and their companions docked in Genoa on 26 August. Shocked and panicked, Jack hesitated about what to do. It took Smathers to shake sense into him, put him on an airplane, and get him to Jackie's side belatedly on 28 August. Crushed yet again, Jackie fell into a state of near clinical depression at the same moment that Mary Meyer was emotionally struggling to come to terms with the accidental death of her son Michael.

***

The fall of 1956 was event-filled. On Tuesday, 23 October, the Hungarian Revolution against Soviet Communist domination began in Budapest with a mass demonstration of 300,000 people, followed by anti-Soviet rioting. Six days later on Monday, 29 October, the British, French, and Israelis intentionally surprised their American allies by starting a war against Egypt in an attempt to regain colonial-era control of the Suez Canal. An additional six days later on Sunday, 4 November, Moscow took advantage of Washington's preoccupation with the Suez crisis to send Soviet tanks into Budapest, brutally crushing any political opposition and killing 30,000 Hungarians.

The next day, Monday, 5 November, incumbent President Eisenhower asserted America's new found authority and power by threatening the British and French with economic sanctions if they did not withdraw from Suez. The day after that, Tuesday, 6 November, Eisenhower won re-election by a landslide, just as Joe Kennedy had predicted he would. In mid-November, British Prime Minister Anthony Eden suffered a nervous breakdown as a result of the Suez fiasco and fled to recuperate at Ian Fleming's personal estate in Jamaica. Eden was replaced by Harold MacMillan, who would eventually become a father-like figure for Jackie Kennedy. These were the dramatic international events that dominated Jack Kennedy's professional attention that fall.

Crisis also loomed on the personal front as the Kennedys' marriage faced its darkest hour. The newly refurbished mansion at Hickory Hill with its cozy nursery no longer held any appeal for Jackie following the stillbirth of their baby girl. Jack had always lived in Georgetown as a bachelor and had never liked the idea of living with Jackie so far out from the city. So, never having slept a single night there, they sold Hickory Hill to Bobby and Ethel. With their fast-growing brood, Bobby and Ethel were better positioned to transform Hickory Hill into a home, which, indeed, they did.

Jack and Jackie rented another little townhouse in Georgetown instead, this one at 2808 P Street. While it lacked size, it was located conveniently close to all the things that mattered to Jack. Coincidentally, former Secretary of State Dean Acheson lived across the street at 2805, and the convicted former State Department officer Alger Hiss lived just down the block at 2905. During this period of mourning,

Jack focused on his work while Jackie recuperated and tried to decide whether their marriage had a future.

Understanding why Mary left Cord at this time is perhaps easier than understanding why Jackie stayed with Jack. On one hand, Jackie indicated years later that her decision was a simple tradeoff, enduring the bad in order to enjoy the opportunities that came with being married and in love with such a powerful character. On the other hand, in alluding to her marriage during an interview just after becoming First Lady, she made the curious comment that "such heartbreak would be worth the pain." Given an opportunity to correct what the interviewer assumed was a misquote, Jackie confirmed the comment as, "such heartbreak would be worth the pain."[7] Perhaps Jackie herself didn't understand why she stayed with Jack; in 1956 she was, after all, only 27 years old.

What is clear, however, is the importance that Jackie placed on children and on her personal responsibility for insuring that her children were raised in the type of nurturing environment that she herself had never enjoyed. So, in the spring of 1957, when she learned that she was again pregnant, there was nothing further for her to decide. Shortly after learning of the pregnancy, the Kennedys committed to the purchase for $82,000 of the stately townhouse at 3307 N Street in Georgetown. Jackie initiated the necessary refurbishing, this time with a particular eye to making it comfortable for busy politicians.

In July, Jackie's father died suddenly of liver cancer. Black Jack Bouvier had been as much a womanizer as her

---

[7] *Jacqueline Bouvier Kennedy Onassis: A Life* by Donald Spoto, p. 96

husband Jack remained. In addition, Black Jack had been an alcoholic and an overall failure professionally. Yet, Jackie forgave her father his weaknesses and loved him dearly until the day he died. Although six months pregnant, Jackie took personal charge to insure that Black Jack's funeral arrangements were worthy of the man she thought he could have been.

On 27 November 1957, Caroline Bouvier Kennedy was born a bit premature but in robust health. To say the birth was a joyous occasion would be an understatement. For Jackie, it confirmed the meaning of her life and the meaning of her marriage to Jack. Only after the happy birth did the young family dare to move into their new Georgetown home. Jack and George Smathers immediately flew off on a short, fun-filled junket to pre-Castro Cuba, but Jack at least was back at home in time for his daughter's first Christmas.

***

That same year, Ben and Tony Bradlee moved into their own stately townhouse a few doors down from the Kennedys. With much in common professionally as well as personally, the new neighbors developed into sincere friends. The only journalist who had better professional access to President Kennedy than Bradlee was the matchmaker Charlie Bartlett. As First Lady, Jackie confided to Tony that she and Ben were also the First Couple's closest personal friends.

Ben Bradlee, like JFK, was born and raised near Boston,

graduated from Harvard, and served in the Pacific as a naval officer during World War II, Bradlee as a naval intelligence officer, JFK as a PT boat commander. After the war, Bradlee worked as a journalist until 1951 when he became a press attaché at the US Embassy in Paris. He did not work for the CIA while at the Paris Embassy, but he did work closely with the Agency, specifically with Cord Meyer and Jim Angleton. In 1953, Bradlee resigned from government service and returned to journalism as the European bureau chief of *Newsweek* magazine. During the summer of 1954, he met Tony, which led to a divorce from his wife of thirteen years, Boston heiress Jean Saltonstall, in 1955. Tony joined him in Paris after the divorce, and they were married in 1956.

In 1957, Bradlee wrote an article based on interviews with Algerian guerrilla leaders about the insurrection then raging in Algeria against the French colonial government. The article angered the French government, particularly in the wake of the Suez fiasco, and raised French suspicions that Bradlee might be involved in some sort of anti-French plotting with his old CIA friends. At the urging of the French government, *Newsweek* pulled Bradlee out of France and promoted him to chief of the magazine's Washington bureau.

According to Bradlee's memoirs, he and Tony first got to know the Kennedys during the late summer of 1958, after Jackie and baby Caroline had returned to Washington from the vacation season in Hyannis Port. The two couples bumped into each other during an afternoon walk around the neighborhood, Jackie pushing Caroline in a baby carriage and Tony pregnant with Dino, the first of her two children with Ben. The Kennedys invited them for a cool drink in their garden. Later that same day, the two couples saw each other again at a neighborhood dinner party. Jackie, a francophile, had much to discuss with Tony, who had recently returned from France. Jack, the politician in the midst of campaigning for his second term in the Senate, and Ben, the erstwhile foreign correspondent in the midst of expanding his contacts with well-informed Washington political insiders, immediately recognized their symbiotic professional interests.

Jackie and Tony grew particularly close over the next two years. With both husbands frequently away on business, the two women enjoyed each other's company either at home or while taking walks together along the nearby towpath of the C&O Canal. Not only were their children Caroline and Dino roughly the same age, but both women were pregnant again during Jack's 1960 campaign for the Presidency.

The couples were together on election evening, and as soon as he learned that he was President-elect, JFK quipped to Tony and Jackie, "Okay, girls, you can take the pillows out now. We won."[8] Only weeks later, Marina Bradlee and John F. Kennedy Jr. were born days apart on either side of Thanksgiving 1960.

Almost certainly, her sister Tony introduced Mary Meyer back into the social network of Jack and Jackie Kennedy during late 1958 and early 1959. At the time, Mary was using the Bradlees' alley garage as her art studio and each day after painting was in the habit of taking a brisk walk along the towpath. Given how close the two sisters were, Tony would frequently have joined Mary for those walks. On occasion, Tony would have invited her neighbor and friend Jackie to

---

[8] *Conversations with Kennedy* by Ben Bradlee, p. 32

join them as well. Jackie and Mary would have enjoyed discussing art. The story of young Michael Meyer's death and its devastating impact on Mary would have struck a chord with Jackie who had lost her daughter Arabella at the same time.

Mary was also a useful social asset; well-bred and well spoken, physically attractive, and with time on her hands, Mary was the perfect addition for any Georgetown hostess who needed an unattached woman at the last minute to maintain the expected male/female balance at a proper dinner party.

***

During the summer of 1958, while Jackie and Caroline were away on vacation, Jack began an affair with Pamela Turnure, one of his senate office staff members. Pamela rented a room in a Georgetown house owned by Leonard and Florence Kater at 2733 Dumbarton, across from Joe Alsop's house at 2720 Dumbarton. After several months of late night comings and goings by the young senator and Presidential hopeful, a scandalized Mrs. Kater started sending letters of complaint to the press, to J. Edgar Hoover at the FBI, and to Democratic Party notables including Eleanor Roosevelt.

Wanting to keep the matter out of the press but not wanting to end the affair with Miss Turnure, Kennedy looked around for a less troublesome landlady with a room for rent even closer to his own home in Georgetown. He found his old prep school friend and renewed acquaintance Mary Meyer.

By this time, Mary had sent her boys off to boarding school and was looking to rent out one of the rooms in her house as means to supplement her alimony payments from Cord.

Suggestions for further reading:

1. *Jacqueline Bouvier Kennedy Onassis: A Life* by Donald Spoto, St Martins Press, 2000.

A wonderful biography of a remarkable person. Spoto is sympathetic to his subject yet honest and deeply insightful.

2. *Conversations with Kennedy* by Ben Bradlee, W.W. Norton and Company, 1975.

An important book from one of Jack Kennedy's closest friends. A New Englander and a protective admirer, Bradlee, the vaunted investigative journalist of Watergate fame, is evasive about the relationship between his pal Jack and his sister-in-law, Mary Meyer. Jacqueline Kennedy broke off relations with Ben in part as a result of this book, in part because he divorced her friend Tony.

Chapter 3
A Different World: Washington in the 1950s and early 1960s

Washington, DC in the decade before the Kennedy assassination was remarkably different from the Washington of today. Spies and diplomats, politicians and journalists were all neighbors and sincere friends. They met frequently on Sunday afternoons for convivial dinners at one or another's home, followed by group walks on the towpath of the C&O canal in Georgetown. Spies did not suspect or disdain journalists who were discreetly gay. Journalists did not publish classified information that spies let slip after one too many martinis. Neither spies nor journalists considered the extramarital sex lives of politicians to be newsworthy. Mutual respect, as well as a genteel tolerance for human imperfection, prevailed as long as a person was smart and either powerful or beautiful; being rich was much preferred but not absolutely required.

The most remarkable difference from today's Washington was that everybody, including the fun-loving CIA Director Allen Dulles and his somber brother, Secretary of State John Foster Dulles, considered it perfectly natural to have their home address and telephone number published in the telephone book.

Secretly, the reputation of the CIA was at its zenith, in considerable part due to the leadership of Allen Dulles. With nothing more than cash, panache, and a lot of luck, the CIA had manipulated political events in Third World countries around the globe, including Iran, Guatemala, and the Philippines, in the directions desired by the Oval Office. CIA's shadowy counterintelligence chief, Jim Angleton, was honored by Israel for contributions that he made to the founding of the Jewish state over objections from the cautious State Department. Here at home, the CIA took the lead in standing up to the demagoguery of Joe McCarthy, helping demonstrate that effective counterintelligence within the moral and political context of American democracy is, indeed, possible.

The CIA was less successful against its most determined and ruthless adversaries from the Soviet KGB and its surrogates. Many people, including CIA Chief of Clandestine Operations Frank Wisner, lost their lives because of the arrogantly naïve confidence that pushing back the KGB-enforced Iron Curtain would be almost as easy as manipulating events in poor Third World countries. Yet, even against the Soviets, American technical ingenuity provided a strategically decisive intelligence advantage. In that context, a special place of honor must be reserved for the U-2 spy plane that was fielded under budget in a matter of mere months during 1956, thanks to the organizational genius of senior CIA official Richard Bissell.

Almost inevitably, this run of CIA successes gave birth to hubris, and hubris led to tragedy. Few Americans blamed the CIA for the tragedy in Hungary in 1956. Fewer still even noticed the tragedy in Indonesia during 1957-1958. But, everybody noticed the tragedy of 1961, when an ill-prepared and poorly supported brigade of Cuban exiles challenged the battle-hardened revolutionary army of Fidel Castro at Cuba's Bay of Pigs.

***

Allen Dulles was a deceptive man, which, for a CIA Director, is a distinct advantage. His outward appearance was that of a jovial and good-natured professor, but when his mouth smiled, his eyes did not necessarily follow suit. Jackie Kennedy's cousin by marriage, novelist Louis Auchincloss, knew Dulles well from when they worked together in the same Wall Street law firm. Auchincloss described Allen as outwardly "a hale fellow" but inwardly "cold as ice," just the opposite of his brother John Foster Dulles, who was a partner in that same law firm. Allen lived with his wife, Clover, at 2723 Q Street in Georgetown, adjacent to the Dumbarton House. The character "Clover Wilson" played by Angelina Jolie in the 2006 movie *The Good Shepherd* is based on Clover Dulles. Like Jackie, Clover tolerated her husband's active extramarital social life, which reportedly included intimate relationships with Queen Frederika of Greece, Countess Toscanini Castelbarco of Italy, and American Ambassador Clare Booth Luce.

Dulles's legendary adventures as an American intelligence officer were not all successful. Born in 1893 to a family that already boasted of one Secretary of State and would later boast of two more, Dulles graduated from

Princeton in 1916 and became an honest diplomat. As Sunday duty officer at the American embassy in Bern, Switzerland, during World War I, Dulles fielded a telephone call from a then-unknown Russian named Vladimir Lenin who was seeking an urgent meeting with a representative of the American government. Dulles, the inexperienced 24-year-old junior diplomat, declined to meet the man on a Sunday and, thus, missed the opportunity to hear out Lenin, who departed for Russia the next day on the famous "sealed train" arranged by German military intelligence. Upon arrival in Moscow, Lenin changed history by successfully overthrowing the Russian government and pulling the czar's army out of the war against the kaiser's Germany.

Dulles was more successful during World War II when he was back in Bern, this time working for the Office of Strategic Services (OSS), the forerunner of America's modern CIA. As Chief of Station/Bern, Dulles officially reported to David K.E. Bruce, the chief of all OSS operations in Europe during the war and later one of America's most distinguished ambassadors. In Dulles's eyes, however, Bruce was a rear-echelon administrator while Dulles was a frontline station chief.

As such, Dulles recruited the two best spies the Allies had inside Nazi Germany, the German diplomat Fritz Kolbe and the German military intelligence officer Hans Bernd Gisevius. Kolbe was the more prolific of the two, but the advance word from Gisevius about the July 1944 assassination attempt on Hitler caught the attention of Supreme Allied Commander Dwight Eisenhower. This helped confirm Dulles's reputation as America's most skilled practitioner of the dark art of human espionage. Eight years later in 1952, when Eisenhower was elected President, he appointed Allen Dulles as CIA director and John Foster Dulles, for whom Dulles Airport outside Washington is named, as secretary of state.

As director, Allen Dulles transformed the CIA into a professional intelligence organization, first building the discipline to compete with and then laying the foundation for the CIA's ultimate victory over the KGB. An important key to Dulles' intelligence success was giving our KGB adversaries their due respect from a counterintelligence perspective. Prior to Dulles, the CIA placed top priority on conducting covert military operations inside Eastern Europe in hopes of rolling back the Soviet-imposed Iron Curtain between East and West.

These covert military operations were intellectually arrogant in their underestimation of the ruthlessly effective counterintelligence departments of the KGB and its East European surrogates. The CIA also naively discounted the possibility that these covert military operations might be betrayed before they even started by a KGB spy working inside the CIA's own intelligence planning and coordination groups. Unfortunately, that is exactly what the KGB had succeeded in doing with their master spy, the Englishman Kim Philby.

A pragmatic realist who hated to lose, Dulles decided to change the game. First, he professionalized counterintelligence. This involved increasing awareness amongst influential Americans that our government could, indeed, be penetrated by KGB-backed communist spies. Equally important, it involved pushing back against McCarthyite hysteria that any American with liberal views had to be a KGB-backed communist spy. Second, he shifted the playing field. This involved downplaying covert military operations in East Europe where the KGB and its surrogates were strongest, while increasing covert political operations in the Third World where the KGB and its surrogates were weaker. It also involved expansion of radio broadcasts into Eastern Europe and the Soviet Union to keep hopes of freedom alive for the long term. Finally, he relied on the strength of American ingenuity. This involved increased emphasis on technical intelligence, including overhead imagery, to reinforce essential and continued efforts in the human intelligence arena.

To assure long-term political support for his intelligence strategic plan, Dulles, a life-long conservative Republican, systematically reached out to life-long liberal Democrats. In other words, Dulles reached out to people like Joe Kennedy, whose handsome young son Jack appeared to have a promising political career ahead of him. Dulles was affluent but not exorbitantly wealthy, so for vacations, he frequently made use of the Palm Beach mansion of oil baron Charles Wrightsman, who coincidently was married to Jackie Kennedy's friend and artistic mentor, Jayne Wrightsman. Dulles and Joe Kennedy made it a practice to get together whenever they were both in Palm Beach at the same time. It was during one of these get-togethers in the spring of 1955 that Dulles first met the young Kennedys while Jack was recuperating from back surgery and the couple was working on *Profiles in Courage.*

In 1956, with Jack's political star continuing to rise, Dulles helped get Father Joe appointed a member of President Eisenhower's intelligence advisory board, thus institutionalizing Dulles's intelligence relationship with the Kennedy family. This foresight paid handsome returns the morning after the election in November 1960 when President-elect Kennedy called Dulles to reappoint him as Director of the CIA.

***

Frank Wisner was the senior CIA officer most committed to rolling back the Iron Curtain sooner rather than later. This commitment would eventually cost Wisner his life. Born in 1909 to a wealthy family from rural Mississippi, Wisner was a moralistic man with a deep sense of right and wrong. He witnessed the brutality of Soviet communism first hand as the senior OSS officer serving in Romania for six months in late 1944 and early 1945. Wisner was morally offended during that time when Romanian friends and lovers were rounded up, loaded into boxcars bound for Soviet labor camps, and then simply disappeared. Arthur Schlesinger Jr., President Kennedy's aide and biographer, served as an enlisted man under Wisner in the OSS and remarked that his anti-Soviet passion was notable even within American intelligence circles.

In 1947, Dean Acheson hired Wisner for a senior State Department position in the Office of Occupied Territories, which dealt with Eastern Europe. At that point in time before the McCarthy purges, America's best Soviet experts worked at the State Department, including George Kennan, Chip Bohlen, and Bohlen's brother-in-law, Charles Thayer. Wisner became close to them as well as to David Bruce, a classmate from the University of Virginia. In 1948, Wisner was made director of the innocuously named Office of Policy

Coordination, or OPC. The top secret charter for OPC gave it authority for any and all covert actions aimed at rolling back the Iron Curtain. Administratively, Wisner reported to Kennan at the State Department, but physically, he was housed at CIA. For all practical purposes, the OPC and Wisner were free agents with more or less unlimited budgets and no oversight.

During 1948-1951, Wisner socially gravitated more towards his State policy colleagues than to his CIA intelligence co-workers. He was one of the founding members, along with journalist Joe Alsop, of the Sunday Night Supper Club. They all lived within a few blocks of each other in the eastern half of Georgetown. Wisner and his wife, Polly, lived at 3019 P Street, two blocks over from Dean Acheson at 2805 P Street. Bohlen lived with his wife Avis Thayer Bohlen at 2811 Dumbarton, two blocks down from Acheson and one block over from Joe Alsop at 2720 Dumbarton.

For a time, John Foster Dulles also lived on Dumbarton at 3107, but Foster was not welcome at the Sunday Night Supper Club. When newly-elected President Eisenhower nominated Bohlen to become US Ambassador to the Soviet Union in 1953, Joe McCarthy attacked both Bohlen and his brother-in-law, Charles Thayer, and intimated that he, the Senator, had damaging information of an improper sexual nature regarding the two diplomats. Frank Wisner spoke out publicly in defense of both men. Their new boss, Foster Dulles, however, left them to their own defenses. Bohlen's reputation was bruised, but his career survived; Thayer, on the other hand, was drummed out of the State Department. Feeling unwelcome in Georgetown, Foster eventually moved to 2740 32nd Street, near the Naval Observatory.

An anglophile, Wisner also socialized frequently with the British intelligence officer Kim Philby. Along with several of his classmates, Philby had been an ideologically motivated spy for the Soviet KGB since his student days at Cambridge University. During 1949-1951, Philby served as Britain's senior intelligence liaison officer in Washington, D.C. and lived with his wife, Aileen, as well as with his fellow KGB spy and occasional gay lover Guy Burgess in the handsome home located at 4100 Nebraska Avenue. His liaison job gave Philby official access to all intelligence and counterintelligence exchanges between the two countries.

So, in 1949, when FBI agents working on the top secret code-breaking project called VENONA determined that British scientist Klaus Fuchs was a Soviet atomic spy, they passed that information to British counterintelligence authorities via Philby. Of course, Philby secretly advised the KGB first. Ironically, the "need to know" security around the VENONA project was so tight that Philby and the KGB learned about it long before President Harry Truman, Wisner or anybody else in the CIA ever did.

With Wisner, Philby worked on every joint British-American covert project to roll back communism in Eastern Europe and betrayed them all to the Soviet KGB. Their joint project to infiltrate hundreds of Albanian exiles back into Albania in hopes of overthrowing the communist government there became a particularly sad and bloody failure, thanks to Philby. When CIA counterintelligence concluded in 1951 that Philby was a traitor and kicked him out of the U.S., Wisner was psychologically shaken because he realized that everything he had worked to achieve for three years had been betrayed before it had even had a chance to begin. In 1952, Wisner's OPC was officially merged into the more rigorous counterintelligence culture of CIA; Wisner was made the CIA's deputy director in charge of all clandestine operations, but he reported to his old friend and sometimes rival Allen Dulles.

In 1956, five years after the unmasking of Philby, Wisner was again psychologically shattered by the simultaneous crises in Hungary and Suez. In mid-October, as tensions mounted in Budapest and Jackie Kennedy was trying to recover from the stillbirth of her daughter, Wisner was working to generate policy support in Washington and London for supplying anti-communist Hungarians with American weapons. On 24 October, he visited London to meet with his counterpart in British intelligence but was snubbed. Unbeknownst to Wisner, his counterpart had been secretly called to Paris to help plan the Anglo-French attack on Egypt. When the attack was launched on 29 October, Wisner felt deeply betrayed for a second time by his British counterparts.

After Soviet tanks rolled into Budapest on 4 November, Wisner rushed to Vienna to get as close to the action as possible. He became greatly distressed when he visited the border to witness the flood of bloodied Hungarian refugees. Here was the opportunity that he had been working for nearly a decade to create, but in the event, Washington policymakers turned cautious, ironically punishing the British and French more for Suez than the Soviets for Hungary. Over the next few weeks, Wisner's behavior became increasingly erratic. Finally, on 16 December, just two days before young Michael Meyer was hit by the car and killed, Frank Wisner suffered a nervous breakdown. Despite continuing psychological frailty, Wisner was not formally relieved of his responsibilities as chief of CIA's clandestine operations worldwide until two years later.

***

To provide an objective basis for the professionalization of counterintelligence at CIA, Allen Dulles enlisted White House support to commission a study by General Jimmy Doolittle, the daring aviator who had won the Medal of Honor by leading America's retaliatory bombing of Tokyo just four months after the Japanese surprise attack on Pearl Harbor in December 1941. The 1954 Doolittle Report included a recommendation that CIA be given responsibility for leading a more strategic approach to counterintelligence that would move beyond domestic security and law enforcement actions by taking the fight to the enemy. The core of that new strategy would be offense, i.e. the penetration of foreign intelligence services targeting America in order to disrupt their operations and, ideally, to turn those operations back against the perpetrators.

In other words, Doolittle recommended that the CIA do to the KGB what the KGB had done to the CIA with Kim Philby. To lead this more strategic approach to counterintelligence, Dulles selected a man he considered one of the most gifted intelligence professionals in America, Jim Angleton. The role of Edward Wilson played by Matt Damon in the 2006 movie *The Good Shepherd* is a one-dimensional caricature of Angleton.

In the late 1970s, Angleton became infamous under the menacing moniker James Jesus Angleton, but for most of his life, he was known more commonly as Jim. Earlier in his career as an American intelligence officer, Angleton had, over the objections of State Department diplomats, made important contributions to the successful founding of the state of Israel, contributions that remain classified to this day in the US but are nonetheless publicly honored in Israel with not one but two monuments.[9]

In 1953, Angleton helped his mentor Allen Dulles rebuff the allegations by Joe McCarthy that senior CIA officers Cord Meyer and William Bundy were secret communists. Subsequently, Angleton played an important role in Kennedy's decision as President to exonerate atomic scientist J. Robert Oppenheimer of McCarthyite suspicions that he, too, had been a communist spy.[10] Despite the reputation as a monster that he unfortunately did earn later in life, during the 1950s and early 1960s, Jim Angleton was the American counterintelligence officer that liberals relied on to counter-balance the influence of the more conservative FBI Director J. Edgar Hoover.

The span of Angleton's many friendships was

---

[9] *Myths Surrounding James Angleton: Lessons for American Counterintelligence* by William Hood et al, Consortium for the Study of Intelligence 1994, p. 10

[10] Thanks to VENONA, American counterintelligence knew that Oppenheimer was not a KSG spy. VENONA was America's TOP SECRET project to decrypt KGB cable during the Manhattan Project era. In 1961, after becoming President, John F. Kennedy transferred control of VENONA from J. Edgar Hoover at the FBI to James Jesus Angleton at the CIA in 1961. Viz *A Spy's Guide to Santa Fe and Albuquerque* by E.B. Held, University of New Mexico Press, 2011

remarkable. From communist labor leaders to conservative FBI agents to liberal journalists, from spies and politicians to poets and professors, women as well as men-- in his early years, they all considered Angleton one of the most exotic and charismatic men they had ever met. His father, Hugh, had been a cavalry officer who rode with General Pershing on the hunt for Pancho Villa. While in Mexico, Hugh met and married a teenage beauty named Carmen-Mercedes Moreno. Hugh and Carmen gave Jim, their first son, born in 1917, the common Mexican middle name, Jesus (hay-zoos).

When Angleton was a teenager, the family moved to Italy, and like many expatriate American children, he was sent away to attend boarding school in England. During 1937-1941, Angleton attended Yale University, where he was a mediocre student but was well known as a poet and campus literary figure. It was then that he began life-long friendships with Yale English Professor Norman Pearson and with the famous poets E.E. Cummings and Ezra Pound. Ironically, Cummings had been falsely accused of spying for Germany during World War I, and if not for Angleton, Pound would probably have been hanged for his open collaboration with Mussolini and the Italian Fascists during World War II.

In the autumn of 1941, Angleton met Cicely d'Autremont, a 19-year-old Vassar student and granddaughter of Chester Congdon, the wealthiest man in Minnesota and founder of the historic Glensheen Mansion in Duluth. Cicely confessed years later that she fell madly in love with Angleton at first sight and, despite a roller coaster marriage, never recovered. They married in July 1943 over the objections of Angleton's father, who worried that Jim had just been drafted into the Army and would soon depart for the war. Cicely was one month pregnant when Jim shipped out for England in December. As his father had feared, they would only see each other for one brief period during the next four years.

Unlike Cord Meyer, Angleton did not serve at the front but, instead, was selected to serve as a junior officer in the most secret of all secret compartments within Allied intelligence. Known as XX by the British and X2 by the Americans, this component was responsible for DOUBLECROSS, the remarkable strategic counterintelligence operation that disrupted Nazi intelligence operations and turned them back into a strategic deception operation against Hitler. It was thanks to DOUBLECROSS that Hitler expected the Anglo-American invasion of Europe to occur near Calais in northern France. Thus, he insisted on keeping Germany's best Panzer divisions stationed in Calais for several crucial days even after the Allies launched the real D-Day invasion in Normandy 200 miles to the southwest.

As a result of this successful deception, tens of thousands of Allied lives were spared, and Western Europe was liberated over the following eleven months by the Allied armies rather than occupied by the Red Army of the communist Soviet Union. Angleton was selected to work in London on the Italian desk of the DOUBLECROSS operation because he spoke fluent Italian and, more importantly, because the chief of the X2 unit in London was Norman Pearson, Angleton's professor and friend from Yale.

The intelligence foundation of the DOUBLECROSS operation was ULTRA, the successful British operation in breaking the Nazi's secret communication codes. Thanks to ULTRA, Allied counterintelligence could identify and quietly arrest Nazi spies. After arrest, they would be given a choice:

execution or cooperation with Allied counterintelligence. Most didn't take long in agreeing to cooperate; the others met their fate promptly. Cooperation meant that the co-opted Nazi spies would send Hitler doctored intelligence that would lead him to believe what the Allies wanted him to believe. To close this loop of deception, ULTRA could then confirm whether the orders sent out from Hitler's General Staff were consistent with the doctored intelligence provided. The strategic counterintelligence lessons that captivated Angleton at age 26 working on DOUBLECROSS would control his thinking the rest of his life.

A few months after D-Day, Angleton was given command of his own counterintelligence unit operating in Italy. The cycle of his work there was similar to what it had been in London: identify enemy spies, turn them, doctor their intelligence reports, and thereby manipulate the perceptions and the actions of their masters back home. As the war in Europe began winding down in the spring of 1945, however, the focus of Angleton's counterintelligence concerns expanded from the Nazis and the Fascists to include Italian communists and Jewish Zionists, many of whom were also communist leaning. Like others both East and West, Angleton was already thinking about the great power rivalries to come post-World War II.

Cicely refused to live overseas, but Angleton nonetheless decided to remain in Italy as a US counterintelligence official for two additional years after the war ended. He made a big name for himself by his role in preventing a communist electoral victory in Italy during the chaotic 1945-1948 period. He did so by following the Machiavellian advice of Jay Lovestone, a former American communist who was then head of the American Federation of Labor (AFL, later to become the AFL-CIO), and of American journalist/intellectual Claire Sterling.

The strategy that Lovestone and Sterling recommended was for Angleton to reach out to and provide modest support for relatively moderate Italian left wing groups and even anti-Stalin communists in order to split the overall left wing vote. At the same time, Angleton concentrated considerable financial support on his personal friend Alcide de Gasperi, founder of Italy's conservative Christian Democratic Party, in order to insure a solid financial basis for unity amongst the Italian conservative parties. This strategy was of particular importance to de Gasperi's victory over the communists in the touch-and-go Italian elections of 1948.

Lovestone, who was a Jewish Russian by birth, also served as a bridge between Angleton and Zionists, including Teddy Kolleck, the future mayor of Jerusalem, who were active in promoting the exodus of Jewish holocaust survivors from Europe to Palestine. Besides the moral obligation he felt personally to the holocaust survivors, Angleton's principle intelligence interest in these Zionists, many of whom were also Russian emigrants, was to use them as a source of intelligence from inside the Soviet Union. A second, but over the longer term, more important interest was to help steer any new Jewish state away from dependence on the Soviet Union and towards a close alliance with the United States. Today, few Americans remember that the Soviet Union was the first nation to recognize the new state of Israel and was a key supplier of arms to the Zionists during 1947-1948.

At home, Cicely was still in love with Angleton but increasingly tired of waiting for him. To bring matters to a head, she filed for divorce in 1946 on grounds of abandonment. To her surprise, Angleton refused and asserted his GI legal right to block the divorce. He finally tore himself away from his work in Italy in December 1947 and returned to reconcile with his wife and 3-year-old son in the United States. Their first daughter was born in 1949, the second in 1958. In Washington, their friends and social life became centered in Georgetown, where Angleton became known for his love of dancing to Elvis Presley songs and for his boycott of Wisconsin beer as a protest against McCarthyism. As a career counterintelligence specialist, however, Angleton chose to keep the Georgetown scene at a careful arm's distance by living across the Potomac at 4814 33rd Street in North Arlington, Virginia, near the southern charm-filled Washington Golf and Country Club.

In the fall of 1954, at the same time Cord Meyer was promoted to the senior rank of CIA division chief at age 34, Angleton was promoted to chief of CIA's counterintelligence staff at age 37; he would remain in that powerful position for over 20 years. He performed at his very best during the late 1950s when he worked hand in glove with his FBI liaison partner and close personal friend, Sam Papich, to identify and neutralize a number of KGB spy rings that existed in the United States, most notably the non-official cover or "illegal" spy ring in New York City led by KGB officer Rudolf Abel. The character "Sam Murach" played by Alec Baldwin in *The Good Shepherd* is based on Papich. Abel's illegal network is the historical antecedent of the eleven Russian illegals wrapped up in New York City during 2010.

***

Frank Wisner retained his title as chief of CIA clandestine operations for two years following his 1956 nervous breakdown, but it was common knowledge that his loyal deputy Richard Helms was covering for him. Sadly, in the fall of 1958, Wisner had to be admitted to a private psychiatric hospital near Baltimore, where his treatment included electric shock therapy. All hands expected Dulles to give Helms formal title to the job that had been his de facto for two years, but he did not. Dulles respected Helms for his hands-on experience in clandestine operations as well as his efficiency as a manager, but Dulles wanted someone more visionary to be his clandestine deputy. Passing over Helms, Dulles surprised everybody by giving the job to a man with no hands-on clandestine experience, Richard Bissell.

Jack Kennedy considered Dick Bissell one of the smartest people in Washington, and without being immodest, Bissell agreed. After graduating from Yale in 1932, Bissell pursued advanced studies at the London School of Economics and then returned to Yale in 1934 as a prodigy professor of economics while Jim Angleton, Cord Meyer and McGeorge Bundy were still undergraduates there. During World War II, Bissell won acclaim for his logistical management of all allied merchant shipping. In 1948, he became the administrator on whom Secretary of State George Marshall relied to successfully implement the Marshall Plan.

When Tom Braden of the CIA asked Bissell for assistance in laundering large sums of money through Marshall Plan accounts in order to clandestinely support anti-communist political action in Italy and elsewhere in Western Europe, he considered it his privilege and duty to help. Bissell lived with his family at 3401 Newark Street NW, across the street from

Cord Meyer's friend Paul Moore, the secretly homosexual Episcopelian bishop of Washington Cathedral.

Bissell and journalist Joe Alsop were life-long friends. They were born in the same neighborhood of Hartford, Connecticut, within weeks of each other in 1910. They, along with Jackie Kennedy's relative Louis Auchincloss, were best friends at Groton preparatory school. As a CIA official, Bissell prided himself on having never leaked sensitive information to the press, but when asked about his close friend Alsop, Bissell admitted, "Well, I did talk to Joe."[11] Bissell helped protect Alsop in 1957 when the KGB photographed him in the midst of a homosexual act during a visit to Moscow. In turn, Alsop helped Bissell in 1960 by brokering a personal relationship with President-elect Kennedy.

A brilliant economist with a proven track record as an excellent administrator, Bissell could have made a fortune in business. Instead, he chose the CIA because of the courage Allen Dulles demonstrated in standing up to Joe McCarthy. Bissell and Braden were on a sailing vacation in August 1953 when Braden received word that his deputy Cord Meyer had been suspended due to McCarthyite allegations. Bissell was impressed when Braden cut short their vacation and immediately returned to Washington. He was even more impressed when he learned in November that Dulles had successfully protected Meyer, as well as William Bundy. A few weeks later, Bissell expressed his admiration to Dulles at a Christmas reception hosted by Joe Alsop's brother, Stewart. Dulles pulled Bissell aside and offered to create a job for him as special assistant to the director of CIA. Bissell agreed to

---

[11] *The Very Best Men* by Evan Thomas, p. 105

drop everything and started the following month, January 1954.

To get Bissell's feet wet, Dulles assigned his new special assistant to be his personal liaison officer to PBSUCCESS, the operation that was already underway to overthrow the left wing government of Guatemalan President Jacobo Arbenz and, thereby, protect US economic interests, including those of the New Orleans-based United Fruit Company. The CIA chief of that operation was the dashing psychological warfare specialist Tracy Barnes, who had been a year behind Bissell at Groton and at Yale. Bissell tried to make himself useful by taking care of logistical details while Barnes used smoke and mirrors to create an impression that the Americans had organized an overwhelming force of Guatemalan guerillas against which the small Guatemalan Army stood no chance.

On the eve of the operation's launch in June 1954, President Eisenhower asked Allen Dulles what the odds of success really were for PBSUCCESS; Dulles responded honestly, 20 percent. But, succeed it did with very little loss of life on either side and at low cost to the US taxpayer because Barnes simply frightened Arbenz into stepping down without a fight. This smoke and mirrors victory made quite an impression on Bissell and on another man that Bissell would confront seven years later at the Bay of Pigs, a young Argentine leftist who had been active in Guatemala named Ernesto "Che" Guevara.

Dulles next assigned Bissell to a technical procurement project that was more up his alley, the U-2 photo reconnaissance plane. Since the onset of the Cold War in the late 1940s, the US Air Force had been using RB-47 retrofitted bombers to fly photo reconnaissance missions over peripheral areas of Soviet territory. These flights were provocative because they were illegal incursions into Soviet airspace and, retrofitted or not, the planes were still clearly bombers. The flights also faced great risk of being shot down because their maximum flying altitude was only 40,000 feet. Given the risks, the Truman administration established explicit guidance that, should one of the bombers get shot down, official responsibility would be denied and all blame would be laid on the pilot for navigational error.

Seeing a crisis waiting to happen, President Eisenhower, in November 1954, enthusiastically endorsed a CIA vision to develop a specially designed photo reconnaissance spy plane that would reduce risks by flying on the edge of outer space at 70,000 feet and improve our intelligence collection by flying long range over even the most remote parts of the Soviet Union. Just as George Marshall had charged Bissell to transform the Marshall Plan from vision to reality, Dulles now challenged his administrative genius Bissell to make this new U-2 spy plane a reality. With a staff that never exceeded eight people, Bissell directed teams from the finest companies in America and delivered a fleet of U-2s ahead of schedule and under budget. It was simply brilliant.

On Independence Day, 4 July 1956, an American U-2 spy plane flew over Soviet sovereign territory for the first time. The plane flew directly over Moscow and is rumored to have snapped a photo of Soviet Premier Nikita Sergeyevich Khrushchev attending the Independence Day reception in the garden of Spaso House, the American Ambassador's residence. In the forty-six months between 4 July 1956 and 1 May 1960, American U-2s flew over Soviet territory twenty-two times, producing America's most important and reliable intelligence on the Soviet nuclear threat to the American homeland.[12] President Eisenhower insisted on personally authorizing each flight. Moreover, to insure the legal precision that the flights were acts of espionage, not acts of war, active U-2 pilots were required temporarily to resign from the Air Force and join the CIA.

The person who made the single greatest contribution to the success of the U-2 program was not Bissell, however. It was a Russian named Pyotr Semyonevich Popov. Popov was a colonel in the GRU, the Soviet's military intelligence agency, and the CIA's top spy inside the Soviet Union for six years, from 1953 until the fall of 1959. Thanks to intelligence provided by Popov, the CIA knew where they should fly the U-2s over the millions of square miles of Soviet territory. Popov would report about new missile or nuclear weapon activity somewhere in the USSR. A U-2 would then be dispatched to over-fly the site in order to confirm the accuracy of his reporting, Popov would close the loop by reporting on Soviet reactions to the U-2 flight. In mid-1958 Popov reported to the CIA that the KGB had a new source somewhere with access to technical details about the U-2. This reporting was of particular interest to CIA's counterintelligence chief, Jim Angleton.

From Popov's reporting, Angleton knew that the U-2 over-flights infuriated Soviet Premier Khrushchev; they were an insult to Soviet sovereignty, an insult to Khrushchev's personal dignity and political power, and worst of all, they flew so high that Soviet air defenses could do absolutely nothing about them. On Khrushchev's orders, bringing down the U-2s became the number one mission priority for the

---

[12] www.spyflight.co.uk

KGB. Thus, from 1956 until 1960, the U-2 was the focus of the most intense spy versus spy struggle ever between the KGB and the CIA.

***

Suggestions for further reading:

1. *The Very Best Men: The Daring Early Years of the CIA* by Evan Thomas, Simon and Schuster, 1995.

Excellent biographic sketches of CIA giants Frank Wisner, Richard Bissell, Tracy Barnes, and Desmond Fitzgerald, all of whom met somewhat sad fates.

2. *Gentleman Spy: the Life of Allen Dulles* by Peter Grose, Houghton Mifflin Company, 1994.

The best biography of the man who transformed CIA into a professional intelligence organization.

3. *Myths Surrounding James Angleton: Lessons for American Counterintelligence* by William Hood et al, Consortium for the Study of Intelligence, 1994.

A short monograph in response to Thomas Mangold's book, *Cold Warrior,* which depicts Angleton as a monster.

4. *Cloak and Gown: Scholars in the Secret War, 1939-1961* by Robin Winks, Yale University Press, 1987.

Contains a 117-page section on Angleton that is insightful.

A Spy's Walking Tour of Georgetown

This walking tour is divided in two parts, one west of Wisconsin Avenue and one east. They can be taken separately or woven together. Each part takes an hour at a normal walking pace. If you do both at once, you might want to take a break midway at one of two spy-related restaurants located on Wisconsin Avenue: Five Guys at the southeast corner of Wisconsin and Dumbarton Street or Billy Martin's Tavern at the southwest corner of Wisconsin and N Street.

In November 1985, Five Guys was the French bistro Au Pied de Cochon from which KGB defector Vitaly Yurchenko slipped away from his CIA escorts and re-defected to the Soviet Union.[13] During the 1940s, Billy Martin's Tavern was

[13] Yurchenko had defected to the CIA in Rome during August 1985 and subsequently identified two Americans who had spied in the past for the KGB , Ronald Pelton and Edward Lee Howard, both of whom were arrested and convicted. However, after the arrest of CIA traitor Aldrich Ames in 1994, many came to believe that Yurchenko was a fake defector from the very beginning who sacrificed Pelton and Howard in order to protect the far more important Ames, who had just volunteered to spy for the KGB in April 1985.

where KGB courier Elizabeth Bentley would collect secret documents from American government sources in Washington. It was also a favorite spot for Jack and Jackie Kennedy when they lived up the block at 3307 N Street.

A third restaurant, Chadwick's, on Water Street at the base of Wisconsin is where CIA traitor Aldrich Ames passed the names of twelve KGB officers spying on America's behalf in early 1985. Chadwick's is, thus, of even greater significance in espionage history than either Five Guys or Billy Martin's Tavern, but it requires a detour from this walking tour.

***

West of Wisconsin Avenue

1. 3321 Dent Place, where Jack and Jackie lived as newlyweds during 1953 and 1954 (see Chapter 2). Walk west a block and a half to 35th Street, turn left, walk two blocks south past Georgetown Visitation Convent on the right hand side of the street, and then turn left again onto Volta Place.

2. 3410 Volta Place, where Tracy Barnes and his family lived. Barnes managed the CIA overthrow of Guatemalan President Jacobo Arbenz in 1954 (see Chapter 5) and was a major figure in the Bay of Pigs operation in 1961 (see chapter 6). Continue on Volta Place to the next corner, 34th Street, and turn right.

3. 1523 34th Street, where Mary Meyer lived from late 1957 until she was murdered in October 1964 (see Chapter 1).

JFK's mistress, Pamela Turnure, rented a room from Mary here in 1959 (see Chapter 2). After Mary's death, Cord Meyer assumed ownership of the house and moved into it with his new wife. Continue south on 34th Street another block.

4. 1411 34th Street, where Ambassador David Bruce and his wife Evangeline lived. During World War II, Bruce was assigned to London as the Chief of OSS operations for Europe and, as such, was the direct boss of Allen Dulles and James Angleton (See Chapter 3).

5. 1400 34th Street, where Jack Kennedy lived as a young congressman in 1949-1951. Cross O Street and continue south on 34th for half a block, then turn left into the alleyway that runs to 33rd Street.

6. The garage behind 3321 N Street, where Mary Meyer had her art studio (see Chapter 1). Continue to 33rd Street turn right and then turn again right onto N Street.

7. 3307 N Street, where Jack and Jackie Kennedy lived from the birth of Caroline in November 1957 until they moved to the White House in January 1961 (see Chapter 2).

8. 3321 N Street, where Ben and Tony Bradlee lived when they met Jack and Jackie Kennedy in 1958 (see Chapter 3). Tony was Mary Meyer's younger sister and became Jackie's best friend. Ben and Tony let Mary use their alley garage as her art studio.

The route Mary walked to her murder site

From 3321 N Street, proceed west to the corner of N and 34th Streets. Turn left and walk south down 34th to M Street (where Polly Wisner drove by and waved to Mary). Cross M and continue down 34th until it ends, across the footbridge to the south side of the C&O Canal, and down the ramp to the towpath. Walk west under Key Bridge and by the Potomac Boat Club on your left. After approximately half a mile, you will see a cement stairway and ramp slope off the towpath down to the left. You will then cross over two small bridges as the towpath curves gently to the left.

It was just after she crossed the second bridge, below the merge of Canal and Foxhall Roads, that Mary was ambushed. The murderer fired one bullet from a small caliber pistol into her head, which would have killed her instantly, and then shot another bullet through her heart. Amongst professionals, two bullets to the head are called "a hit;" one to the head and one to the heart are called "a message."

Presumed escape route of the murderer

From the murder site, a professional who had pre-cased the area could have quickly been out of sight and down the hill south of the towpath well before any bystanders could have reacted. The murderer would then have passed beneath the canal via the underpass near the cement stairway and then back up onto Canal Street all within ninety seconds of the shooting. He/she would probably have disposed of the incriminating murder weapon north of the canal and then resumed a normal walking pace back towards Georgetown. Police responding to the reports of an incident several minutes later probably drove right past the murderer as he/she was walking calmly back into Georgetown.

For the purposes of this walking tour, retrace your steps back across the two small bridges and then take the cement stairway down the hill to the underpass. You will see that even at a normal walking pace you can pass underneath the canal and be back up on Canal Road in just a few short minutes. For a professional with a pre-arranged plan, a covert escape from the murder scene would have been quite easy.

9. Walk back along Canal Road towards Georgetown. If you are up to it, climb the steep, "Exorcist"[14] stairway that leads from the Canal Road Exxon Station up to the intersection of Prospect Place and 36th Street; alternatively, walk up 35th Street to Prospect Place. Turn left.

10. 3615 Prospect Place, where Cord Meyer, Mary's estranged husband, lived in a rented room (see Chapter 1). Turn right from Prospect Place onto 37th Street and enjoy the nice view of Georgetown University on your left. Turn right on N Street and then left onto 36th Street.

11. Holy Trinity Church on 36th Street at N where Jack and Jackie attended Sunday Mass. It was on the street here after Mass on 13 March 1960 that Jack and Jackie bumped into Georgetown socialite Oatsie Leiter and spy novelist Ian Fleming and invited them for dinner at the 3307 N Street house later that same day. Hatched at that dinner was the CIA plot to make the hair of Fidel Castro's beard fall out (see Chapter 2). Turn right at the intersection of 36th and O

---

[14] This stairway played a role in the final, climatic scene of the 1973 movie, *The Exorcist*.

Streets.

This ends the first part of the walking tour. If you choose to continue, proceed along O Street to Wisconsin Avenue, cross over and veer slightly to the right onto Dumbarton Street.

***

East of Wisconsin Avenue

12. 3107 Dumbarton, where Secretary of State John Foster Dulles lived before fleeing the social whirl of Georgetown for the more sedate neighborhood of 2740 32nd Street NW, near the Naval Observatory (see Chapter 3). Continue east along Dumbarton Street to 31st Street, turn right, go one block to N Street and turn left.

13. 3038 N Street, the former home of Averill Harriman where the widowed First Lady and the Kennedy children lived temporarily after leaving the White House on 6 December 1963 through January 1964.

14. 3017 N Street, where Jackie and her children lived during February-September 1964 when they moved to New York City (see Chapter 12).

15. 3014 N Street, the Todd Lincoln House purchased in 1983 by Ben Bradlee and his new young wife Sally Quinn. Turn left at 30th Street, go one block, and turn right back onto Dumbarton.

16. 2811 Dumbarton, where Ambassador Chip Bohlen lived (see Chapters 3 and 8).

17. 2733 Dumbarton, where JFK's aide and mistress Pamela Turnure rented a room from Florence and Leonard Kater during 1958-1959 until Mrs. Kater began publicly complaining about JFK's late night comings and goings (see Chapter 2).

18. 2720 Dumbarton, journalist Joe Alsop's home, the headquarters of the Georgetown Sunday Supper Club (see Chapter 3, 6, 8 and 12). Turn left on 27th Street, continue three blocks to Q Street, and turn left.

19. 2723 Q Street, where CIA Director Allen Dulles and his wife, Clover lived (see Chapter 3). Turn left on 28th Street, go one block, and turn right onto P Street.

20. 2805 P Street, where Secretary of State Dean Acheson lived. Acheson's son-in-law was William Bundy, the CIA officer who, like Cord Meyer, was accused of being a communist by Joe McCarthy (see Chapters 1 and 3).

21. 2808 P Street, where Jack and Jackie Kennedy lived during 1956-1957, the darkest period in their marriage (see Chapter 2).

22. 2905 P Street, where Alger Hiss, the Soviet spy inside the State Department, lived. Hiss was convicted of perjury in 1950 for having lied under oath about his membership in the Communist Party and served 44 months in prison. Secretary of State Dean Acheson as well as future democratic presidential candidate Adlai Stevenson continued to defend Hiss's innocence. Joe McCarthy exploited the Hiss case to launch his campaign to purge communists from the US

government (see Chapters 1-3). Continue to 30th Street and turn right.

23. 1511 30th Street, where Desmond Fitzgerald lived. During 1963, Fitzgerald was the senior CIA official working under Bobby Kennedy's oversight to organize the assassination of Fidel Castro (see Chapters 4, 10 and 11). Return to P Street and turn right.

24. 3019 P Street, where Frank Wisner lived. During the 1950's, Wisner was the deputy director in charge of CIA clandestine operations worldwide (see Chapter 3). He suffered a series of nervous breakdowns in the late 1950s and early 1960s, which led to his suicide in 1965. Continuing along P Street, cross over Wisconsin Avenue.

25. 3271 P Street, where Jack Kennedy lived when he was courting Jackie (see Chapter 2).

This ends the tour.

1. The home at 2237 48th St. NW where Charlie Bartlett matched Jack and Jackie

2. Mary Meyer's home in Georgetown at 1523 34th St. NW

3. Mary's art studio in the alley garage behind the Bradlee residence

4. Jack and Jackie Kennedy's home in Georgetown at 3307 N St NW

5. Ben and Tony Bradlee's home in Georgetown at 3321 N St NW

6. The spot on the towpath where Mary was murdered

7. The underpass through which the murderer probably escaped

8. The widowed First Lady's home in Georgetown at 3017 N St NW

9. Journalist Joe Alsop's home in Georgetown at 2720 Dumbarton St NW

10. The Georgetown home of Allen and Clover Dulles at 2723 Q St NW

11. The Georgetown home of Des Fitzgerald at 1511 30th St NW

12. Jim and Cicely Angleton' s home at 4814 33rd St in North Arlington

13. View from the President's grave in Arlington Cemetery across Memorial Bridge

Chapter 4
Enter Lee Harvey Oswald

On 12 September 1957, a 17-year-old American kid named Lee Oswald walked smack into the middle of the CIA-KGB spy versus spy struggle over the U-2s, on his tragic way into the lives of Washington's power elite. Oswald reported on that day to his post as a US Marine radar operator at Atsugi Naval Air Station, 35 miles south of Tokyo, Japan. Atsugi was of historical interest because it had served as the headquarters for the Japanese kamikaze squadrons at the end of World War II. In 1957, Atsugi was of current interest to the KGB officers working inside the Soviet Embassy in central Tokyo because it was one of two CIA operational bases worldwide from which U-2 flights were launched.

Everybody assigned to Atsugi was a top recruitment target for KGB-Tokyo because of the U-2s based there. A Marine radar operator like Oswald, who openly professed to be a devoted communist, would have been a particularly tempting recruitment target. If the KGB foreign intelligence directorate did not recruit Oswald in late 1957 or early 1958 to serve as a low-level source regarding the U-2s at Atsugi, then they were either incompetent or incredibly unlucky. But, the KGB foreign intelligence directorate, known as the First Chief Directorate, was anything but incompetent. Quite the contrary, officers of the First Chief Directorate were exceptionally professional, thorough, and skilled in making luck work in their favor.

When Oswald returned stateside on 15 November 1958, the KGB probably thought they would never see him again. Like a bad penny, however, he showed back up in Moscow eleven months later on 16 October 1959 hoping to defect to the USSR and become a Soviet citizen. The KGB's first reaction was to do everything they could to quietly expel Oswald from the country before American counterintelligence became aware of the situation. To resist expulsion, Oswald walked into the American Embassy in Moscow on Saturday, 31 October, and alerted American counterintelligence of his intentions and his willingness to earn Soviet citizenship by sharing with the KGB everything he knew, including whatever classified information he might have learned as a US Marine radar operator at Atsugi.

Oswald's visit to the American Embassy prompted an absolutely remarkable about-face on the part of the KGB. Just four days later, on Wednesday, 4 November, an officer of the First Chief Directorate, probably Department 13, using only his given and patronymic names, "Andrei Nikolayevich," met with Oswald in his hotel room to discuss opportunities for Oswald to work abroad as a KGB spy. On Monday, 16 November, the KGB concurred that Oswald could remain in the Soviet Union for the time being. Eleven days later, on Friday, 27 November, the Central Committee of the Communist Party of the Soviet Union approved a written request signed by Chairman of the KGB Aleksandr Nikolayevich Shelepin and by Soviet Foreign Minister Andrei Andreyevich Gromyko to formally grant Oswald residency in the isolated city of Minsk as well as a KGB stipend, a luxury apartment, a guarantee of employment, and attractive young people to entertain him.[15]

In short, in late October, the KGB issued orders for Oswald to be quietly but, if necessary, forcibly ejected from the Soviet Union. A month later, the chairman of the KGB and the Foreign Minister of the USSR personally sponsored Oswald as a Soviet resident. What a remarkable change one short visit to the American Embassy in Moscow can make.

***

Lee Harvey Oswald was born in New Orleans on 18 October 1939 to a poor family. His father, Robert E. Lee Oswald, died before he was born. His mother was a difficult person with grandiose views of her position in life. Her son was not unintelligent, but he was dyslexic and poorly educated. He dropped out of high school before completing the tenth grade, by which time he had attended twelve different schools and resided in twenty-two different locations, including a short period in an orphanage. Oswald desperately wanted to make a big name for himself one way or another. Such people, if they get into a position that merits targeting, are easy for intelligence services to recruit, but they can be difficult to control and discipline. The intelligence service wants them to maintain a low, clandestine profile, but they want to exploit their relationship with the powerful intelligence service to make themselves famous.

---

[15] The stipend was nominally paid by the Soviet Red Cross, but in his diary Oswald recognized that the true source was Soviet intelligence.

Oswald was an impressionable teenager living in the Bronx during the highly publicized espionage trial and execution of Julius and Ethel Rosenberg. He felt outrage over the case, just as KGB propaganda specialists in Moscow hoped young Americans would be.[16] From that point on, Oswald fancied himself a street-smart Marxist intellectual. As soon as he was of age, this would-be Marxist enlisted in the US Marine Corps in order to escape his domineering mother. After completing basic training as a Marine and advanced training as a radar operator, Oswald was sent to Japan.

Shortly after reporting to Atsugi Naval Air Station south of Tokyo, his barrack mates introduced the newcomer to a hostess club called the Blue Bird Café, which was located in nearby Yamato and catered to US enlisted personnel. The hostesses at the Blue Bird may have seemed exotic to the American servicemen, but like most of the hostesses throughout Japan, they were just young farm girls trying to save some money. Their job was to pour the men's drinks and laugh at their jokes. By paying a separate fee to the bar owner, a guest could take one of the girls for a date outside of the bar. For another separate fee arranged directly with the girl, they could have sex. Thus, it was that Oswald lost his virginity.

During one of his first visits to the Blue Bird, the teenager Oswald became light-headed after one too many beers and loudly caused a small scene by proclaiming himself a Marxist and blaming President Eisenhower for millions of

---

[16] The Rosenbergs' KGB control officer, Aleksandr Feklisov, complained in his post-Cold War memoir, *The Man Behind the Rosenbergs,* about the KGB decision to use the couple as propaganda pawns rather than negotiate to free them.

innocent deaths during the war in Korea-- unusual behavior for a Marine which did not go unnoticed. Subsequently, Oswald befriended some Japanese socialists who also frequented the Blue Bird. Via these Japanese socialists, he met a high-class Japanese hostess from the Queen Bee hostess club in downtown Tokyo. An hour of flattery and witty conversation-- nothing more-- with a hostess from the Queen Bee would cost more than a young Marine earned in a month. Oswald's barrack mates never could understand what an expensive and high-class hostess from the Queen Bee would see in any low-paid Marine private, much less one as socially awkward as Lee Oswald. Professional intelligence officers, on the other hand, would tell you that Oswald had probably gotten himself involved with a KGB spotting and assessment operation.

All American military bases in Japan were high priority targets for the KGB. The bases were central to America's ability to project military force in times of crisis onto the Korean Peninsula or into the Taiwan Straits. Therefore, the KGB mission was to monitor sensitive activities on the bases and disrupt or sabotage them during those same times of crisis. KGB officers responsible for such sabotage operations were assigned to Line F in field offices like KGB-Tokyo. Line F officers in the field reported to Department 13 of the First Chief Directorate back at KGB headquarters in Moscow. Besides sabotage operations, Department 13 was also responsible for the occasional KGB assassination operation, which generally targeted Soviet defectors and dissident Russian émigrés.

Atsugi Naval Air Station was of particular interest to KGB-Tokyo because it was a closed base. The only people allowed to enter Atsugi were U.S. military assigned there or

American civilians with top secret security clearances. The most important reason Atsugi was closed was because it served as one of only two bases worldwide for the CIA's U-2 spy planes that flew over the Soviet Union. Soviet Premier Khrushchev had ordered the KGB to do everything in its power to either sabotage the U-2s or collect sufficient intelligence to enable the Soviet Air Force to shoot them down.

Targeting Atsugi directly was difficult for the KGB because it was located in a suburb 35 miles south of Tokyo. Any Soviet diplomat casually hanging about trying to meet American enlisted personnel would be easily spotted by the Japanese police or by American military counterintelligence. In such situations, the standard KGB modus operandi was to use friendly local nationals to conduct the initial spotting and assessment of potential American targets. A first friendly local who spotted a prospective target would introduce the mark to a second friendly local whose job would be to assess whether the target was legitimate or perhaps a provocation by American counterintelligence. If the target was assessed to be legitimate, then the second friendly local would introduce the mark directly to a KGB officer for advanced assessment and eventual recruitment. This common operational approach is called a "daisy chain."

Seen through the eyes of a professional intelligence officer, this appears to be what happened to Oswald in Japan. The Japanese socialists would have spotted him at the Blue Bird when he loudly declared himself a Marxist and criticized President Eisenhower. The socialists would have arranged an occasion for Oswald to meet the alluring and high-priced hostess from the Queen Bee. Her job would have been to assess Oswald more intimately and to generate a need on

Oswald's part for additional money. Then, a professional KGB officer would have moved in for the recruitment. Ideologically compatible and appreciative of additional money to keep his expensive girlfriend happy, Oswald would have accepted.

Given the high priority that Premier Khrushchev placed on neutralizing the U-2s, we can be certain that such KGB operations targeting enlisted personnel assigned to Atsugi were attempted. If, in fact, Oswald came up on the radar screen of KGB-Tokyo, then we can be equally certain that they would have made a run at him. To the KGB, a radar operator like Oswald would have represented a low-level but nonetheless very useful spy to report on U-2 flights out of Atsugi. It is not known with absolute certainty that he did come up on the KGB radar screen. During the fourteen months that he was based in Atsugi, Oswald was on deployments outside of Japan for seven months, so any KGB recruitment process would have had to have been somewhat quick, but it would not have been difficult. The manner in which the KGB handled Oswald when he unexpectedly arrived in Moscow during the fall of 1959 left strong telltale clues that, indeed, they did have a previous relationship with him.

***

The two deployments that Oswald participated in during his fourteen months in Japan were of high interest to the CIA. His first deployment, from mid-November 1957 until March 1958, was an exercise in gunboat diplomacy in support of a

CIA operation to overthrow Indonesian President Sukarno. In the late 1940s after World War II, Sukarno, who by custom used only one name, had led Indonesia to independence from Dutch colonial rule. During the mid-1950s, he seemed to be drifting into the anti-American, communist camp. He visited the Soviet Union and "Red" China in 1956, brought the Indonesian Communist Party into his government, and began receiving Soviet arms shipments in early 1957. Thus, in August 1957, a worried White House authorized the CIA to spend $10 million to repeat in Indonesia what they had done successfully in Guatemala during 1954, i.e. overthrow a Third World leader by using psychological warfare to create the impression that America had covertly organized an overwhelming force of Indonesian rebels backed by US Marines floating just offshore.

This time, however, the targeted Third World president and his army did not frighten so easily. They fought back and exposed the CIA's clandestine role when they shot down a "rebel" bomber and captured the pilot, a former American Air Force officer flying for the CIA. Washington disavowed any official knowledge or responsibility but, to Lee Oswald's great delight, quickly backed down.

Oswald's second deployment, during August-November 1958, was to Taiwan, in response to threats of war from Beijing unless the Chinese Nationalist government on Taiwan withdrew from Quemoy and Matsu, two small islands within artillery range of the Chinese mainland. When U-2s out of Atsugi revealed that the Chinese threats were just bluster, President Eisenhower was confidently able to calm the crisis. He first pushed back against the Chinese threats by deploying the Marines from Japan to Taiwan and then by threatening the use of nuclear weapons if the Chinese pushed further. When Moscow distanced itself from Beijing's brinkmanship, it became Chinese leader Mao Zedong's turn to quickly back down.

Both the Indonesia operation and the U-2 involvement in the Quemoy/Matsu crisis were overseen by the senior CIA official for East Asia, Desmond Fitzgerald. Des, as he was known, was another charter member of Joe Alsop and Frank Wisner's Sunday Night Supper Club. He lived in Georgetown at 1511 30th Street, just around the corner from Frank Wisner, in a stately townhouse that rivaled that of Jack Kennedy at 3107 N Street.

Fitzgerald was likewise an Irish-American from Massachusetts, born in 1910, seven years before Kennedy. After graduating from Harvard and Harvard Law, Fitzgerald joined a prestigious Wall Street law firm and married his first wife, Marietta Peabody, the daughter of Endicott Peabody, the founder of Groton.[17] A romantic by nature, he enlisted as an army infantryman following the Japanese attack on Pearl Harbor, despite his age of 31. After his basic training, the army decided to send him to Officer Candidate School and subsequently put him in charge of training black recruits. Bored by that training assignment, Fitzgerald persistently lobbied for a combat assignment. Finally, in August 1943, he

---

[17] Marietta Peabody Tree, as she became known, was famous in her own right. While Des Fitzgerald was off at war, she had a passionate affair with film director John Huston. After divorcing Fitzgerald in 1947, she married the homosexual British billionaire Ronald Tree. She became mistress to Adlai Stevenson in 1952 and served as US Delegate to the UN Commission on Human Rights during 1961-1964 while Stevenson was President Kennedy's Ambassador to the UN. Stevenson died in her arms in 1965.

got his wish and was sent to serve under General Joe Stilwell as an intelligence liaison officer to a Chinese infantry regiment fighting the Japanese under incredibly harsh conditions in Burma and Southern China.

After the war, Fitzgerald returned to his lucrative law practice for five years, but he became bored again. When the Korean War broke out in 1950, Frank Wisner recruited Fitzgerald to join the element of CIA responsible for East Asia. He made a name for himself in 1953 working with an Air Force Colonel named Edward Lansdale to counter a communist-backed insurgency in the Philippines and to manipulate the Philippine Presidential elections to come out the way that the White House hoped they would. Lansdale would later become the model for *The Quiet American* by Graham Greene and *The Ugly American* by Eugene Burdick and William Lederer. For his part, Fitzgerald would become the CIA's point man for Cuba in 1963 with the specific responsibility of assassinating Fidel Castro.

***

Lee Oswald proved a disciplinary problem for the Marines at Atsugi, spending an unusual amount of time off base with his Japanese friends. After a tour in the brig, he was sent back to the United States in November 1958. Ten months later, on 4 September 1959, Oswald was granted an early dependency discharge in response to his claim that he needed to return home to Fort Worth, Texas and support his mother. The same day his discharge was granted, however, Oswald applied for a US passport. He spent only two days in

Fort Worth "supporting" his mother. He then traveled to New Orleans and booked passage on a Europe-bound freighter. Following up on discussions that he had with his socialist friends back in Japan, Oswald was defecting to the Soviet Union.

Oswald arrived in Moscow on 16 October 1959 ostensibly for a five-day tourist visit. Upon arrival, he handed a letter to his government-provided tourist guide, a nice looking 18-year-old blond named Rimma Shirakova. In the letter, Oswald requested that he be granted citizenship in the Soviet Union.

Surprised, the KGB general in charge of the Second Chief Directorate, Oleg Mikhailovich Gribanov, the Soviet equivalent of the FBI director, conferred with the KGB general in charge of the First Chief Directorate, Alexsandr Mikhailovich Sakharovsky,the Soviet equivalent of the CIA Director, with the result that the KGB issued an order for Oswald to be quietly but, if necessary, forcibly ejected from the USSR. Accordingly, on the morning of 21 October, an officer of the KGB's Second Chief Directorate, who used the alias "Abram Shaknarazov," met with Oswald and tried to convince him to leave the Soviet Union quietly. When he declined to leave on his own volition, "Shaknarazov" advised Oswald that he nonetheless would be leaving the Soviet Union later that day, until which time he would be under house arrest.

When Rimma Shirakova and some KGB officers arrived at Oswald's hotel to escort him to the train station on the afternoon of 21 October, they found him unconscious in the bathtub of his room with superficial cuts on his wrists. Oswald had written a suicide note stating, "I have made such a long journey to find death, but I love life."[18] Oswald never was in any danger of death as a result of the scratches to his wrists, but the Soviet authorities did take him to Moscow's Botkin Hospital and put him under watch in a psychiatric ward. Given the time and expense this American was causing for the Soviets, it is highly unusual that they did not pass responsibility for the nuisance over to the American Embassy.

Oswald was released from the hospital on 28 October and placed under observation at another hotel with the expenses paid for by the Soviets. On Saturday, 31 October, Oswald left his hotel and took a taxi to the American Embassy in Moscow. He walked into the consular section and met with the Saturday duty officer. Oswald told this American diplomat that he had come to Moscow to seek Soviet citizenship, that he had served as a Marine radar operator in Japan, and that in order to earn Soviet citizenship, he was prepared to share with Soviet authorities any sensitive information he had learned as a Marine radar operator.

In such a situation, standard operating procedure would be for the consular officer to send an immediate message alerting CIA and the Naval Criminal Investigative Service (NCIS). CIA and NCIS officers in Washington and Japan would promptly investigate to determine what classified or sensitive information from Atsugi was in danger of compromise. The U-2s at Atsugi would have immediately jumped to their attention. Any consideration of further U-2 over-flights would be postponed until the new risks could be

[18] *Reclaiming History* by Vincent Bugliosi, p. 571-585

thoroughly assessed. Indeed, the Americans did not fly U-2's over the Soviet Union for the next five months, despite a critical intelligence requirement to do so.[19]

As noted previously, Oswald's visit to the American Embassy prompted a remarkable about-face on the part of the KGB. The KGB has long claimed that this about-face in their attitude was because they were embarrassed about Oswald's attempted suicide and did not want it to disrupt the "warming trend" in Soviet-American relations following Premier Khrushchev's September 1959 visit to the US. Anyone who believes that claim must believe that the KGB was a charity. But, the KGB was not a charity, nor for that matter is America's own CIA.

If an intelligence service invests time and money in a person, it is because that intelligence service thinks that person can provide something useful in return. Had the KGB only been concerned about how a half-hearted suicide attempt by a psychologically unstable American kid might impact Soviet-American relations, they simply would have returned the kid to American authorities in a polite and friendly fashion.

No, one does not need to be a professional intelligence officer to see what really happened here. At first, the KGB tried to get Oswald out of the USSR quietly without drawing the attention of the American authorities. Then, after his visit to the American Embassy and his threat to reveal what he had learned as a Marine radar operator in Japan, the KGB abruptly decided that they needed to isolate Oswald from the American authorities.

---

[19] www.spyflight.co.uk

The common sense reason the KGB wanted to isolate Oswald from American authorities was to deny American counterintelligence the opportunity to question him about exactly what sensitive information he had provided to the KGB and exactly when. Jim Angleton from CIA counterintelligence would have been particularly anxious to question Oswald about any information he might have provided relating to the super-secret U-2 flights out of Atsugi. As discussed in the previous chapter, Angleton had learned from the CIA spy inside Soviet military intelligence, Colonel Popov, that the KGB had recruited a source on the U-2 in mid-1958. Moreover, U-2 #360 had just crashed under suspicious circumstances outside of Atsugi in September 1959, just weeks prior to Oswald's arrival in Moscow. Might Oswald know anything about that suspicious crash? Might he be the source the KGB recruited in mid-1958?

To add one final element to the intrigue, at the time of Oswald's arrival in Moscow, the KGB knew that the CIA knew that the KGB had recruited a new source on the U-2 in mid-1958. The KGB knew this because they had arrested Colonel Popov in early 1959, and under brutal interrogation, Popov had told them so.

***

With the endorsement of KGB Chairman Shelepin as well as Foreign Minister Gromyko and the Central Committee, the 20-year-old Oswald was given VIP treatment when he arrived in Minsk on 7 January 1960. He was officially welcomed by the Mayor of Minsk and assigned a prestigious apartment in central Minsk with a beautiful view of the Svislach River. The apartment was being refurbished for him by direct order of the Central Committee of the Communist Party of the USSR. While awaiting completion of this refurbishing, he resided free of charge in the city's finest hotel, the Hotel Minsk. He received a salary from a cushy "job" arranged for him by the KGB in an electronics factory, as well as a generous KGB monthly stipend. Together, his salary and stipend provided him an income equivalent to what a high-ranking Communist Party official received at the time.

The KGB also assigned three young people to befriend Oswald, tutor him in Russian, and report back to them on everything he did and said. The three young people were Rosa Kuznetsova, an attractive blond, Ella German, an equally attractive brunette, and Pavel Golovachev, the wayward son of a famous Soviet Air Force general. With all the money he could need, a beautiful apartment, stunning and willing women, as well as social recognition, Oswald in Minsk enjoyed a lifestyle far beyond anything that he ever experienced in America.

Meanwhile, back in the United States, Jack Kennedy was preparing for the November 1960 Presidential elections against his Republican opponent, Vice President Richard Nixon. One of Kennedy's principal campaign themes was that the fiscally conservative Eisenhower/Nixon administration had under-spent on national defense and, thus, allowed the Soviets to take the lead in the deployment of Intercontinental Ballistic Missiles (ICBMs) which could deliver nuclear weapons to the American homeland within a matter of minutes. Kennedy asserted that a missile gap had developed between the US and the USSR that left Americans vulnerable.

Through mid-1959, Eisenhower and Nixon had been fully confident that talk of a missile gap was nonsense, thanks to the combined efforts of the U-2s and Colonel Popov. To protect these strategically important intelligence sources, however, they could not responsibly reveal the secret basis of their confidence to the American people.

By late 1959, the Pentagon began echoing the claims that the Soviets were accelerating deployments of new ICBMs, Colonel Popov had been arrested and would soon be executed, and the U-2 flights over the Soviet Union had been placed on indefinite stand down because of the perceived risks. Unable to convince the White House to authorize new U-2 flights using American pilots, the CIA's Dick Bissell turned to the British for help. Until this point, the British had been happy to receive the U-2 intelligence but had been distinctly skittish about getting involved directly, even refusing basing rights in the UK for the U-2 over-flights. Nonetheless, Bissell succeeded in convincing the UK government to allow British pilots to fly American U-2s from a base in Pakistan over the Soviet Union on two occasions, 6 December 1959 and 10 February 1960. Both flights went smoothly.[20]

With the missile gap campaign rhetoric mounting and the Pentagon breaking ranks with the White House on the issue, President Eisenhower finally authorized an American-piloted U-2 over-flight from Pakistan on 9 April, which likewise went smoothly. At Bissell's request, the president authorized a second U-2 over-flight from Pakistan, weather permitting, up until a cutoff date of 1 May. The President did not want any flights after that date because he was scheduled

[20] www.spyflight.co.uk

to meet with Soviet Premier Khrushchev in Paris on 15 May. The plane designated for this second flight was U-2 #360, the same plane that had mysteriously crash-landed outside of Atsugi the previous September. The designated pilot was Francis Gary Powers.

When Powers failed to arrive at his designated landing point in Norway, Bissell understood that he had either crashed or had been shot down over Soviet sovereign territory. Bissell calmed a nervous White House by noting that this would not be a repeat of the 1958 embarrassment in Indonesia. Bissell assured them that neither the pilot nor the plane could survive a crash from an altitude of fourteen miles. Moreover, Bissell assured the White House that unlike Sukarno, Premier Khrushchev would handle the matter quietly so as not to disrupt the 15 May Paris Summit. After all, Khrushchev had never made a public issue of earlier U-2 flights or even of the earlier over-flights by the retrofitted RB-47 bombers. Why would he do so now and disrupt the "warming trend" in Soviet-American relations?

Accordingly, the American government executed the pre-arranged cover story, announcing publicly that an experimental weather aircraft had suffered navigational problems, disappeared, and presumably crashed. The Soviet government responded that an American plane had indeed crashed a thousand miles deep inside Soviet sovereign territory, but it was a spy plane, not an experimental weather aircraft. The American government indignantly retorted that it was a weather plane. When President Eisenhower himself publicly stuck to the pre-arranged cover story, Premier Khrushchev pounced. In a public speech, he announced to the world that the pilot of the American spy plane was "alive and kicking" inside a Soviet prison cell. Khrushchev went on to exploit the incident to scuttle the 15 May Paris Summit.

The CIA had committed a cardinal sin; they had gotten caught. Moreover, they had allowed the President of the United States to be caught out in a public lie. Allen Dulles offered to resign, but the offer was declined. Eisenhower was not the type to make any of his subordinates a scapegoat. However, the White House did direct Dulles to provide a comprehensive, classified briefing to a closed session of the publicly outraged leadership of the Senate and House, who had been kept completely in the dark about the U-2 program.

Dulles did not expect to politically survive the Congressional briefing. Dutifully, he and his aides showed the Congressional leadership the incredible U-2 photography and explained how the photography confirmed the President's continued confidence in America's nuclear supremacy. Then, an amazing thing happened. The congressional leadership rose and gave the CIA a secret standing ovation. Further accusations of a missile gap quietly disappeared from Presidential campaign speeches.

***

There was, of course, no real warming trend in Soviet-American relations at the time of Oswald's arrival in Moscow. Khrushchev's visit to the United States in September 1959 had served the political objective of confirming the Soviet premier's legitimacy as a world leader. Once that objective had been achieved, it was back to business as usual, especially for the KGB.

For example, just a few weeks after Khrushchev's visit to the US in September and days before Oswald's unexpected arrival in Moscow in October, the Soviet government sent a delegation of energy experts to conduct exchanges with American energy experts. Hidden on the delegation were sabotage specialists from Department 13 of the First Chief Directorate of the KGB, who were assigned to conduct reconnaissance of oil and gas pipelines as well as electric power grids in Texas and the American Southwest that would be targets for sabotage during a time of war. [21] Khrushchev's decision to make a fanfare of the U-2 shoot down and to scuttle the Paris Summit is additional evidence that the Kremlin saw no further advantage in diplomatic dealing with the lame duck Eisenhower administration and, instead, was establishing a hard line in anticipation of the next president.

The pampered treatment afforded Lee Harvey Oswald after his visit to the American Embassy in Moscow was not because of the non-existent "warming trend," but rather because Oswald was a pawn in the CIA-KGB spy versus spy contest regarding the U-2. Once that contest had been decided, the KGB had no further need to keep him isolated, and thus, he became more expendable. This worried Lee Harvey Oswald as he confided to his KGB supplied "friend" Ella German.

***

---

[21] *The Sword and the Shield* by Christopher Andrew and Vasili Mitrokhin, p. 360

Suggestions for further reading:

1. *Legend: The Secret World of Lee Harvey Oswald* by Edward Jay Epstein, Reader's Digest Press, 1978.

A ground-breaking book based on extensive conversations with James Jesus Angleton. A must read.

2. *Reclaiming History: The Assassination of President John F. Kennedy* by Vincent Bugliosi, W.W. Norton, 2007.

Essential reading for anyone interested in a factual understanding of the Kennedy assassination tragedy. Bugliosi's scholarship is awe-inspiring, but he does not have an accurate feel of the deceptive world of clandestine intelligence.

3. *Ike's Spies: Eisenhower and the Espionage Establishment* by Stephen Ambrose, Doubleday, 1981.

A bit dated in places but remains essential reading for anyone who wishes to understand the early history of the Cold War.

Chapter 5
Cuba: The KGB "Bridgehead"

On New Years Day 1959, Lee Harvey Oswald had just returned stateside from Japan, Mary Meyer was helping Jack Kennedy lower the publicity on his sexual affair with Pamela Turnure, and Dick Bissell was settling into his new job as chief of CIA clandestine operations. Meanwhile, Fidel Castro, his brother, Raul, Che Guevara and their band of a few hundred bearded revolutionaries entered Havana and seized control of the Cuban government. Without significant help from any foreign intelligence service, the Cuban people had risen up, overthrown the corrupt military dictatorship of General Fulgencio Batista, and installed a left wing, revolutionary government just 90 miles from the United States.

Fidel was nearly as surprised as both Washington and Moscow clearly were. Cuba became an emotional inspiration to would-be revolutionaries worldwide, including Lee Oswald. Moreover, Cuba became a strategic inspiration for Cord Meyer's old nemesis from the international student movement, Aleksandr Nikolayevich Shelepin, as he ascended to become the ambitious new chairman of the Soviet KGB.

Shelepin, as a well-informed KGB officer, understood that

the Soviets were losing the battle for the hearts and minds of Europe, both East and West. He, like Eisenhower, knew that in a nuclear confrontation, the United States would suffer grievously yet survive, while the USSR would be totally and utterly annihilated. In contrast, the Cuban Revolution offered a more promising strategy for communist underdogs to defeat corrupt international imperialism from within. Cuba inspired Shelepin's strategic vision of using sabotage and subversion "to bring imperialism to its knees in the Third World."[22]

Just as the KGB Chairman understood the opportunity, President Eisenhower and, in turn, President Kennedy understood the broad strategic threat that Castro's Cuba represented to the United States. If an indigenous revolution could succeed in Cuba, then one could succeed in Central America and in Mexico as well. That, in turn, could threaten political stability in America's own Southwest. To both presidents, Castro's Cuba represented "a clear and present danger" to US national security. Both Presidents were equally determined to respond to that danger.

Given the strategic stakes, Shelepin moved forcefully to assert KGB control over the entirety of Soviet relations with Cuba. He assigned to Havana a senior KGB officer Aleksandr Ivanovich Alekseyev and had him named to serve concurrently as the Soviet Ambassador to Cuba, moving aside the cautious career diplomats from the Soviet Foreign Ministry. Shelepin, having himself made a name as a successful saboteur and guerilla leader against the Nazis during World War II, was personally at ease in directing Department 13 of his KGB's First Chief Directorate to work with the new Cuban

[22] *The World Was Going Our Way* by Andrew and Mitrokhin, p. 33-57

intelligence service in recruiting, training, and deploying sabotage and guerilla warfare specialists beyond Havana to Mexico and Nicaragua in search of other indigenous revolutionaries who might, in time, develop into another Castro. Finally, to underscore his determination to defeat America in its own backyard, Shelepin changed the KGB code name for Cuba from "YOUNTSIE" ("youngsters" in English) to "AVANPOST" ("bridgehead").

KGB documents from 1959 that have become public since the end of the Cold War describe the profile of the potential saboteurs that Department 13 was ordered to recruit for this important mission. The desired profile matched exactly the profile of Lee Harvey Oswald when he arrived in Moscow in October 1959. One of the sabotage and assassination specialists from Department 13 that Shelepin assigned to Mexico City was Valeri Vladomirovich Kostikov. The KGB has long, albeit reluctantly, conceded that Oswald met clandestinely with Kostikov and his KGB colleagues, Oleg Maximovich Nechiporenko and Pavel Antonovich Yatskov, in Mexico City during late September 1963, seven weeks before Oswald assassinated President Kennedy.

***

According to his official biography, Fidel Castro was born on 13 August 1926, but in fact, he was born a year later on 13 August 1927. In 1941, Fidel's father, Angel Castro, paid a bribe to get a new birth certificate that listed Fidel's date of birth as 1926 versus 1927 because the fourteen-year-old Fidel needed to be fifteen to gain admittance as a boarding student to the most prestigious high school in Havana. For some reason, Fidel never bothered to correct this small deception when he got older.[23]

Fidel's father was a self-made businessman. Born a peasant in Spain, Angel served in colonial Cuba as a Spanish soldier and subsequently emigrated there after independence. He settled in Oriente Province in the eastern part of the island where the dominant landowner was the New Orleans-based United Fruit Company. Thanks to hard work and austere living, Angel saved enough money first to lease a plot of land from United Fruit and then to buy his own farm in Biran. Eventually, Angel came to own 5,000 acres of his own land and lease an additional 25,000 from United Fruit. Fidel's mother, Lina Ruz, was a servant girl in Angel's home who eventually bore him three sons and four daughters. When Fidel turned seven, Angel and Lina had an official church marriage to facilitate the boy's entrance into the best Catholic grade school in nearby Santiago, then Cuba's second largest city.

As a child, Fidel grew up hating United Fruit Company and the "ugly American" expatriates who worked there. The American executives lived in their own gated enclaves in the Oriente Province town of Banes, the hometown of General Fulgencio Batista. Young Fidel was particularly resentful that he and other normal Cuban citizens were excluded from entry to nearby Puerto Rico Beach, United Fruit's private resort. One of Fidel's very first acts after seizing power in 1959 was to force United Fruit to open Puerto Rico Beach to the Cuban general public.

---

[23] *The Real Fidel Castro* by Leycester Coltman, p. 9

As World War II ended with the atomic attacks on Hiroshima and Nagasaki, Fidel was a seemingly conventional eighteen-year-old entering the Havana University School of Law. Last minute cramming aside, he paid little attention to his studies, preferring instead to focus his time on becoming prominent politically amongst his fellow students. He opposed American economic and political domination of Cuba, as did virtually all Cuban university students. He married in conventional fashion at the age of twenty-one to Mirta Diaz-Balart, the daughter of a conservative politician from Banes with business ties to United Fruit and political ties to Batista. The general gave the young newlyweds $1,000 to help pay for their honeymoon in the United States. The couple's first child, Fidelito, was born eleven months later. Fidel seemed to be settling down. But, unlike most other students, Fidel was comfortable in actually using violence as a political tool, not just talking about it. As a nineteen-year-old, Fidel had tried to assassinate a student political rival, and two years later, a second student political rival had tried to assassinate Fidel.

After graduation in 1950, he could have landed a high paying job with a prestigious Havana law firm, but instead, Fidel committed himself to politics. His ambition to run for Congress in June 1952 was cut short by the March 1952 coup d'etat that overthrew the democratically elected Cuban President Carlos Prio and returned the military to power under General Batista. Thereafter, Fidel became increasingly radicalized, seeing violent revolution as the only path to real political change in Cuba. Sixteen months later, on 26 July 1953, Fidel and a group of 138 other boys, with no military training and armed only with pistols, shotguns, and a few rifles, launched an attack on the Moncada Military Barracks in Santiago, home to a heavily armed Cuban Army Regiment,

400 soldiers strong.

Lacking an essential intelligence source inside the barracks, the attack was a fiasco from the start. The rebels were surprised to find the 400-man regiment reinforced by an additional 50 soldiers brought in from outlying districts to help with a festival that day in Santiago. Only one group of rebels made it inside the barracks, and they could not find their objective, the barracks' communication room. The other rebels still outside were immediately pinned down by heavy machine gun fire. Some, including Fidel, succeeded in escaping the immediate scene, but virtually all the rebels were either killed or arrested within days.

Then, to his considerable credit, Fidel turned military disaster into political success. In the immediate aftermath of the attack, the army soldiers sought revenge for the deaths of nineteen comrades by brutally torturing and executing the rebels captured at the scene. This became widely known to the Cuban public thanks to journalists who succeeded in surreptitiously photographing rebel corpses with evident signs of torture, including gouged out eyes. When the government tried to bring Fidel to trial in the fall of 1953, he succeeded in turning the tables and putting the government on trial for its use of torture. This trial transformed Fidel in the eyes of Cuban public opinion from an obscure extremist to a seemingly well-intentioned Cuban patriot.

Fidel was sentenced to twenty years in prison, his brother Raul to thirteen years. They were sent to Cuba's Model Prison on the Isle of Pines and kept in humane conditions by Third World standards. They could exercise, read books, send and receive letters, as well as receive family visits once a month. Fidel found the prison confinement frustrating personally but not without its advantages politically; he was becoming more famous in prison than he had ever previously been in freedom. In May 1955, General Batista succumbed to American political pressure and declared a general political amnesty, which led to the release of Fidel and Raul after only eighteen months. In the summer of 1955, while Jack Kennedy was finishing up work on *Profiles in Courage* and then heading off for one last tryst with Gunilla von Post in Europe, Fidel Castro and his brother Raul fled into exile in Mexico City.

***

Shortly after arriving in Mexico City, Fidel met the Argentine Che Guevara and his Peruvian wife, Hilda Gadea. Che and Hilda had themselves met in 1953 while both were working in Guatemala for the left wing government of Jacobo Arbenz. When Tracy Barnes, Dick Bissell, and the CIA's PBSUCCESS operation succeeded in toppling Arbenz during June 1954, Che and Hilda had fled to Mexico City to avoid prison. Radicalized by the Guatemala experience, they, too, became communists committed to violent revolution as the only path to real political change in Latin America.

The first meeting between Fidel and Che during the fall of 1955 lasted from dinner one day until dawn of the following day. Che recounted his experiences in Guatemala. Fidel discussed his plans to return to Cuba with an armed group of revolutionaries to overthrow the Batista regime and free Cuba from American economic and political domination. Both shared intense animosity towards the United Fruit

Company, which they believed called the shots on US government policy towards Latin America, including Cuba and Guatemala. As an Argentine, Che accepted Fidel's natural leadership of the Cuban revolutionary movement, and the two became ideological partners forever after.

Fidel and Che had big plans, but they both recognized that they had no money, no weapons, and, importantly, no military training to successfully carry out their plans. To help out on the latter two points, the 28-year-old Fidel approached a 63-year-old retired Spanish Army Colonel named Alberto Bayo. During the 1936-1939 Spanish Civil War, Colonel Bayo sided with the Soviet-backed Republicans against the Nazi-backed forces of Francisco Franco. Although it is not known whether Bayo himself cooperated with the KGB during the Civil War, he was certainly close to known KGB operatives like Vittorio Vidali.

Following the Republican defeat, both Bayo and Vidali fled to exile in Mexico City. Vidali is known to have remained in contact with the KGB and participated with the famous KGB operative Josef Grigulevich in planning the KGB's 1940 assassination of Leon Trosky in Mexico City. Bayo earned his living by teaching and running a furniture business. At their very first meeting, Bayo agreed to Fidel's request that he resign from his teaching position and sell his business in order to train and support the young Cuban revolutionaries. One of Bayo's key precepts for the young revolutionaries was the KGB mantra, "Death to spies."[24]

---

[24] SMERSH, the evil organization of the early James Bond novels, was the true name of the Soviet counterintelligence organization during World War Two responsible for eliminating spies. SMERSH is an acronym for "death to spies."

To raise funds, Fidel visited the United States for six weeks in October and November 1955 and met with Cuban exile groups opposed to the Batista military dictatorship. Batista's intelligence operatives in the US, as well as America's own security services, kept a close eye on Fidel's progress in fundraising with the intent to disrupt any concrete operational planning. In early 1956, Mexican authorities temporarily detained Fidel and Che at the request of the American Embassy. Subsequently, in June 1956, Mexican police raided two safe houses and confiscated most of Fidel's stockpile of weapons.

Likewise for the purpose of fundraising, in late 1955, Raul Castro introduced Che to Nikolai Sergeyevich Leonov, a KGB Latin American specialist assigned to the Soviet Embassy in Mexico City. Raul had first befriended Leonov during early 1953 in Prague at an international youth conference sponsored by the Prague-based International Union of Students and its then Vice President, Aleksandr Shelepin. After the conference, Raul, 22, and Leonov, 25, traveled across the Atlantic together on an Italian freighter bound for Cuba and Mexico. Raul disembarked in Havana and joined Fidel in the final preparations for the Moncada attack while Leonov continued on to his KGB assignment in Mexico City. They reconnected two years later when Raul and Fidel were released from prison and fled into exile.

The Soviet Embassy turned down the request for funding from Che, so sometime in 1956, Raul introduced Leonov directly to Fidel. Although he considered Raul and Che more reliable ideologically, Leonov was impressed with Fidel's charisma and revolutionary zeal. Leonov established regular clandestine communications with Fidel and offered encouragement as well as moral support. However, Leonov's

KGB superiors continued to disapprove funding for Fidel, at least directly.

Fidel's funding problems were finally solved in August 1956 by former Cuban President Carlos Prio, who was then living in exile in the United States. The left wing Prio detested the right wing usurper Batista. Prio also had access to plentiful funding, generally believed to be monies absconded from official Cuban coffers while he was president. At a clandestine meeting just across the border into Texas, Prio agreed to fund Fidel's effort to overthrow Batista with $100,000-- an enormous sum of money in 1956.

Later that same August, Fidel received a visit from Jose Antonio Echeverria, a rival for leadership of the revolutionary movement in Cuba. Echeverria had formed a new group based inside Havana University named the Revolutionary Directorate (DR) that had much in common with Fidel's own 26 July Revolutionary Movement (MR-26-7) but was separate from it. This attempt at conciliation amongst like-minded groups opposed to Batista was probably encouraged by the joint paymaster, ex-President Prio.

Both Fidel and Echeverria agreed that a unified effort would have greater chances of success than a divided effort, but as is common in such circumstances, neither man would agree to cede leadership to the other. A few weeks after this meeting, one of Echeverria's lieutenants, Rolando Cubela, assassinated Batista's intelligence chief, Antonio Blanco Rico. Fidel publicly condemned the assassination as unjustified, but his objective was as much to reduce the revolutionary credit gained by the rival DR as it was to express moral outrage.

***

The $100,000 from ex-President Prio enabled Fidel to replenish his cache of weapons, train more rebels, and buy a decrepit old yacht appropriately named the *Granma*. Purchased on 10 October 1956 via a clandestine intermediary in order to camouflage its purpose, the *Granma* would transport Fidel's rebels back to invade Cuba. The 50-foot yacht was outfitted for 12 people comfortably and 20 maximum; Fidel had 82 rebels plus their weapons and equipment.

The Mexican police were again tipped off that Fidel was preparing an imminent armed action against Cuba. A police officer friendly to Fidel's cause warned him on 21 November that he had 72 hours to leave Mexico or face arrest and deportation. So, Fidel slipped out of Mexico City on 23 November, heading for the Caribbean port of Tuxpan where the *Granma* was still completing repairs. The police tracked him and alerted the Batista government that he was about to depart by sea. His enemy forewarned and with an overloaded yacht of questionable seaworthiness, Fidel's chances of success seemed slim, indeed, but he had no other option. Shortly after midnight of 24-25 November, the *Granma* slipped out of port into the Caribbean on its way to a beach in Southeastern Cuba near the town of Niquero.

Fidel expected the voyage to take five days. Thus, he had signaled to MR-26-7 operatives already inside Cuba to launch a series of attacks on government buildings in Southeastern Cuba to coincide with his expected landing on 30 November. As it turned out, the voyage took seven days, so the attacks proved premature and served merely to provide further warning to the Cuban military in the area.

The *Granma* finally reached its destination at dawn on 2 December. The yacht ran aground several hundred yards from the beach. Waist-deep water and soft sand made it impossible for the men to offload their heavy weapons. Within a few hours, a Cuban naval patrol boat had spotted the grounded *Granma* and alerted the army to the rebels' location. Forced to move inland with no further delay, Fidel had to abandon the yacht with much of their ammunition, medical supplies, and communications gear still on it.

On 5 December, the rebels were ambushed by a Cuban militia detachment. Forty-six of the 82 rebels were killed or captured, and the others were forced to scatter in small groups. The army deployed search planes and more troops to the area in an effort to wipe out the rebel band entirely. The landing had been another military disaster for Fidel. By the end of December, only 19 of the original 82 had managed to regroup, including Fidel, Raul, Che, and the group's intelligence chief, Ramiro Valdes.

Fidel's rebel band had survived politically, however. In January, they made their presence known by coming down out of the hills to launch a successful attack on the small ten-man militia post located at the coastal village of La Plata, 70 miles west of Santiago. The rebels killed two of the soldiers during the attack but won public support by releasing the remaining eight unharmed after confiscating their weapons and food. Then, with crucial support from local peasants, Fidel and his men started about the mundane task of establishing a secure base of operations deep inside the rugged Sierra Maestra Mountains, which they proudly referred to as the "Liberated Zone."

His revolutionary rival, Jose Antonio Echeverria, disdained Fidel's slow and pretentious guerilla efforts in the isolated Sierra Maestra. Echeverria and his DR faction preferred to go straight for the jugular via sabotage and assassination operations in the capital, Havana. In retaliation for these DR operations, the Batista regime "temporarily" closed Havana University on 30 November 1956; it would not re-open until early 1959. Echeverria and his lieutenant, Rolando Cubela, then attempted to topple the government by mounting a direct attack to assassinate Batista.

On 13 March 1957, Cubela coordinated an attack on the Presidential Palace while Echeverria took control of a Havana radio station; their plan was to kill Batista and then announce to the nation the formation of a new government of national unity. A spy inside the DR group forewarned Batista, however. Echeverria and thirty-five other DR militants were killed. Cubela managed to escape Havana and within a year had established his own group of DR guerillas operating from the Escambray Mountains of central Cuba.

Three weeks later on 6 April, a group of career Cuban Army officers who understood that the Batista regime was fast losing legitimacy in Cuban as well as international eyes, launched their own coup d'etat attempt against the general. This, too, failed after being betrayed to Batista by another spy inside that group. A major purge of the officer corps followed, which made the army increasingly unwilling to risk their lives in fighting for the corrupt government.

Although Fidel's small band of rebels was even now only 120 men strong, he was again winning on the political battleground. He publicly criticized the efforts by Echeverria and the officers as misguided. Then, in May, he attracted international press attention by coming down out of the hills again to launch another successful guerilla attack on the fifty-man coastal militia post at Uvero, fifty miles west of Santiago.

***

The corrupt Batista regime collapsed of its own weight in 1958, leaving Fidel Castro alone to fill the political vacuum. The collapse began in March when the US government announced an embargo on further shipments of weapons to the Batista government. In an attempt to regain Washington's confidence, General Batista ordered an all-out summer offensive to crush Castro's Liberated Zone in the Sierra Maestra once and for all. The offensive pitted 10,000 soldiers supported by artillery, planes, and tanks against Fidel's lightly armed rebels, now 300 men strong. Given the 33 to 1 correlation of forces, success of the offensive should have been pre-ordained. The rebels were, indeed, pressed at one point. However, the offensive eventually failed, in good part because the rebels fought bravely and smartly, but in even larger part because the corrupt and brutal Batista regime no longer commanded the loyalty of the government's own troops.

When the summer offensive collapsed, army morale disintegrated. The soldiers' reluctance to fight allowed Fidel's rebels to break out from the Sierra Maestra and maneuver westward toward Havana. At this point, Cubela's DR guerillas in the Escambray agreed to a unity manifesto drafted by Fidel that recognized the revolutionary leader of the MR-26-7 group. By November, the rebel union controlled most of

Oriente and Las Villas provinces outside of the provincial capitals of Santiago and Santa Clara.

Recognizing that the Batista regime had lost legitimacy, Washington maneuvered to find a viable alternative that would be more compatible with US interests than the avowed revolutionary Fidel Castro. To that end, President Eisenhower sent a special envoy in early December to advise Batista that he had irrevocably lost Washington's confidence and support. With American encouragement and Batista's reluctant concurrence, senior Cuban Army officers began organizing a new government and sent an emissary to Fidel on 28 December to probe whether he would be willing to join as a cabinet member.

Fidel saw the maneuver for what it was, an attempt to sideline him, and ordered Che to join up with the DR guerillas under Rolando Cubela in an attack on Santa Clara, the capital of Las Villas province. Together, Che and Cubela commanded 340 guerillas to confront 4,000 Cuban Army soldiers garrisoned in Santa Clara. The army enlisted men in particular were sympathetic to the rebel cause, however, so after a few minor skirmishes, the soldiers surrendered. The Battle of Santa Clara, including a photo of Che standing in front of a tank with his arm in a sling, has become part of the legend of the Cuban Revolution. In fact, there were only a handful of casualties on either side, and Che only hurt his arm by falling off a wall.

Nonetheless, the rebel capture of Santa Clara had the political effect intended by Fidel. Batista resigned minutes after midnight on 31 December and fled the country with hundreds of millions of Cuban government dollars. Batista had hoped to settle at his home in Daytona Beach, Florida, but President Eisenhower, trying to salvage some credibility with the Cuban people, denied Batista asylum in the US. He was eventually accepted by Portugal.

Fidel ordered Che to get to Havana as quickly as he could and specified that Cubela and the DR guerillas were not to enter the capital until after the MR-26-7 guerillas. Ignoring Che's orders that they remain in Santa Clara, Cubela and his men raced into Havana and seized the presidential palace. The DR militants were well-armed and enjoyed considerable support amongst Havana University students. Hence, two days of delicate negotiations between Che and Cubela were required before the DR rebels agreed to evacuate the Presidential Palace without a fight. Fidel himself proceeded across the island at a careful and measured pace, receiving a hero's welcome at each stop. He finally entered Havana on 9 January after Che had established firm control of the capital.

***

Soviet Premier Khrushchev and the Kremlin leadership were taken by surprise by Fidel's successful seizure of power. KGB Latin American specialist Leonov had maintained regular clandestine communications with Fidel's group since 1956, and the Kremlin had naturally voiced political support for the heroic efforts of the Cuban people. But, realistically, the Soviet Foreign Ministry had not assessed Fidel's chances of overthrowing Batista as being very good. As a result, for three years, the Kremlin had denied requests for concrete military assistance that Fidel had communicated to Moscow via the KGB's Leonov. The first time the Kremlin did overrule the cautious Foreign Ministry and approve an arms shipment was on 27 December 1958, just five days before Fidel declared victory.[25]

Khrushchev moved quickly to recover from this surprise and take advantage of the turn of events, however. He named the aggressive, 40-year-old Aleksandr Shelepin as the new Chairman of the KGB. Shelepin had won his reputation in World War II as a commando conducting daring sabotage and assassination operations behind German lines. He then went on to run KGB operations targeting the international youth movement. Khrushchev designated the new KGB Chairman to lead a government-wide review of Soviet foreign policy towards the Third World. This was an important loss of power and influence for the cautious Foreign Minister Andrei Andreyevich Gromyko vis-à-vis Shelepin and for Soviet diplomats in general vis-à-vis KGB officers.

Chairman Shelepin, who did not hide his own ambitions to succeed Khrushchev as Soviet premier, believed that the worldwide struggle between imperialism and communism was a fight to death. Because of nuclear weapons, he believed that the struggle could not be won in a direct military confrontation. Rather, it would be an indirect fight led by the intelligence services of the opposing sides. The frontlines of this fight would be in the Third World, not in Berlin or on the plains of Europe. Convinced that the KGB could "bring imperialism to its knees" in the Third World, Shelepin's first target was Central America, the backyard of the United

---

[25] *The World Was Going Our Way* by Christopher Andrew and Vasili Mitrokhin, p. 33-57

States. Specifically, his targets were Nicaragua in the South and Mexico in the North. Fidel's Cuba would be "the bridgehead," the Soviet launching pad into Central America in the same way that Japan was America's launching pad into the Asian mainland.

Immediately upon becoming KGB Chairman, Shelepin created the first ever Cuba Office at KGB headquarters with Castro's KGB contact, Leonov, in charge, assisted by Oleg Nechiporenko. In July 1959, he dispatched Leonov to Mexico City to meet with Fidel's intelligence chief, Ramiro Valdes. They agreed that the KGB would open a clandestine office in Havana as soon as possible. In October, Aleksandr Ivanovich Alekseyev transferred from his post as the senior KGB officer in Buenos Aires and became the KGB's first "Man in Havana." Alekseyev had made his name within the KGB as a result of his close relationship with left wing Argentine President Arturo Frondizi.

Fidel and Alekseyev hit it off personally at their first meeting that October. They agreed to establish trade relations as an initial step towards full diplomatic relations between Cuba and the USSR. Details of a long-term trade agreement under which Cuba bartered sugar in exchange for Soviet oil were worked out in Mexico City when Khrushchev's deputy Vice Premier Anastas Ivanovich Mikoyan visited in November 1959. When Mikoyan paid a subsequent visit to Cuba in February 1960 to formally sign the trade agreement, he came away deeply impressed by the revolutionary zeal of Castro and his leadership colleagues. In March, Alekseyev succeeded in putting Castro on the KGB payroll via a commonly used cover guise of royalties for the rights to publish Fidel's speeches in Russian.[26] Payments like these don't allow an intelligence operative to give orders to a foreign head of state; rather, they are designed to build friendship and influence with the target.

In May 1960, US-Soviet relations turned publicly sour after the shooting down of Francis Gary Powers and his U-2. In the aftermath of that incident, Soviet Premier Khrushchev declared in July that the Monroe Doctrine was "dead" and that "Soviet artillerymen could support the Cuban people with rocket weapons" if the Americans intervened in Cuba.[27] Khrushchev and Castro met face to face for the first time in New York City during the September 1960 General Assembly of the United Nations, at which Khrushchev famously denounced the West while pounding his shoe on the table. Khrushchev publicly declared himself a *fidelista* and referred to Fidel as a beacon of socialism in Latin America.

In short order, the KGB's man in Havana, Alekseyev, was promoted and given the additional title of Ambassador Alekseyev, the senior-most Soviet envoy to the Cuban government. Alekseyev's Cuban intelligence counterpart, Ramiro Valdes, was soon sending young Cuban intelligence officers to the KGB training school in the isolated Soviet city of Minsk where, by honest coincidence, they became neighbors with the young American, Lee Oswald.[28]

---

[26] *One Hell of a Gamble* by Aleksandr Fursenko and Timothy Naftali, p. 45

[27] Ibid, p. 52, quotes Khrushchev's 1960 threat to defend Cuba with Soviet based missiles.

[28] *Legend* by Edward Jay Epstein, map preceding p. 93

***

Washington did not know what to make of Fidel during the first half of 1959. Was he a communist or not? Conservatives within the Eisenhower administration quickly concluded that he was a communist and, thus, that the CIA should be given the green light to work with more reliably pro-American elements in the Cuban Army to overthrow him. Others, including some inside the CIA, thought that Fidel was a pragmatic Cuban nationalist who would soon come to understand Cuba's economic dependency on US markets and, thus, gradually adopt responsible policies. Fidel, for his part, wanted to keep the Americans guessing for as long as possible to give himself time to solidify his political power base.

In April 1959, Fidel agreed to pay an unofficial visit to the United States at the invitation of the Society of Newspaper Editors. By tacit agreement between the two governments, President Eisenhower arranged to be out of Washington during the time that Fidel visited the city. However, Fidel did meet "unofficially" with Vice President Richard Nixon, as well as secretly with the CIA's top analytic expert on Latin American communism, Frank Droller, who used the alias Dr. Frank Bender. Nixon concluded that Fidel was either very naïve about communism or very clever in hiding his communist views; whichever, Nixon reported to President Eisenhower that Fidel was irrevocably anti-American. "Dr. Bender" spent three hours talking with Fidel and concluded that he was not only not a communist but was actually an anti-communist with whom the CIA could work to mutual benefit. For his part, Fidel came away with the understanding that Washington didn't care what he was as long as he was not a communist.

Events during the second half of 1959 gave greater credence to Nixon's political judgment than that of "Dr. Bender." In October, at the same time that the KGB's Alekseyev arrived in Havana, Fidel promoted the two most prominent communists in his government to key positions; Raul Castro became Minister of Defense, assuming control of the national security elements of the government, and Che Guevara became Central Bank Governor, assuming control of the economy. A well-regarded anti-communist revolutionary, Huber Matos, immediately resigned as military governor of Camaguey province in protest. An angry Fidel traveled to Camaguey personally to arrest Matos who was sentenced to 20 years in prison for treason in a show trial during December 1959. After serving out his full term, Matos was released in 1979 and fled to Miami.

Fidel's public shift towards communism during late 1959, coupled with Mikoyan's visit to Havana in February 1960 to sign the Cuban-Soviet long term trade agreement, settled the policy debate within Washington's power elite. On 13 March, Senator Jack Kennedy asked his Sunday supper guest Ian Fleming what James Bond would do about Fidel. Four days later, on 17 March, President Eisenhower signed the covert order designating the communist government of Cuba as a clear and present danger to US national security and, accordingly, directed the CIA to overthrow Fidel Castro.

***

Suggestions for further reading:

1. *The Real Fidel Castro* by Sir Leyster Coltman, Yale University Press, 2003.

A thoughtful and balanced biography of Fidel by the late Ambassador Coltman, the UK's envoy to Havana during 1991-1994.

2. *One Hell of a Gamble: Khrushchev, Castro, and Kennedy 1958-1964, The Secret History of the Cuban Missile Crisis* by Aleksandr Fursenko and Timothy Naftali, W.W. Norton and Company, 1997.

An outstanding history of this period which draws extensively on declassified Russian archives to provide a Soviet perspective Balanced and insightful. The cover photo of JFK is from the personal archives of Jim and Cicely Angleton.

3. *Cuba: The Pursuit of Freedom* by Hugh Thomas, Harper and Row, 1971.

A dated history of Cuba that remains insightful regarding Fidel during the later 1950s and early 1960s.

Chapter 6
Camelot Meets Communism

On Inauguration Day, 20 January 1961, the contrast between the outgoing Eisenhower White House and the incoming Kennedy White House could not have been more palpable. The Eisenhowers represented experience and reliability: the Kennedys, youth and promise. The Eisenhowers personified the staid, domestic image of a Grant Wood painting: the Kennedys, the style and cosmopolitan flair of a Renoir. An uncertain American electorate had split exactly down the middle on which style they wanted to carry the country into the new decade. In the end, Kennedy had eked out a victory by the slimmest of electoral margins, some say thanks to vote fraud engineered with the help of Chicago mafia boss Sam Giancana.

As a gesture of respect to the New Deal of iconic Democratic President Franklin Delano Roosevelt (FDR), Kennedy adopted the moniker JFK and christened his own Presidency the New Frontier. Thanks largely to the grace and beauty of the 31-year-old First Lady, however, the image of the new administration that truly captured America's heart and imagination was Camelot.

President Kennedy's speech that day, drafted by his faithful scribe Ted Sorensen, remains arguably the most inspiring inaugural address in American history to date. Starting with, "Let the word go forth from this time and place, to friend and foe alike,that the torch has been passed to a new generation of American," and culminating in, "And so, my fellow Americans, ask not what your country can do for you, ask what you can do for your country," the new President's words catalyzed a rebirth of our nation's optimistic idealism and reenergized our belief in American exceptionalism.

With Cuba and the Soviet Union on his mind, Kennedy's inaugural address also suggested hope for a new era of international relations with the words, "To those nations who would make themselves our adversary, we offer not a pledge but a request that both sides begin anew the quest for peace... Remembering on both sides that civility is not a sign of weakness and sincerity is always subject to proof... Let both sides join in creating a new endeavor, not a new balance of power, but a new world of law, where the strong are just, and the weak are secure, and the peace preserved."

Just eight days later, however, President Kennedy gave Allen Dulles and his deputy Dick Bissell the green light to continue preparations for a CIA-backed invasion of Cuba with the objective of overthrowing the Soviet-backed communist government of Fidel Castro.

The decision to support an invasion of Cuba was one of those tough decisions that, in the final analysis, only the President can make. There were three possible outcomes for President Kennedy: (1) say yes and commit to winning but thereby belie the sincerity of his inaugural words; (2) say no and demonstrate the sincerity of those words but be cast as a weakling in the same way that his father had been during World War II; or worst of all, (3) say yes but prevaricate and lose, thereby appearing both insincere and weak. It is not uncommon in Washington, even today, for people with exceptionally high IQs to let themselves get trapped into outcome number 3, and so it was with President Kennedy in the case of the Bay of Pigs.

Observing the indecisiveness in Washington that helped doom the invasion, Soviet Premier Nikita Khrushchev virtually dismissed Kennedy as a serious adversary. Khrushchev was a graduate of Josef Stalin's school of hard knocks. He had been Stalin's ruthless political commissar to the Red Army during the bloody World War II battle of Stalingrad. Winning was all that mattered to him; losing was a sign of weakness. Two months later, in June 1961, during his Vienna Summit meeting with Kennedy, Khrushchev used threats of war in an effort to intimidate the young President into abandoning West Berlin to communist control. Kennedy stood his ground with Khrushchev but admitted later that "he beat the hell out of me."[29] *Two months after that, in August, Khrushchev presented Kennedy a* fait accompli *by building the Berlin Wall to isolate West Berlin from the remainder of the city. Then, underestimating Kennedy as nothing more than a young playboy, Khrushchev made the most important miscalculation of the Cold War: he tried to present Kennedy with another* fait accompli *by ordering the secret deployment of Soviet nuclear missiles to Cuba.*

***

[29] *Mrs. Kennedy* by Barbara Leaming, p. 128

On 2 January 1960, 42-year-old Jack Kennedy formally declared his candidacy for the Democratic presidential nomination. His main opponents were Senator Hubert Humphrey of Minnesota, Senator Wayne Morse of Oregon, and Governor Pat Brown of California, as well as the powerful Senate Majority Leader Lyndon Johnson. A number of party elders, including former President Harry Truman and former First Lady Eleanor Roosevelt, suggested that Kennedy was too young and inexperienced to be President and encouraged him to think about the Vice Presidency. Kennedy moved promptly to nip off that disrespect by the party elders, declaring that he was not interested in the Vice Presidency and was running only for the Presidency. Its vaunted experience notwithstanding, Kennedy also alleged that the Eisenhower administration had miscalculated and allowed a missile gap to develop by not authorizing sufficient funding for America to keep pace with Soviet deployments of intercontinental ballistic missiles (ICBMs).

In March, around the same time Jack met spy novelist Ian Fleming, Jackie became pregnant again. Jackie did not enjoy campaigning under any circumstances, and the pregnancy gave her all the more good reason to limit her participation further. While Jack was off on the campaign trail that spring, Jackie stayed in Georgetown reading the works of Protestant ethicist Reinhold Niebuhr and enjoying the company of her neighbor and best friend, Tony Bradlee. Tony was also pregnant, so for exercise, the two young mothers took regular walks along the towpath of the C&O canal, frequently accompanied by Tony's sister, Mary Meyer. At this time, Mary was earning some extra spending money by renting out a room to Jack's senate staff aide and mistress, Pamela Turnure.

The constant travel around the country required of a presidential candidate meant that Jack and Jackie saw each other infrequently during much of 1960. Jack took that liberty to get to know many available young women. One named Judith Campbell was an attractive 26-year-old divorcee and member of Frank Sinatra's Las Vegas entourage. Sinatra introduced Judy to Kennedy in early February, and their intimate relationship continued for the next two years and well into his Presidency. A month later, Sinatra also introduced Judy to Chicago mafia boss Sam Giancana, with whom she remained involved throughout her affair with Kennedy. Her relationship with Giancana quickly brought Judy onto the radar screen of the FBI. In turn, the FBI stumbled upon her intimate relationship with Kennedy in July, just prior to the Democratic convention.

During May, the headlines were dominated by the Soviet shooting down of Francis Gary Powers in his U-2 spy plane and Premier Khrushchev's political decision to disrupt his scheduled Paris summit meeting with lame duck President Eisenhower. That same month, Jack Kennedy was facing a make or break Democratic primary in West Virginia against Hubert Humphrey. Jack's age was no longer an issue-- Humphrey himself was only 49-- but Jack's religion was.

Family patriarch Joe Kennedy had opposed Jack's running in West Virginia, arguing strenuously that a Roman Catholic could not win in the heavily Protestant state. Jack rarely ignored his father's advice but did so in this case. Jack was convinced that his chances of winning the Democratic nomination depended on his ability to demonstrate that he could win in a Protestant state despite being Catholic. Jack's game plan to win in West Virginia relied heavily on the tireless campaign support of Franklin Delano Roosevelt, Jr.

His father, FDR, was still worshipped by the coal miners and blue collar workers of the state. Moreover, the high profile support for Kennedy from FDR Jr. helped offset criticism from his mother, Eleanor.

Jack and Jackie waited out election night of the West Virginia primary in Georgetown with their friends Ben and Tony Bradlee. After dinner, the foursome tried to see the new Tennessee Williams movie *Suddenly Last Summer,* starring Elizabeth Taylor and Montgomery Clift, but the theater was sold out, and even a serving senator couldn't get tickets. Instead, the two husbands and their pregnant wives went to an adjacent porn theater and saw *Private Property,* featuring the 1950s porn star Katie Manx.[30] When Bobby Kennedy called with the news of a big victory, the two couples took their leave of Ms. Manx, raced to the airport, and flew up to Charleston on the Kennedy family's private plane to join Bobby for the early morning victory celebration. As Jack had predicted, victory in the West Virginia primary virtually assured his subsequent nomination by the Democratic convention the following August.

During the fall presidential campaign itself, Jack faced Richard Nixon, Eisenhower's Vice President of eight years. Nixon had also been a naval officer in the Pacific during World War II, and both men were elected to Congress in 1946. Jack's main campaign theme was to get America moving again, while Nixon promised to continue the peace and prosperity that America had enjoyed under Eisenhower. Only 47 himself, Nixon tried to use his eight years as vice president as proof of his greater experience than the junior

---

[30] *Conversations with Kennedy* by Ben Bradlee, p. 27

senator from Massachusetts. However, a glib comment by Eisenhower during August completely undercut Nixon's strategy. Asked by a reporter to give examples of important contributions that Nixon had made to decision-making during his administration, President Eisenhower joked, "If you give me a week, I might think of one."[31]

On election evening, 8 November, the Kennedys again invited the Bradlees to join them, this time at the Kennedy clan compound at Hyannis Port, Massachusetts. The election was one of the closest in American history and was not decided in Jack's favor until the afternoon of 9 November. Republican Party elders were convinced that vote fraud gave Kennedy victories in Texas and Illinois, without which Nixon would have won. The possibility of fraud was greatest in Illinois, where Jack won by just nine thousand votes out of almost five million cast. Mayor Richard Daley, the Democratic Party boss of Chicago, suspiciously withheld the Chicago election results until late on the morning of 9 November. Before doing so, he told Jack, "With a little bit of luck and the help of a few close friends, you are going to carry Illinois."[32] Subsequently, there was widespread suspicion that Daley's "close friends" included mobster Sam Giancana and that Judy Campbell had played a role as courier between the Kennedy campaign and the Chicago mafia.

Kennedy's inauguration took place Friday, 20 January 1961. After Mass on Sunday, 22 January, he stopped by the Bradlee home and found the front door unlocked as was not uncommon in Georgetown at that time. Ben and Tony

---

[31] *Eisenhower: Soldier and President* by Stephen Ambrose, p. 525

[32] *Conversations with Kennedy* by Bradlee, p. 33

Bradlee were upstairs in their Georgetown home when they heard a familiar voice call out from the first floor. "Isn't there anybody in this house who is going to greet the President of the United States?" [33]

That same evening, the new President and Mrs. Kennedy hosted the first of their many small dinner parties for personal friends in the White House residential quarters. The honored guests at that very special first dinner party were Franklin Delano Roosevelt Jr. of the West Virginia primary and influential journalist Joe Alsop of the Georgetown Sunday Supper Club. About the same time, Mary Meyer's renter, Pamela Turnure, was transferred from her job on Jack Kennedy's senate office staff to become press secretary to the First Lady.

***

In August 1960, Joe Alsop had arranged a dinner at his Georgetown home shortly after the Democratic convention in order to reacquaint the Democratic nominee with Alsop's old school chum and CIA clandestine operations chief, Dick Bissell. Alsop arranged a second, more private meeting between Kennedy and Bissell in October, during which Bissell offered to support Kennedy. Both men came away from these discreet meetings mutually impressed. Afterwards, Bissell compared Kennedy to Caesar in that he was both a superb orator and a man of action, willing to

[33] Ibid, p. 38

make tough decisions. For his part, Kennedy told foreign policy aides who hoped to steal Bissell away from CIA for the number three position at the State Department that they couldn't have him. Kennedy told his aides that he thought it more important for Bissell to remain at CIA as heir apparent to the aging director, Allen Dulles.

During these tête-à-têtes in the midst of a tense presidential election campaign, Bissell may have tipped off Kennedy to the status of CIA plans for an invasion of Cuba. What is certain is that during the campaign, Kennedy aggressively criticized Eisenhower and Nixon for not doing enough to support non-communist Cubans opposed to the Castro regime. These criticisms had special political impact amongst conservative Americans, coming as they did at the same moment as Soviet Premier Khrushchev's theatrical pounding of the table at the United Nation and his public embrace of Fidel in New York City for all the American media to see and report during September 1960. This infuriated Nixon because he could not defend the administration's record without giving away the secret details of ongoing CIA support and training for an invasion force of anti-communist Cuban exiles.

To Nixon, Kennedy's criticism regarding Cuba smacked of the earlier Kennedy allegations of a missile gap, which could not be refuted without giving away the secret U-2s. Not able to respond in detail to Kennedy's criticism but not willing to remain passive in the midst of a neck-and-neck presidential race, the Eisenhower administration reacted by impounding the Cuban airline jet that had brought Castro to New York on the grounds that the Cuban government owed money to US oil companies. Castro was forced to borrow a Soviet jet to take him back to Havana. In October, the

Eisenhower White House placed an embargo on most US exports to Cuba, severely disrupting the Cuban economy. Then, in early January 1961, just days before leaving office, outgoing President Eisenhower formally broke off American diplomatic relations with Cuba.

President-elect Kennedy received his first official brief on the CIA's Cuban invasion operation from Allen Dulles and Dick Bissell on 18 November 1960 at the Kennedy family mansion in Palm Beach. Kennedy learned officially that in March 1960, Eisenhower had authorized $4.4 million of covert funding for the CIA to overthrow Castro in response to Fidel's decision to align Cuba with Moscow. The CIA's initial plan was to establish contact with and provide arms to indigenous anti-communist opposition groups that had sprung up in the Escambray Mountains of South Central Cuba after the arrest and trial of Huber Matos for daring to voice opposition to the increasing communist influence over Castro's government.

These efforts to support internal opposition had progressed too slowly, however, in large part due to the surprising effectiveness of Castro's intelligence chief, Ramiro Valdes, and his deputy in charge of counterintelligence, Manuel "Redbeard" Pineiro. Much later, the CIA would learn that at least some of the "anti-communist opposition groups" were actually double agents working with Redbeard to disrupt American intelligence operations and turn them back against the US.

In August 1960, encouraged directly by President Eisenhower to pick up its pace and authorized an additional $13 million of covert funding, CIA made two important and related decisions: to train a brigade of Cuban exiles to invade the south central coast of Cuba near the city of Trinidad and to contact Chicago mobster Sam Giancana to explore whether the Mafia could help the CIA assassinate Castro. The Cuban exile force, recruited in Florida and trained at a secret base in Guatemala, was 200-men strong by October and had grown to nearly 600 by the time of the November briefing for President-elect Kennedy. During that briefing, Dulles and Bissell stressed that the invasion's chances of success would be minimal without command of the air; there is, however, no record of any mention of the assassination plans. Since Kennedy was only President-elect, the briefing was informational. He was not expected to decide yea or nay. According to Bissell's memoirs, Kennedy's only reaction was to express surprise at the scale of the operation.

***

On Saturday, 28 January 1961, eight days after his inaugural address, now-President Kennedy was expected to make a decision on whether to proceed with preparations for the invasion of Cuba. Allen Dulles and Tracy Barnes, by then Bissell's Deputy, briefed the invasion details to the principal members of the National Security Council, including the president, the vice president, the secretaries of state and defense, the chairman of the Joint Chiefs of Staff, the national security advisor to the president, as well as Assistant Secretary of Defense Paul Nitze. Secretary of State Dean Rusk expressed strong reservations about the propriety of the CIA operation and the negative impact that, win or lose, it would have on US standing in Latin America. National Security Advisor McGeorge Bundy was nervous but deferential to any plan endorsed by Dick Bissell, who had been his professor at Yale.

President Kennedy never had any realistic option to cancel the operation outright after he had made Cuba such an issue during the election campaign. After all his tough talk, it would have been politically disastrous for him to begin his presidency by backing down. Thus, the President maneuvered for time by ordering the CIA to continue and accentuate its planning and the Pentagon to review the CIA planning and report back to the White House on the feasibility of the operation.

In late February, the cautious Pentagon reported ambiguously that the operation had a "fair" chance of success. They agreed with the CIA assessment that command of the air would be essential to the chances of the invasion force getting successfully off the beach. Thereafter, the ultimate success of the operation would depend on either supportive action by other anti-communist elements of the Cuban population or the ability of the invasion force to establish a base of operations in the Escambray Mountains in much the same fashion that Fidel himself had established a base of operations in the Sierra Maestra.

On 11 March, one month prior to the anticipated invasion date, Bissell briefed the President and the other NSC principals on the results of the Pentagon report as well as on the CIA plan to land 750-1,000 men on beaches near the city of Trinidad, close to the Escambray Mountains. At this point, President Kennedy expressed concern that the operation was "too spectacular."[34] He directed that a more remote invasion

---

[34] *The Very Best Men* by Thomas, p. 246

beach be identified. He also stressed that there should be no overt US military action in support of the Cuban exiles and that the CIA covert hand should remain plausibly deniable.

Pursuant to the President's orders, Bissell and his deputy Tracy Barnes selected as the new invasion beach an isolated area 100 miles west of Trinidad with the unfortunate name of the Bay of Pigs. This spot was too distant to allow any realistic chance that the invaders could make it to the Escambray Mountains and establish a base of operations there. Thus, the switch to the Bay of Pigs meant that the invading force would have to stand and fight the Cuban Army long enough for the hoped-for supportive action by other anti-communist elements of the Cuban population.

Bissell and Barnes clearly hoped that this supportive action would include the assassination of Castro, although it has never been clear whether President Kennedy understood this. During the waning months of the Eisenhower administration, Sam Giancana had put the CIA in contact with Santos Trafficante, another mobster, who had lost lucrative gambling interests in Cuba after Castro came to power. Trafficante, in turn, had recruited Castro's personal secretary, Juan Orta Corvado, to poison Fidel. The CIA passed water-soluble poison pills via Giancana and Trafficante to Orta in February 1961, after JFK's assumption of the Presidency. Orta panicked at the last minute, however, and fled to refuge in the Venezuelan Embassy just days before the Bay of Pigs landing. [35]

---

[35] *The Dark Side of Camelot* by Seymour Hersh, p. 205. Related CIA documents that were declassified in 2007 can be found on the CIA website at "Family Jewels/Johnny Rosselli section: FOIA Electronic Reading Room."

In the final weeks leading up to the planned 17 April invasion, leaks to the press eliminated any remaining tactical surprise that might have helped the chances of the exile invasion force. On Friday, 7 April, journalist Tad Szulc published an article in the *New York Times* reporting that a CIA-backed invasion of Cuba by Cuban exiles was imminent. President Kennedy himself had to speak with Times publisher Orvil Dryfoos to prevent publication of precise details. On Tuesday, 11 April, James Reston, Paul Nitze's next-door neighbor in Georgetown, published a report in the *Times* about the sharp policy dispute within the Kennedy administration about how much support the CIA should provide Cuban exiles intent on overthrowing Castro. The next day, 12 April, President Kennedy stated during a press conference that US armed forces would not intervene in Cuba under any circumstances. In a follow-up article on Friday, 14 April, Reston reported that a key policy question within the administration was whether the US government would rescue the Cuban exiles if they got in trouble after invading the island. A frustrated JFK told aides that Castro didn't need spies in the US; all he had to do was read American newspapers.

Castro did have spies in the US, however. The Cuban counterintelligence service under Redbeard Pineiro had successfully penetrated all the major Cuban-exile groups in the US. These spies were able to keep Redbeard advised of the pace of recruitment for the exile army, the location of the training camps, the combat readiness of the invasion force, and even the details of CIA assassination plots against Fidel. They did not have access to policy debates amongst the senior-most officials of the Kennedy administration, however; for that, Cuban intelligence did have to read American newspapers. Moreover, Redbeard's spies could not tell him the exact location of the planned invasion because the CIA trainers did not entrust their Cuban trainees with that secret.

On Thursday, 13 April, the brigade of Cuban exiles set sail from Guatemala on seven ships, five of which were leased by the CIA from Castro's old nemesis, the United Fruit Company. On Friday, 14 April, with press interest running high, President Kennedy authorized an air strike by the exiles for the following day to knock out the small Cuban air force, but he also ordered Bissell to reduce the number of B-26 bombers involved in the strike from sixteen to eight. Politically, eight bombers cause as much controversy as sixteen, but militarily, eight are far less than half effective as sixteen. As a result, when the seven ships pulled into the Bay of Pigs on the morning of Monday, 17 April, and began disembarking the exile brigade, Fidel still retained control of the air. Cuban air force planes made their first attack on the invasion flotilla at dawn, forcing one ship aground and damaging a second. During a second attack at 0930, they made a direct hit on the exile freighter *Rio Escondido,* which exploded in a fireball and sank. At that point, the remaining ships fled to the safety of the open sea, leaving the brigade stranded on the beaches with only the ammunition and supplies on hand.

For three days, both sides fought to a deadlock. Cutoff from their supply ships, at the mercy of the Cuban air force, and far too distant from the safety of the Escambray Mountains, it was only a matter of time before the exile brigade had to capitulate. On the evening of Wednesday, 19 April, 1,189 men of the exile brigade surrendered. Over 100 exiles had died during the battle, as well as some 200 Cuban troops.

***

In the weeks prior to the Bay of Pigs, Soviet-American relations had seemed poised to take their first step forward since the shooting down of Francis Gary Powers and his U-2 a year earlier. President Kennedy had spoken of a new beginning during his inaugural address. Premier Khrushchev was anxious to size up the young American president and was confident that the world was going in the Soviets' direction. Cuba had become an outpost for communism in Latin America, and Laos was becoming one in Southeast Asia. Moreover, the Soviets scored another first in the Soviet-American space race on 12 April by putting Cosmonaut Yuri Gagarin into orbit around the globe. It was in this context that on 1 April 1961, Premier Khrushchev agreed to an American proposal for a 3-4 June summit meeting in Vienna, Austria.

Following the 17-19 April Bay of Pigs fiasco, Khrushchev became even more confident because President Kennedy had put himself on the defensive both at home and abroad. In contrast to the 1960 Paris Summit, Khrushchev concluded that the 1961 Vienna Summit offered the Soviets more than just an opportunity to make some propaganda points; it seemed to offer Moscow an opportunity to extract important substantive concessions from an inexperienced American president. Thus, on 22 April, just three days after the Cuban exiles surrendered to Fidel, the Kremlin signaled to the American Embassy in Moscow that the Soviets remained committed to the Vienna Summit. On 4 May, Foreign Minister Gromyko himself called in US Ambassador Llewellyn Thompson to reiterate Soviet interest in proceeding with the summit.

In response, President Kennedy directed his brother Bobby to establish a secret communications channel to Khrushchev via a senior Soviet military intelligence officer serving in Washington, Georgi Nikotovich Bolshakov. On the evening of 9 May, the attorney general of the United States met the Soviet colonel in front of the Justice Department at the corner of Constitution Avenue and 10th Street and then walked over to the National Mall for a private conversation. Bobby warned sternly that the events in Cuba should not lead the Kremlin to underestimate the resolve of his brother, the President, to defend American interests. At the same time, if the Soviets were serious about concluding a nuclear test ban at Vienna, then the Americans were willing to proceed with the summit. Bobby underscored that the White House was not interested in a summit for the mere purpose of a general exchange of views. [36]

Khrushchev chose to send his response in a 12 May letter via the officially designated Soviet Ambassador to Washington. Khrushchev wrote that in the wake of the unfortunate events in Cuba, it seemed a good time for the general exchange of views between the leaders of the two superpowers, which Bobby Kennedy had just said was of no interest. For his part, Colonel Bolshakov was not allowed to speak in Khrushchev's name but, instead, was given instructions on the "personal opinions" that he could express to Bobby when they met again unofficially on 19 May. Accordingly, Bolshakov told Bobby that the President's inaugural words were a signal of hope to all Soviets that

---

[36] *One Hell of a Gamble* by Fursenko and Naftali, p. 109-114

relations with America could return to the level they had enjoyed during President Roosevelt's administration. However, before any progress could be made on nuclear arms control, Bolshakov stressed that the status of Berlin had to be resolved.[37]

Despite these two, dismissive rebuffs from Khrushchev, President Kennedy decided to proceed with the summit in hopes of making some progress on a nuclear test ban treaty.

But, Khrushchev had no intention to discuss arms control. He went to Vienna looking to bully JFK into abandoning the city of Berlin to communist control. One hundred miles inside East Germany and still occupied by the Allies of World War II, Berlin was the embarrassment of international communism. The sharply higher standard of living in the western-occupied zone of the city was obvious to any East German who took the time to walk over and take a look. As a result, nearly three million East Germans-- the best educated, most qualified people in the country-- had just continued walking and fled communism. To stop this hemorrhage, Stalin had tried to seize control of the city in 1948 but was thwarted by President Harry Truman and the Berlin Airlift. In 1958, Khrushchev had tried to intimidate President Eisenhower with threats of war over the city, but the old general, confident in American nuclear dominance, had not blinked an eye. Now, in 1961, Premier Khrushchev intended to settle the issue once and for all with President Kennedy.

Khrushchev warned that unless Kennedy was prepared to reach a diplomatic settlement regarding Berlin by

---

[37] Ibid.

December, the Soviets would wash their hands of the issue and allow the East Germans to proceed with plans to blockade western access to the city. The Americans would then be left with the choice of acquiescing in a *fait accompli* or war. Khrushchev told Kennedy, "If you want war, that is your problem." JFK probably surprised Khrushchev when he replied, "Then there will be war."[38]

In July, Soviet-American tensions continued to mount. Describing Berlin as the testing ground of western courage, President Kennedy called Khrushchev's bluff by announcing preparations to deploy six additional combat divisions to Europe. For his part, Premier Khrushchev told a secret gathering of the Soviet leaders, "We helped elect Kennedy last year. Then we met with him in Vienna, a meeting that could have been a turning point. But what does he say? 'Don't ask for too much. Don't put me in a bind. If I make too many concessions, I'll be turned out of office.' Quite a guy! He comes to a meeting but can't perform. What the hell do we need a guy like that for? Why waste time talking to him?"[39]

Despite this tough talk by Khrushchev, the KGB advised the leadership in the Kremlin that they could not win a nuclear confrontation with America over Berlin. The Soviets also knew, however, that communism in East Germany would collapse if they did not do something soon to stop the westward exodus of talented East Germans via Berlin. So, the Kremlin backed away from the risk of war that would have resulted by cutting off western access to the city. Instead, the Kremlin decided to cut off East German access to West Berlin.

---

[38] *Mrs. Kennedy* by Barbara Leaming, p. 128

[39] *One Hell of a Gamble* by Fursenko and Naftali, p. 134

To that end, construction of the Berlin Wall began on the night of 12-13 August. America was shocked but, pragmatically, no more prepared to start a war over Berlin than they had been over Hungary five years earlier.

In the fall, Khrushchev directed resumption of Soviet nuclear tests as another direct snub of Kennedy. Khrushchev ordered a test in the open atmosphere of the "Tsar Bomba," the most powerful nuclear weapon in history. Originally designed by Andrei Sakharov for 100 megatons, the test was scaled back to 54 megatons because Sakharov feared it might go totally out of control and destroy the world. Still, 54 megatons was more than five times the explosive power of all the bombs, artillery shells, hand grenades, and dynamite used by all combatants in World War I and World War II combined. Indeed, the "Tsar Bomba" was the model for "The Dooms Day" machine made famous in the 1964 movie, *Dr. Strangelove.*

***

The only bright light that offset these gloomy events during the first year of the Kennedy presidency was the elegant and soft-spoken First Lady. The cultured young mother turned the White House into both a home and a national showcase. The American people looked upon her with affection and admiration while remaining blissfully unaware of the pain she endured due to her husband's philandering. The President's long-time political aides, who had feared that Jackie would be seen as a spoiled rich girl detached from the daily lives of common Americans, were taken by complete surprise as her popularity transformed the First Lady into a powerful political asset both at home and abroad. The President was also surprised but deeply pleased as well as sincerely proud of her.

Jackie truly grabbed the spotlight first in Paris during 31 May - 2 June 1961, as she and the President were on their way to the difficult Vienna Summit. In a motorcade from the Arc de Triomphe to the Place de La Concorde, French President Charles De Gaulle rode with the President while De Gaulle's wife, Yvonne, rode in a separate limousine with the First Lady. To the surprise of all the Americans present, the welcoming French crowds chanted "Vive Jacqueline, Vive Jacqueline!" They had been enchanted the night before when French television had broadcast a pre-recorded interview with Jackie from the White House in which she spoke in perfect French of her love for France, its long history, and its rich culture. For the next three days, all eyes were on Jackie, which was a matter of evident pride for Jack. He summed up the visit with the self-effacing comment, "I am the man who accompanied Jacqueline Kennedy to Paris and I have enjoyed it."[40]

***

Suggestions for further reading:

1. *Mrs. Kennedy: The Missing History of the Kennedy Years* by Barbara Leaming, Simon and Schuster, 2001.

---

[40] *Mrs. Kennedy* by Leaming, p. 121

A thoughtful look into the private lives of President and Mrs. Kennedy during their years in the White House. It provides compelling insight into the depth of the First Lady's character and into Mary Meyer's special significance to the President as a social companion as well as a sexual partner.

2. *The Dark Side of Camelot* by Seymour Hersh, Little Brown and Company, 1997.

Hersh confirms what everyone suspected but nobody wanted to say about the private life of the assassinated president. It's hard to dispute Hersh's investigative reporting, although there is an unpleasant and perhaps unnecessary edge to his negative sentiments towards the Kennedy family.

3. *The Crisis Years: Kennedy and Khrushchev, 1960-1963* by Michael Beschloss, Harper Collins, 1991.

Thoroughly researched and balanced, as always with Beschloss.

4. *Bay of Pigs Chronology, Forty Years After,* The National Security Archive, 2001.

A detailed chronology of events drawn up for an international conference held in Havana, 22-24 March 2001.

5. *Jacqueline Kennedy: Historic Conversations on Life with John F. Kennedy* by Jacqueline Kennedy, Arthur Schlesinger, and Caroline Kennedy, Hyperion, 2011.

Seven interviews of the widowed First Lady conducted just months after the assassination at her 3017 N Street home in Georgetown. They reveal a worldview that is remarkably different than that of most young American women today.

Chapter 7
Sleeper Agent with Insomnia

The KGB always claimed that Lee Harvey Oswald lived in the Soviet Union as a normal resident. Immediately after the Kennedy assassination, the KGB denied having any direct contact with him whatsoever during the time that he resided there. They even denied asking about his service at the top secret U-2 base in Atsugi, Japan, although he had volunteered to tell them anything he knew. Since the end of the Cold War, the Kremlin has reluctantly come to admit that, yes, the KGB did have direct contact with Oswald in Moscow as well as in Minsk, but ostensibly only for the purpose of assessing whether he was a spy for the CIA. None of these stories fit plausibly with known facts, however.

We know that on 4 November 1959, an officer of the KGB First Chief Directorate, using only his first and patronymic names, Andrei Nikolayevich, visited Lee Harvey Oswald in Room 214 of the Metropole Hotel in Moscow to discuss opportunities for Oswald to work abroad for the KGB in some unspecified capacity. Twelve days later, on 16 November, the KGB concurred with granting Oswald permission to remain indefinitely in the Soviet Union. Eleven days after that, on 27 November, KGB Chairman Aleksandr Shelepin personally sponsored Oswald for residency in the isolated city of Minsk, along with a generous stipend, a prestigious apartment, and a cushy job, as well as attractive young people assigned by the KGB to watch and entertain him. We know this from a variety of sources, but in 1993, KGB officer Oleg Nechiporenko admitted it all in his book Passport to Assassination.[41]

So, what type of work abroad did the KGB have in mind for Oswald? Obviously, they understood that he would never again be given access to US government secrets after telling the US embassy in Moscow on 31 October of his readiness to reveal classified information to the Soviets. As noted in Chapter IV, the KGB's first objective in sending Oswald to Minsk would have been simply to isolate him from American counterintelligence officials interested in questioning him about what sensitive information regarding the U-2s he might already have shared with the Soviets and when. But, since they had this young American on their hands in any case, the ever-practical KGB sent Andrei Nikolayevich to see if he could find some other useful purpose for Oswald to earn his keep.

Coincidently, KGB Chairman Shelepin was placing top priority on sabotage and subversion operations as part of his grand strategy to "bring imperialism to its knees in the Third World." Shelepin's first objective was to use Fidel Castro's Cuba as the KGB's bridgehead to launch sabotage and subversion operations in Central America, Mexico, and the southwest of the United States. In support of Shelepin's strategy,

---

41 *Passport to Assassination: The Never-Before-Told Story of Lee Harvey Oswald by the KGB Colonel Who Knew Him* by Oleg Maximovich Nechiporenko, Carol Publishing Group, 1993

Department 13 of the KGB's First Chief Directorate was looking for young Americans fitting Oswald's exact profile to serve as "sleeper agents" in the American southwest. These sleeper agents were supposed to keep a low profile until called upon by the KGB to sabotage critical infrastructure like oil pipelines and electric power grids during a time of war between the Soviet Union and the United States. Thus, Andrei Nikolayevich was almost certainly a representative of Department 13 and would have been interested in Oswald as a saboteur, not as an assassin.

During his time in Minsk, Oswald picked up a number of clandestine operational skills that he would demonstrate back in Dallas a few years later, including surveillance-detection techniques, escape-and-evasion techniques, counter-interrogation techniques, and the creation of alias documents. Moreover, in the tightly controlled Soviet Union, the KGB permitted Oswald to own a gun and to experiment with bomb making. Such skills are hardly indicative of a normal resident of any country, but are common and very useful skills for prospective saboteurs.

In June 1962, Oswald, his Russian wife, and child reluctantly departed the Soviet Union and returned to Texas. He kept a low profile, as would be expected, until October 1962 when the Cuban Missile Crisis erupted. On 19 October, President Kennedy put the US military on war alert, with Premier Khrushchev promptly following suit. Such war alerts were the reason KGB Department 13 existed and why it had sleeper agents like Oswald in the first place. Probably not by accident then, every night from 19 October through 2 November, during the height of the Cuban Missile Crisis, Lee Harvey Oswald mysteriously disappeared without even his wife knowing his whereabouts or activities.

***

On 25 December 1958, as Fidel's rebels were closing in on Havana, Soviet Premier Khrushchev promoted the dynamic 40-year-old Aleksandr Shelepin to the position of KGB Chairman, replacing the lackluster 53-year-old Ivan Serov. Less than three years later, in 1961, Shelepin was again promoted to become by far the youngest member of the Central Committee of the Soviet Communist Party, where he retained oversight responsibility for the KGB. In 1962, he added the title of first deputy prime minister, and in 1964, he became a member of the ruling Politburo of the Communist Party.

Initially, these promotions were recognition of Shelepin's intelligence work battling the CIA's Cord Meyer for influence over the international youth movement. Subsequently, the promotions were in recognition of the young Shelepin's innovative strategic thinking regarding the ideological struggle between communism and imperialism. The Supreme Soviet of the USSR formally adopted Shelepin's strategic thinking as Soviet national policy on 1 August 1961, eleven days prior to construction of the Berlin Wall.[42]

Because of America's absolute dominance in nuclear weapons, Shelepin recognized that the victory of communism could not be won in an armored confrontation on the plains of northern Europe or in Berlin. Despite electoral campaign rhetoric in the United States, Shelepin knew that America enjoyed a 10 to 1 advantage in the

---

[42] *The World Was Going Our Way* by Andrew and Mitrokhin, p. 40

number of nuclear warheads and even greater superiority in the ability to deliver those nuclear warheads to their intended targets. Shelepin knew, as did President Eisenhower, that in a nuclear confrontation, Europe would be devastated and America grievously wounded, but the Soviet Union would be utterly and completely annihilated. From KGB spies inside NATO, Shelepin also received alarmist reporting that aggressive US military leaders, like Air Force Chief of Staff Curtis LeMay, were hoping that Moscow would give Washington some pretext so that America could exploit its advantage and launch a nuclear first strike against the Soviet Union.[43]

In this strategic context, Shelepin argued that the ultimate victory of communism would depend less on Red Army tanks and more on KGB sabotage and subversion operations to undermine the legitimacy of western governments. Shelepin believed that corrupt imperialist regimes would decay from within; all the KGB had to do was direct its Department 13 to help the process along a bit. The first battlegrounds would not be in Europe but rather in the vulnerable Third World. Fidel Castro's revolutionary success against overwhelming military odds in Cuba was evidence that Shelepin's strategy could work in America's own backyard.

Two days after Shelepin became KGB Chairman, the Kremlin approved for the first time a KGB request to supply arms to Fidel so that Cuba's fledgling revolutionary government could defend itself. In short order, Shelepin created the KGB's first ever Cuba office, placing Raul Castro's

---

[43] *One Hell of a Gamble* by Fursenko and Naftali, p. 51-52

friend Nikolai Leonov in charge, with Oleg Nechiporenko as one of Leonov's key lieutenants. Senior KGB officer Aleksandr Alekseyev was transferred to Havana and put in charge of all aspects of Soviet-Cuban relations. Fidel's intelligence chief, Ramiro Valdes, began sending young Cuban intelligence officers to the KGB training school in Minsk. Then, in 1961, Nechiporenko and Department 13 sabotage and assassination specialist Valery Kostikov were assigned to the KGB office in Mexico City with orders to cooperate with Cuban intelligence—first, to overthrow the US-backed government of Nicaragua; second, to destabilize the US-backed government of Mexico; and third, to lay the foundation for sabotage operations in the southwest of the United States itself.

In October 1959, just weeks after Premier Khrushchev's "good will" visit to America in September, Shelepin inserted a group of KGB sabotage specialists from Department 13 into a Soviet energy delegation that had been invited to visit Texas. It's known from KGB documents that have become available since the end of the Cold War that the mission of these Department 13 sabotage specialists was to conduct reconnaissance of critical oil and gas pipelines between Texas and US military facilities in southern California that would be targets of KGB sabotage during a time of war. We also know from KGB documentation that during this time Department 13 was looking to recruit Americans for sabotage operations who fit the following profile: "People who are suitable as special agents for Line F operations are 20 to 45 years old. Persons from aristocratic and bourgeois-conservative backgrounds are of no interest. Preference is given to the following professions: electricians, mechanics, toolmakers, chemists, qualified engineers, technicians and highly skilled workers-- primarily citizens of the United

States."[44] "Line F" refers to the representatives of Department 13 assigned to a KGB office overseas.

At the very moment these Department 13 sabotage specialists were in Texas and issuing the above recruitment profile, a 20-year-old American citizen, a professed communist from a solidly proletarian family background,and technically trained by the US Marines as a radar operator, arrived in Moscow willing to do anything he needed to do in order to earn Soviet citizenship. His name was Lee Harvey Oswald. Under these circumstances, it would have been absolutely remarkable if the KGB had not recruited Oswald as a prospective saboteur.

***

Remember that Oswald arrived in Moscow on 16 October 1959. On 21 October, the KGB tried to get him out of the country quietly without alerting American counterintelligence, but Oswald stymied them by feigning a suicide attempt. On 31 October, on his own initiative, Oswald walked into the US Embassy in Moscow and alerted American counterintelligence to his intentions. Then, beginning with the 4 November visit from Andrei Nikolayevich, the KGB reversed course and moved to isolate Oswald from American authorities.

On 15 November, Pricilla Johnson, a young American

---

[44] *The Sword and the Shield* by Christopher Andrew and Vasali Mitrokhin, p. 360

scholar and reporter living in Moscow on the third floor of the Metropole Hotel, returned from a business trip to the US. Since she resided at the same hotel as Oswald, a consular official at the American Embassy asked her to check up on his well-being. Oswald agreed to an interview in Johnson's hotel room on the evening of 16 October, which lasted for six hours. The KGB probably suspected that Johnson was cooperating with the CIA because as a university student, she had been a member of Cord Meyer's United World Federalists and, in 1953, had applied for a job as a CIA research analyst. In any case, immediately after his interview with Johnson, Oswald dropped out of sight. American authorities had no further communication from him for the next fifteen months.

On 7 January 1960, Lee Oswald arrived in Minsk and soon moved into his comfortable, rent-free apartment with the balcony overlooking the Svislach River. The apartment was easy walking distance from the Byelorussian Radio and Television Factory, where he was ostensibly employed doing electrical work, and from the KGB training school in Minsk, where Cuban intelligence officers would soon arrive. As evidenced by the clandestine operational skills that he demonstrated a few years later back in Dallas, it is likely that Oswald received his own clandestine basic training from that very same KGB school.

But, Oswald was not a good student. He settled into womanizing and the bourgeois life style typical of a senior Soviet Communist Party official of the time. During October and November 1960, he was having sex regularly with an Estonian woman named Inna Tachina, who had been introduced to him by his KGB contact, Pavel Golovachev. From December 1960 through February 1961, Oswald was having sex regularly with another woman named Nellya Korbinka. According to KGB files, Oswald was also having sex during this same period with a KGB informant referred to in the files by the alias "Anna Byeloruskaya" (presumably, "Byeloruskaya" was either Tachina or Korbinka). In her report to the KGB, "Byeloruskaya" stated, "The general mental development of Oswald is low."[45]

In late 1960, the KGB evidently decided that it was time to send Oswald back to the US. They terminated his monthly stipend effective January 1961. On 1 February, somebody clearly helped him draft a letter to the US Embassy in Moscow that was unusually well-written for Oswald and absent any indication of his dyslexia. The letter claimed that Oswald wanted to return to the United States because he had become "disillusioned" with his life in the Soviet Union.

Just a few weeks later, however, in March 1961, Oswald had a chance meeting with a young American tourist visiting Minsk named Katherine Mallory. He told Mallory that he despised the US and hoped to stay in Minsk the rest of his life. Given that the quality of his lifestyle in Minsk was far beyond anything that Oswald ever experienced in the US, his unrehearsed comment to Miss Mallory is more credible than the coached letter to the Embassy.

As with his feigned suicide attempt in Moscow in October 1959, Oswald resisted the renewed KGB efforts to send him back to the US. On 2 January, in the midst of his sexual affair with "Byelorusskaya" and the termination of his KGB monthly stipend, Oswald abruptly proposed marriage to his KGB contact, Ella German; Miss German rejected his

45 *Reclaiming History* by Bugliosi, p. 604

proposal out of hand. Then, on 17 March 1961, just as he was telling Katherine Mallory how he hoped to stay in Minsk for the rest of his life, Oswald met Marina Prusakova for the first time. He proposed marriage to Marina just 34 days later, on 20 April, the day after the CIA-backed Cuban exiles surrendered to Castro's army at the Bay of Pigs.

Oswald never told Marina that he loved her; she has admitted that she agreed to marry him because he lived in such a prestigious apartment with that beautiful view of the Svislach River. In proposing marriage to her, Oswald also told Marina that he wanted to spend the rest of his life in Minsk. He avoided any mention that he had already written the American Embassy of his disillusion with life in the Soviet Union and his desire to abandon that beautiful apartment in order to return to the United States. The 21-year-old playboy also became, according to Marina, very anxious to father a Russian child. In June 1961, as Khrushchev and Kennedy were rattling their war sabers in Vienna, Marina indeed became pregnant.

Oswald's abrupt desire to marry a Soviet citizen-- any Soviet citizen-- and father a Soviet child are clear indications that he was trying anything possible to establish permanent residence in Minsk for the rest of his life, just as he told Marina and Katherine Mallory that he wanted to do. Oswald would have known that obtaining both Soviet and American government permission for Marina and child to emigrate with him to the United States would be an uncertain and time-consuming process. Indeed, from the time Oswald first re-contacted the US Embassy in Moscow in February 1961 until their final reluctant departure to Texas in June 1962, the process took seventeen months.

***

During the fall of 1961, while Oswald was resisting KGB efforts to deploy him back to America and the Soviets were testing the Tsar Bomba, President Kennedy was experiencing a crisis of confidence. The first seven months of his presidency had resulted in the Bay of Pigs, the Vienna Summit, and construction of the Berlin Wall. When asked for a background interview for a book about his first year in office, Kennedy quipped, "Why would anyone write a book about an administration that has nothing to show for itself but a string of disasters." His friend British Prime Minister Harold MacMillan confided to Queen Elizabeth that JFK appeared "completely overwhelmed" and that Kennedy versus Khrushchev reminded him of "Neville Chamberlin trying to hold a conversation with Herr Hitler." International alarm bells about JFK's health were set off by television pictures of him being lifted out of Air Force One by a crane due to severe back pain. Finally in December, his touchstone and father, Joe, was felled by a stroke.[46]

Jackie and Bobby rose to the President's rescue. With enhanced self-confidence after her success in Paris, Jackie responded to JFK's crisis, just as she had during *The Profiles in Courage* period, in a fashion calculated to promote an image of her husband's presidency as one of power and grandeur. She asserted her authority as First Lady as well as her own intelligence and charm to more effectively orchestrate JFK's personal interactions with foreign heads of state, including the Prime Ministers of India, Jawaharlal

---

46 *Mrs. Kennedy* by Leaming, p. 130-172

Nehru, and Pakistan, Ayub Khan. More important still, she expanded her high visibility efforts to transform the White House into a proud American national showcase. That effort culminated on Valentine's Day, 14 February 1962, with the famous *Television Tour of the White House with Mrs. John F. Kennedy,* broadcast on all three major networks to the acclaim of millions of American voters.

Meanwhile, Bobby pursued the Boston political dictum, "Don't get mad, get even," in becoming his brother's point man on all decisions related to Cuba. CIA legend Allen Dulles was allowed to step down as director immediately after the 28 November 1961 opening ceremony for CIA's new headquarters building in Langley located half way between Bobby's mansion at Hickory Hill and Jackie's girlhood home at Merrywood. The next day, Dulles was replaced by John McCone, the former Chairman of the Atomic Energy Commission. The brilliant dilettante and U-2 mastermind Dick Bissell was eased out as CIA's clandestine operations chief in February 1962 and replaced by the stolid and experienced operative, Dick Helms. Lead responsibility for Cuba was moved to the Defense Department under the military intelligence legend Colonel Edward Lansdale, with CIA relegated to a support role. Although Lansdale was officially assigned to the Pentagon, he lived at 4503 McArthur Boulevard, which made it convenient for him to visit CIA's new headquarters at the beginning and end of each day.

Bobby ordered an urgent, all-out effort to foment an internal Cuban uprising to unseat Castro and his communist regime. The politically astute Lansdale promised that, with good leadership, this could be achieved before the mid-term elections in November 1962. The professional operative Helms pointed out that following the Bay of Pigs, the Cuban counterintelligence service under Redbeard Pineiro had arrested over 20,000 Cuban dissidents, leaving CIA with few, if any, agents on the island. It would take time to rebuild CIA clandestine capabilities, and thus, Lansdale's November 1962 target was unrealistic unless the White House was prepared to commit US forces directly. The pragmatic Joint Chiefs of Staff developed top secret contingency plans to invade the island if and when ordered by the Commander-in-Chief to do so.[47]

On the personal front, JFK asked Jackie to arrange a White House lunch on 21 September 1961 for some Hollywood notables as a favor for his brother-in-law, actor Peter Lawford. The lunch invitees included, amongst others, film director Otto Preminger and actors Henry Fonda, Charles Laughton, Walter Pidgeon, and Gene Tierney. At the last minute, Frank Sinatra wrangled his own invitation, leaving Jackie to find one more woman in order to strike the expected gender balance at the table. As she had done frequently back in Georgetown, Jackie called Mary Meyer to ask if she could help out. Mary was naturally pleased to be invited to the White House, and the opportunity to chat with her old paramour, Walter Pidgeon, only added to her delight.

That September lunch would also lead to a two-year affair between Mary and the President. Eleven days later, on Monday, 2 October, while Jackie and the children were away, he invited Mary to the White House for drinks. She arrived assuming that the invitation was to join another small gathering for cocktails. Surprised when she realized that she was the only guest, Mary got out of the situation with polite

---

[47] *One Hell of a Gamble* by Fursenko and Naftali, p. 156-158

excuses; she was, after all, a family friend of social standing in her own right. On Saturday, 11 November, in the midst of a White House dinner dance including eighty-nine guests, Mary coquettishly rejected a direct proposition from JFK. Eventually, on Monday 22 January 1962, while Jackie and the children were away, JFK again invited Mary to the White House for drinks, and the affair was consummated.[48]

On 9 February, the President and First Lady hosted another White House dinner dance with over a hundred guests. In the midst of the party, JFK pulled aside Ben Bradlee and gave him the scoop that U-2 pilot Francis Gary Powers had just been exchanged for KGB spy Rudolph Abel at the Glienicker Bridge in Berlin. A bit later, JFK and Mary, Bradlee's sister-in-law, snuck away from the party for a brief tryst upstairs. Other guests did not fail to notice nor, of course, did the Secret Service.[49]

***

Meanwhile, in Moscow, events were driving decisions that would lead to the Cuban Missile Crisis. On 21 February, KGB headquarters advised the Kremlin about the Pentagon's top secret contingency plans to invade Cuba and warned that the invasion could occur in the months prior to the November 1962 mid-term elections. The senior KGB officer in Washington, Aleksandr Feklisov, took exception to the

---

[48] *Mrs. Kennedy* by Leaming, p. 152-164

[49] Ibid, p. 181-182

headquarters' assessment, reporting to Moscow in March 1962 that, barring a pretext provided by the Soviets or Cubans themselves, the White House had no real enthusiasm for directly committing US troops to another invasion of Cuba any time soon. In April, however, Kremlin leaders were alarmed when Kennedy responded to the Tsar Bomba by ordering a resumption of America's own nuclear testing and became even more so when the US military conducted a large scale exercise of the Cuban invasion contingency plans, including an amphibious landing of 30,000 troops on Vieques Island in Puerto Rico. Uncertain whether JFK had full control of the Pentagon and with so much at stake politically in Cuba, Khrushchev and Shelepin were prepared to do whatever necessary to protect Fidel's hold on power.[50]

Khrushchev and Shelepin recalled Ambassador cum KGB chief Alekseyev from Havana to participate in a 20 May meeting of the Politburo. At that meeting, the Minister of Defense explained that the Soviet Union had ample quantities of medium- and intermediate-range nuclear missiles capable of striking Western Europe or China, but that it would take at least a decade to build up the arsenal of intercontinental ballistic missiles (ICBMs) that Moscow needed to strike the US. To fill this gap, Khrushchev proposed the idea of deploying Soviet medium and intermediate range nuclear missiles to Cuba, where they would be within striking range of the US. There was unease among civilian elements of the Politburo, so the discussions were continued the next day, 21 May, at which time Khrushchev argued additionally that deployment of Soviet nuclear missiles would protect Moscow's "bridgehead" in Cuba, as well as reinforce the

---

[50] *One Hell of a Gamble* by Fursenko and Naftali, p. 165-183

Soviets' strategic nuclear position vis-à-vis America. Finally, at a third meeting on 24 May, the Politburo unanimously endorsed "the *concealed* movement of troops and military technology by ship to Cuba."

On 28 May, the commander of Soviet strategic rocket forces, traveling under the alias "Engineer Petrov," flew secretly to Cuba along with the chief of operations for the Soviet General Staff and Ambassador Alekseyev to meet with Fidel. The Soviets did not inform Castro about the visit of the two general officers until after they had arrived in Havana on 29 May. Nonetheless, on 30 May, Castro readily agreed to host the Soviet nuclear missiles for the dual purpose of defending the Cuban revolution and strengthening the Soviet strategic position. He also agreed to dispatch his brother, Raul, to Moscow in early July to work out the detailed logistics and security arrangements required to keep the missile deployment secret from the Americans, as Khrushchev insisted be done, until after the US mid-term elections in November 1962.

The planned deployment was large and complicated, however. It included a total of sixty missiles divided into five nuclear missile regiments that would be transferred to Cuba from the Ukraine and European Russia. Thirty-six missiles were medium-range SS-4 missiles with a range of 1,000 miles, and twenty-four were intermediate-range SS-5 missiles with a range of 2,000 miles. All of the missiles carried one-megaton nuclear warheads, fifty times more powerful than the atomic bombs of Hiroshima and Nagasaki. In addition, to protect the missiles, the Soviets planned to deploy four motorized infantry regiments, two tank battalions, a jet fighter wing, a light bomber wing, two cruise missile regiments, anti-aircraft missiles, and gun batteries. In total, 51,000 Red Army troops would be sent to Cuba.[51]

The KGB knew that keeping such a large military deployment from the Soviet Union to Cuba secret from the CIA would be exceptionally difficult, no matter how much Premier Khrushchev insisted upon it. The KGB knew that the CIA had spies in Cuba. By August 1962, the KGB also suspected that Soviet military intelligence Colonel Oleg Penkovsky, a protégé of Soviet military intelligence chief and former KGB Chairman Ivan Serov, was a CIA spy inside the Red Army, but they did not yet have sufficient proof to arrest an officer of his standing. The KGB knew that American surveillance aircraft closely monitored Soviet ships sailing to and from Cuba and that U-2 spy planes regularly overflew Cuba itself. Moreover, the KGB knew that U-2 flights over the Soviet Union which had ended on 1 May 1960 had been replaced in August 1960 by even more effective over-flights by American spy satellites.

The KGB got additional clues that the Americans were on alert directly from the President of the United States and his brother, the attorney general. In a May interview with Stewart Alsop, JFK directly warned that, "In some circumstances we must be prepared to use the nuclear weapon at the start, come what may." Soon thereafter on Sunday, 3 June, Bobby invited military intelligence Colonel Georgi Bolshakov and his family to spend a relaxed day at Hickory Hill. Bobby confided to Bolshakov that, "Recently, the Joint Chiefs of Staff had offered the President a report in which they confirmed that the United States is currently ahead of the Soviet Union in military power and that *in*

---

[51] *One Hell of a Gamble* by Fursenko and Naftali, p. 184-197

extremis it would be possible to probe the forces of the Soviet Union." Bobby did not explain what he meant by "probe" but added that the President "had decisively rejected any attempt by zealous advocates of a clash between the United States and the Soviet Union to force him to accept their point of view." Carefully, Bobby also asked Bolshakov, "Tell me, Georgi, is there anyone in the Soviet leadership who advocates a decisive clash with the United States?" Bolshakov's report of these comments was sent directly to Khrushchev on 4 June.[52]

Hence, by late spring 1962, the KGB had strong reason to believe that the CIA would learn of the missile deployments almost as quickly as the KGB had learned of the Pentagon's top secret"contingency plans for invading Cuba and that the risk of war would increase dramatically during the height of the missile deployments to Cuba in September and October 1962. Given these increased risks of war, the sabotage and subversion specialists working for KGB Department 13 would be put on heightened alert during this period.

***

On 24 May, the same day that the Politburo met in the Kremlin to unanimously approve the deployment of Soviet nuclear missiles to Cuba, Lee and Marina Oswald visited the US Embassy in Moscow to receive the required documents

---

[52] *One Hell of a Gamble* by Fursenko and Naftali, p. 184

for their travel to the United States. Along with their three-month-old baby girl, they departed Moscow by train on 1 June bound for the Dutch port of Rotterdam. On 4 June, they departed on the freighter Maasdam, arriving in New York City on 13 June.

During their transit across the Atlantic, Lee, who was very worried that he might be prosecuted by American authorities for treason, wrote two separate responses to a series of eleven possible questions he might be asked. The first response to each question appears to be Lee's true and honest answer, the second response a more legally correct cover story. The questions and separate responses follow verbatim (emphasis author's):[53]

Q1: Why did you go to the USSR?

1. I went as a mark of my discuss and protest against American political policies in forenign countrys, my personal sign of discontent and horror at the misguided mind of reasoning of the U.S. Government.

2. I went as a citizen of the U.S.(as a tourist) residing in a foreing country which I have a perfect right to do. I went there to see the land, the people, and how there system works.

Q2: What about those letters?

1. I made serval letters in which I expressed my above feelings to the American Embassy when in Oct 1959 I went there to legally liquate my american citizenship and was refused this legalle right.

---

53 *Reclaiming History* by Vincent Bugliosi, p. 634-636

2. I made no letters deriding the US!! In correspondence with the U.S. Embassy I made no anti-american statements, any critizem I might have had was of policies not our government.

Q3: Did you make statements against the U.S. there?

1. yes

2. no

Q4: What about that type recording?

1. I made a recording for Radio Moscow which was broadcast the following sunday in which spoke about the beauiful capital of the Socialist work and all its progress.

2. I made a recording for the Moscow Tourist Radio travel log, in which I spoke about sight-seeing and what I had seen in Moscow tourist circles. I expressed delight in all the interesting places, I mentioned in this respect the University, mesuem of art, Red Square, the Kremlin I rember I closed this 2 minute recording by saying I hoped our peoples could live in peace and fr.

Q5: Did you break laws by residing or taking work in the USSR?

1. **I did in that I took an othe of allignce to the USSR.**[54]

2. Under U.S. law a person may lose the protection of the U.S., by voting or serving in the armed forces of a foringn state or taking an othe of alligence to that state. I did none of

---

[54] KGB Department 13 typically required its saboteurs and agents to sign an oath of secrecy.

these

Q6: Isn't all work in the USSR considered State work?

1. Yes of course in that respect I allso broke US law in accepting work under a forign state.

2. No. Technically, only plants working directly for the State, usually defense, all other plants are owned by the workers who work in them.

Q7: What about the statements you made to UPI agent Miss Mosby?

1. I was approched by Miss Mosby and other reporters just after I had formally requested the American Embassy to legally liquate my U.S. citizenship, for a story, they were notified by the U.S. Embassy, not by me. I answered questions and made statements to Miss Mosby in regard to my reasons for coming to the USSR, her story was warped by her later, but in barest esscens it is possible to say she had the truth printed.

2. I was approcaed just after I had formally notified the U.S. Embassy in Moscow of my future residence in he USSR by the newspaper agenties in Moscow including U.P.I. API and time inc who were notified by the Embassy. I did not call them. I answered questions and gave statements to Miss Mosby of U.P.I. I requested her to let me OK. her story before she released it, which is the polite and usual thing. She sent her version of what I said just after she sent it. I immially called her to complant about this, at which time she apolizied but said her editor and not her had added serval things. She said London was very excited about the story (there is how I deduced that she had allready sent it) so there wasn't much

else I could do about it. And I didn't relize that the story was even more blown out of shape once it got to the U.S.A. I'm afriad the printed story was faricated sensenlionilizism.

Q8: Why did you remain in the USSR for so long if you only wanted a look?

1. **I resided in the USSR from Oct 16 1959 to sprig of 1961 a period of 2 ½ years I did so because I was living quite comfortably. I had plenty of money, an apartment rent free lots of girls, etc...why should I leave all that?**

2. I resided in the USSR until February 1961 when I wrote the Embassy stating that I would like to go back. (My passport was at the Embassy for safekeeping) they invited me to Moscow for this purpose however it took me almost ½ year to get a permit to leave the city of Minsk for Moscow. In this connection, I had to use a letter from the head consular, to the Russian authrities in Minsk (the Russians are very beaurocratic and slow letting foreingrs travel about the country hence the visa) when I did get to Moscow the Embassy immiately gave me back my passport and advised me as to how to get an exit visa from Russia for myself and my Russian wife, this long and ardous process took months from July 1962 untill _ 1962, therefore you see almost 1 year was spent in trying to leave the country. that's why I was there so long not out of desire!

Q9: Are you a communits?

1. Yes basically, allthough I hate the USSR and socialist system I still thank marxism can work under different circumstances.

2. No of course not.

Q10: have you ever now a communist?

1. not in the U.S.A.

2. I have never know a communist, outside the ones in the USSR but you can't help that.

Q11: What are the othestanding differants between the USSR and USA?

1. **None, except in the USA the living standard is a little higher, freedoms are about the same, medical aid and the educational system in the USSR is better than in the USA.**

2. freedom of speech travel outspoken opposition to unpopular policies freedom to believe in god.

***

On 14 June 1962, the Oswalds arrived back in Texas. They lived with Lee's brother Robert for almost a month at 7313 Davenport Avenue in what is now the Ridglea Hills section of Fort Worth. In mid-July, they moved in with Lee's mother, Marguerite, for a few weeks at 1501 West Seventh Street in the West Side section of Fort Worth. In late July, Lee got a job at the Leslie Welding Company and developed a reputation as a good employee. He earned sufficient money there to rent a modest one-bedroom apartment for himself, Marina, and the baby at 2703 Mercedes Avenue in the Linwood section of Fort Worth. They lived there through September 1962.

FBI Special Agent John Fain interviewed Oswald for the first time on 26 June at the FBI office in downtown Fort Worth. Oswald stuck closely to the second set of responses noted above. He denied any cooperation with the KGB during his residence in the USSR, but he declined Fain's invitation to take a lie detector test on that question. Fain interviewed Oswald again on 16 August at the apartment on Mercedes Street. On one hand, Fain did not believe that Oswald was honest about his time in the USSR. On the other hand, Fain did not believe that the immature young man constituted a serious counterintelligence threat to US national security. Only weeks away from his own retirement, Special Agent Fain closed his investigation of Oswald after this second interview.

Eight weeks after the FBI closed its investigation of him and with no further sign of Special Agent Fain, Oswald abruptly severed contact with his mother and brother, abandoned his job at Leslie Welding without notice, and departed his Mercedes Street apartment in Fort Worth to an unknown location in Dallas, leaving Marina and the baby in Fort Worth with friends. His very first day in Dallas, 9 October, Oswald rented post office box #2915 at the main Dallas Post Office on Ervay Street, giving as his own address the 3519 Fairmont Street address of an acquaintance named Alexandra de Mohrenschildt, the daughter of Baron George de Mohrenschildt.

Oswald checked in to the Dallas YMCA on 15 October and departed on 19 October, the same day that President John Kennedy put the US military on a war alert because of the Cuban missile crisis. Nobody, including his wife, knows where Oswald resided during 9-14 October or from 19 October until 3 November. We do know that during the latter period he was working daytime hours at a graphics art firm in downtown Dallas named Jaggers-Chiles-Stovall.

If Oswald returned to Texas as a low-level spy for KGB Department 13, then it is not hard to see what was happening during this period. Oswald stayed in Fort Worth until FBI interest in him died down. He then moved to Dallas and set up a covert communications mail drop at the main post office. This would be standard operational procedure for the KGB. The key question about Oswald's activities during this period, from the perspective of a professional intelligence officer, is the nature of Lee's relationship with Baron de Mohrenschildt.

***

George de Mohrenschildt was a Russian of minor nobility from Minsk, the same city where Oswald had just lived. In 1931, at age 20, he emigrated to Belgium, and in 1938, he emigrated again to New York City. Although broke, de Mohrenschildt's good looks and noble title made him popular with American socialites, including the recently divorced Janet Bouvier. His first marriage lasted from 1942 until 1944. His second marriage lasted from 1947 until 1949.

His third marriage, 1951-1956, was to a wealthy woman from Philadelphia. They had two children, both of whom suffered from cystic fibrosis. De Mohrenschildt used his third wife's money to found the National Foundation for Cystic Fibrosis. The honorary chairwoman of the foundation was his friend Janet Bouvier's daughter, Jacqueline, who had since become the wife of the junior senator from Massachusetts, John Kennedy.

In 1959, at age 48, de Mohrenschildt was living in Texas where he met and married his fourth wife, Eugenia Fomenko, another member of the Russian émigré community in Dallas, who went by the name Jeanne LeGon. Jeanne was wildly unconventional, especially by the staid standards of Dallas in 1959. In her mid-40s and a bit plump, she had platinum blond hair, dressed in tights pants and tight tops, and was well-known for playing tennis in her bikini.

Always seeking adventure, Jeanne convinced her new husband to embark on a two-year walking trek from Mexico, through violence-torn Guatemala and Nicaragua, all the way to Panama. In Mexico City, they met with officials from the Soviet Embassy and, in November 1959, were even honored with an introduction to Khrushchev's deputy Anastas Mikoyan, who was there negotiating the first Soviet trade agreement with Castro's Cuba.[55] Then, for several months, de Mohrenschildt and Jeanne literally disappeared into Central America. In autumn 1961, they reappeared and returned to Dallas, short on money, and rented a pleasant but by no means luxurious apartment at 6624 Dickens Avenue near Southern Methodist University.

In mid-August 1962, de Mohrenschildt heard about the young Oswald family that had recently arrived in Fort Worth from his hometown of Minsk. Promptly, he drove the thirty miles all the way out from Dallas to Oswald's modest apartment at 2703 Mercedes Street in Fort Worth to introduce himself and invite the young family over for

---

[55] See p. 124 in Chapter 5 of this text.

Sunday supper. Over the next eight months, the urbane Baron de Mohrenschildt would meet with the hopelessly awkward Lee Harvey Oswald two or three times per month and spend hours talking with him. Oswald was immensely flattered that a man of de Mohrenschildt's social stature would show such interest in him.

Gadflies like de Mohrenschildt and Jeanne are not uncommon on the fringes of the clandestine intelligence world. They seem to like the idea of "having people" inside that world. In turn, intelligence operatives find such people useful as social brokers and as low-level sources of intelligence and gossip. De Mohrenschildt appears to have been in contact with a number of intelligence services over the years including the Nazis, the French, and the CIA. Given his background, it would be surprising if he did not have some contact with the KGB as well, especially during his trip with Jeanne to Mexico and Central America.

KGB Department 13, responsible for sabotage and assassination, may not have been directly interested in de Mohrenschildt because of his aristocratic background and his age.[56] However, KGB counterintelligence officers, with responsibility for monitoring Russian émigré communities, would have been quite interested in someone of his social stature. Such counterintelligence officers are frequently assigned "undercover" in Soviet consular sections because that is where Russian émigrés must visit to take care of their routine consular matters. The three KGB officers assigned to the closest Soviet Consular Section, Mexico City, during this period were the previously mentioned Oleg Nechiporenko

---

[56] See p. 156 of this text for the profile of prospective saboteurs of interest to Department 13.

and Valery Kostikov, as well as Pavel Antonovich Yatskov.[57] It is quite likely that they were in clandestine contact with de Mohrenschldt and via de Mohrenschildt with Oswald.[58]

***

Suggestions for further reading:

1. *The World Was Going Our Way: The KGB and the Battle for the Third World* by Chistopher Andrew and Vasili Mitrokhin, Perseus Book Group, 2005.

Documentary evidence of the KGB world view in the years leading up to the Kennedy assassination. Essential reading for anybody who wishes to understand how the KGB would have looked at Lee Harvey Oswald in 1959-1962 when he lived in the Soviet Union.

---

[57] Pavel Yatskov's brother, Anatoli, was the KGB's lead atomic spy against America's Manhattan Project in 1944-1945. See *A Spy's Guide to Santa Fe and Albuquerque* by E.B. Held, 2011.

[58] Kostikov is known to have been Line F, the local representative of KGB headquarters Department 13, responsible for sabotage and assassination operations in Central America. Yatskov, a veteran of the war-era SMERSH organization, is known to have been Line KR, the local counterintelligence representative of KGB headquarter Directorate K (Counterintelligence). Nechiporenko was the Line KR officer responsible for émigrés and the local community of Soviet officials but was also active in Line F operations. See John Barron's book *KGB*.

2. *The Sword and the Shield: The Mitrohkin Archive and the Secret History of the KGB* by Chistopher Andrew and Vasili Mitrokhin, Perseus Book Group, 1999.

The companion volume to *The World Was Going Our Way.*

3. *KGB: The Secret Work of Soviet Secret Agents* by John Barron, Reader's Digest Press, 1974.

One of the classic Cold War studies of the KGB written with assistance from the CIA. See in particular the chapter regarding Mexico on pages 230-257.

Chapter 8
Desperately Seeking Fidel

That the CIA promptly detected the attempt to deploy Soviet nuclear missiles to Cuba did not surprise the KGB in the least. Premier Khrushchev, however, was totally surprised by JFK's decisive response to this Soviet strategic challenge. Despite all the warnings to the contrary that the White House had sent the Kremlin, Khrushchev misjudged JFK as nothing more than a shallow politician and playboy. Khrushchev was convinced that JFK, distracted by the Marilyn Monroe sex scandal and by civil rights turmoil at the University of Mississippi, would not have the gravitas to risk nuclear war with the USSR over Cuba.

When JFK called Khrushchev's bluff, the Soviet Premier was himself forced to back down from a nuclear confrontation that he and the KGB knew the Soviets could not win. From the youthful perspective of both Fidel Castro, only 35 at the time, and Lee Harvey Oswald, 23, nuclear war, no matter what the cost, would have been justified and preferable to humiliation. They considered Khrushchev, the 68-year-old veteran of Stalingrad, a cowardly old man for caving in to Kennedy, and they felt personally betrayed by the Soviet Union.

Oswald, for his part, first vented his anger and frustration on the nearest Soviet citizen at hand, his young and fragile wife, Marina Prusakova Oswald. Then, he decided to strike a blow to demonstrate, at minimum, his own courage, as well as his personal support for Cuba in its struggle against world imperialism. On his own initiative, Oswald decided to assassinate a rabidly anti-Castro, retired American army general who lived in Dallas named Edwin Walker. Walker, who had been prosecuted for sedition due to his role in the civil rights turmoil at the University of Mississippi, would later become the model for the mentally unstable character, General Jack D. Ripper, played by actor Sterling Hayden in the 1964 movie Dr. Strangelove.

When his attempt to assassinate General Walker narrowly failed, Oswald fled Dallas to his hometown, New Orleans. Once confident that the FBI was not hot on his trail, Oswald began trying to make clandestine contact with the Cuban government by establishing a New Orleans chapter of the Fair Play for Cuba Committee of America. Oswald would appear to have succeeded in making clandestine contact with Cuban intelligence operatives in late August 1963.

Shortly thereafter, on 7 September, Fidel Castro told an American reporter that Cuba was prepared to retaliate "in kind" for persistent CIA efforts to assassinate Cuban leaders, including Castro himself. These persistent assassination efforts were directed by the Kennedys' social acquaintance at the CIA, Des Fitzgerald. Castro knew all about Fitzgerald's effort, because Rolando Cubela, the Cuban "agent" that Fitzgerald and his operatives were working with, was really a double agent working for Cuban intelligence. Castro's threat to retaliate "in kind" was thus well informed. On 9 September 1963, Castro's threat was reported in all the major American newspapers, including the New Orleans Times-Picayune *that*

Lee Oswald read daily. Just a few days later, unemployed and broke, Oswald decided to leave New Orleans and spend his remaining funds on a trip to Mexico City for the purpose of meeting with Cuban Embassy officials assigned there.

***

In late July and early August 1962, the CIA detected an abrupt increase in the shipment of military personnel and materiel from the USSR to Cuba. On 10 August, CIA Director McCone briefed the President's special advisory group on Cuba about this turn of events. In doing so, McCone expressed suspicion that Moscow was trying to secretly deploy Soviet nuclear missiles to Cuba. The president's national security adviser, former Harvard Professor McGeorge Bundy, strongly doubted that Moscow would take such a high-risk political gamble, as did Secretary of State Dean Rusk and Secretary of Defense Robert McNamara. Attorney General Bobby Kennedy shared McCone's concerns. To clarify the facts of the situation, a U-2 spy plane was sent over Cuba on 29 August. It discovered at least eight different sites under construction for SA-2 anti-aircraft missiles, the same anti-aircraft missile that succeeded in shooting down the U-2 of Francis Gary Powers, but provided no conclusive evidence regarding nuclear missile deployments.[59]

As former chairman of the Atomic Energy Commission, McCone had an intimate understanding of American nuclear

---

[59] *One Hell of a Gamble* by Fursenko and Naftali, p. 198-204 and *Mrs. Kennedy* by Leaming, p. 217-236

dominance over the Soviets, both in terms of warheads and long-range delivery systems. As current director of the CIA, McCone was also privy to the clandestine reporting from the Agency's top spy inside the Red Army, military intelligence Colonel Oleg Penkovsky. Understanding the hard facts and, thanks to Penkovsky, the Kremlin's perspective on those hard facts, McCone assessed that Moscow had a compelling strategic motivation to re-deploy medium- and intermediate-range nuclear missiles from western districts of the USSR to Cuba, where they would be within striking range of the US, including Washington DC. McCone understood clearly that if the Soviets could successfully keep the missile deployment secret until it was a *fait accompli*, then they would succeed in fundamentally altering the strategic balance between the US and the USSR.

In late May, after making the decision to deploy the missiles to Cuba, Khrushchev had assured nervous Politburo colleagues that the decision was based on his personal assessment of JFK's character. Khrushchev was confident that JFK, faced with a *fait accompli,* would have no alternative but to accept the missiles just as he had accepted the Berlin Wall. He said that JFK was "intelligent" and "would not set off a thermonuclear war if our warheads are there."[60]

Khrushchev made these comments only eight days after JFK was forced to divert considerable time and attention to damage control when a scantily clad Marilyn Monroe created a scandal by singing her famous rendition of "Happy Birthday" to JFK at Madison Square Garden in front of a televised audience of some forty million Americans. After JFK

[60] *One Hell of a Gamble* by Fursenko and Naftali, page 182

subsequently stopped taking her telephone calls, Monroe asked Peter Lawford to "say goodbye to Jack" for her and then committed suicide on 5 August.[61]

To further divert JFK's attention, Khrushchev sent him a letter, which Soviet Ambassador Dobrynin personally delivered to Bobby Kennedy on 4 September. Both the letter and Dobrynin's comments floated the tempting possibility that Khrushchev was beginning to support JFK's long sought objective of a ban on nuclear tests in the open atmosphere. Moreover, Moscow promised not to take any initiative in US-Soviet relations that might cause controversy prior to the American mid-term congressional elections in November. On 6 September, Dobrynin met with Ted Sorensen to reiterate these offers and to assure the White House that Soviet military support to Cuba was purely defensive in nature.

These were all bald-faced lies, of course. Khrushchev knew full well that the first Soviet medium- and intermediate-range missiles were scheduled to arrive at Cuban ports during the weekend of 8-9 September.[62] Moreover, he knew that a shipment of forty-five one-megaton nuclear warheads would depart the USSR on 16 September aboard the Soviet freighter *Indigirka* and arrive at Mariel Cuba on 4 October.[63] On 5 October, Georgi Bolshakov met with Bobby Kennedy at Khrushchev's direction and provided additional assurances that Soviet military support to Cuba was purely defensive in nature.

---

[61] *Mrs. Kennedy by* Leaming, p. 211

[62] *Mrs Kennedy* by Learning, p. 219

[63] *One Hell of a Gamble* by Fursenko and Naftali, p. 213-217

JFK was yet further distracted by an outbreak of civil rights turmoil at Ole Miss: in late September, a federal court had ordered the University of Mississippi to accept its first black student, Air Force veteran James Meredith. When Mississippi Governor Ross Barnett refused to do so, the extreme right wing retired army major general Edwin Walker publicly called for 10,000 volunteers to rally at Ole Miss and block the federal court order. Rioting broke out, and US Army troops had to be called in to reinforce the US Marshals. Two people died and hundreds were injured; Walker was arrested and charged with inciting insurrection and conspiracy to commit sedition. As federal officials escorted Meredith into his university dormitory on 1 October, Walker's supporters chanted, "Go to Cuba, nigger lovers, go to Cuba."[64]

Lulled by repeated Soviet assurances and fearful of another U-2 shoot-down by the dangerous SA-2s during the run-up to the congressional elections, Bundy, Rusk, and McNamara had successfully opposed any further U-2 flights over Cuba during the month of September. When McCone returned from a honeymoon in France with his second wife (his first wife having died), he insisted that additional U-2 flights over Cuba were strategically imperative regardless of the tactical and political risks. With the support of Bobby Kennedy, McCone received JFK's concurrence to proceed with the over-flight.

At 11:30 PM on Saturday, 13 October, a U-2 piloted by Major Richard Heyser took off from Edwards Air Force Base in California and flew over western Cuba without incident on

---

[64] Ibid, p. 224

Sunday morning, 14 October. On Monday evening, 15 October, McCone presented Bundy conclusive photographic evidence of Soviet SS-4 medium-range missiles being readied for deployment at San Cristobal Cuba, thirty miles southwest of Havana. Bundy authorized briefings of this new intelligence for the secretaries of state and defense that same evening but decided to let the President get a good night sleep. The next few weeks would be busy.

***

At 8:45 Tuesday morning, Bundy advised JFK of the missiles. Appointments had to be rearranged that morning to permit the President to receive detailed briefings and see the photographic evidence himself. One of the protocol appointments that JFK did not postpone, however, was the official farewell call by the outgoing US Ambassador to France, Chip Bohlen. A former US Ambassador to Moscow and the translator for FDR during his 1945 meetings with Stalin at Yalta, Bohlen's reputation had recovered from the McCarthyite allegations directed at him in 1953, and he had remained one of America's premier experts on the Soviet Union. Moreover, JFK personally trusted Bohlen as a result of their many conversations on the Georgetown dinner circuit.

Indeed, JFK and Jackie were to attend a farewell dinner in Bohlen's honor that same evening at Joe Alsop's home. Although JFK had publicly warned during mid-September that any attempt to turn Cuba into an offensive Soviet military base would prompt an American military strike on the island, Bohlen now cautioned JFK to proceed with diplomatic care.[65]

On Thursday morning, 18 October, the CIA advised the President that additional U-2 photographic evidence indicated that Soviet nuclear warheads were already in Cuba and, thus, that the missiles could be armed and ready for launch within days. In other words, the *fait accompli* for which Khrushchev was aiming was almost a reality, with only two weeks left until the mid-term Congressional elections. Later that same morning, JFK met in the Oval Office with Soviet Foreign Minister Andrei Gromyko, who persisted for over two hours in the lie that Soviet military assistance to Cuba was purely defensive in nature. That evening, with strategic and political disaster looming, the State Department proposed a blockade of Soviet shipments of offensive military equipment to Cuba, coupled with a demand for the removal of the missiles and warheads already in place. With the clock running out, American Air Force Chief of Staff Curtis LeMay countered the State Department proposal with a personal jab at the President's father, Joe, saying that a time-consuming blockade would be "almost as bad as appeasement at Munich."[66]

When JFK accompanied the First Lady to Mass on Sunday morning, he was still weighing his options. He recognized that a surprise air attack as proposed by General LeMay was America's best hope of wiping out all of the Soviet missiles before they became an operational threat. Alternatively, announcement of a blockade as proposed by the State Department would give peace a chance but would

---

65 *Mrs. Kennedy* by Leaming, p. 232-233

66 *Mrs. Kennedy* by Leaming, p. 234-235

forfeit the element of surprise, vastly increasing American casualties should war prove unavoidable. JFK made the decision in favor of a blockade that Sunday evening, 21 October, after the chairman of the Joint Chiefs of Staff, General Maxwell Taylor, conceded that even a surprise air strike would destroy at best only 90 percent of the Soviet missiles. [67] Even in Taylor's best-case scenario, Washington and New York City would remain in extreme peril.

On Monday, 22 October, the White House announced that the President would make a televised address to the nation that evening. Knowing that the Soviet missiles in Cuba were capable of hitting Washington within minutes after the address, JFK suggested cancellation of a previously planned dinner that evening with four friends in the White House residence so that Jackie and the children could depart Washington early and secretly position themselves closer to the Presidential bunker. Jackie declined, insisting that the family would stay by his side and share his fate. A short while later, before he went to the Oval Office for the speech, JFK added Mary Meyer and his friend Bill Walton to the list of dinner guests. Upon arrival at the White House after the President's televised address, Mary and Walton were quietly assured that they would be evacuated to the Presidential bunker along with JFK and the First Lady should there be an emergency.[68]

In this crisis atmosphere, the KGB chief in Washington did exactly what he was trained to do. First, he took

---

[67] Ibid, p. 238-239. Bobby and Ethel Kennedy named their son born in 1965 after General Taylor.

[68] *Mrs. Kennedy* by Leaming, p. 240-242

contingency precautions in preparation for war, such as destroying sensitive files, assuring critical supplies, and putting Department 13/Line F sabotage agents within the United States on alert. Then, he sought out all possible sources of information to determine the plans and intentions of the Kennedy White House.

The Washington KGB chief was known to Americans as Aleksandr Fomin, but his true name was Aleksandr Semyonovich Feklisov. He had first made a name for himself in New York City during 1944-1945 as the KGB officer responsible for handling the trained spy Julius Rosenberg.[69] On Friday, 26 October 1962, Feklisov/Fomin reached out to one of his contacts in Washington code named MIN. MIN was not a trained spy; rather, he was the well-connected ABC newsman John Scali, who years later would become America's Ambassador to the United Nations during the Nixon and Ford administrations. Feklisov found Scali a useful source of information and gossip; Scali, for his part, provided the FBI insight about what questions were on the mind of the local KGB chief. Such relationships are quite common in the clandestine world.

On this Friday, Scali and Feklisov met openly for a late lunch at the Occidental Restaurant next to the Willard Hotel, just 200 meters from the White House.[70] After the lunch, Feklisov reported back to KGB headquarters in Moscow that Scali had been authorized by the Kennedy administration to propose a deal: the USSR would withdraw its nuclear

---

[69] *A Spy's Guide to Santa Fe and Albuquerque* by Held, p. 60

[70] The table they sat at is marked and can be specially reserved by history buffs.

missiles from Cuba in exchange for a US pledge not to invade the island, directly or indirectly. In addition, the US secretly would agree to withdraw outdated American intermediate-range nuclear missiles deployed in Turkey against targets inside the USSR. Although considerable drama would continue for another 48 hours, it was this deal that became the basis for Khrushchev to publicly announce on 28 October the Soviet decision to withdraw the missiles from Cuba under UN oversight.

The world had averted nuclear Armageddon, but Fidel Castro was furious. On 27 October, sensing that Khrushchev was about to back down, Fidel called an urgent meeting with his KGB friend Soviet Ambassador Alekseyev and conveyed a message to Moscow urging a surprise nuclear first strike against the Americans. After Khrushchev backed down, Castro sent a second message criticizing Moscow's handling of the crisis, noting the "surprising, sudden, and practically unconditional decision to withdraw the weapons." Alekseyev warned Moscow that it was going to take at least two years of careful political work to assuage Castro's anger.[71]

***

As noted in Chapter VII, in early October, Lee Harvey Oswald severed contact with his brother and mother, abandoned a job he seemed to enjoy, abruptly moved from Fort Worth to Dallas, and then disappeared for three weeks

---

[71] *One Hell of a Gamble* by Fursenko and Naftali, p. 288-292

at the peak of the Cuban Missile Crisis. On 3 November, Oswald reappeared and rented an affordable apartment at 604 Elsbeth Street in the modest Oak Cliff section of Dallas, a short bus ride from downtown. Marina became deeply depressed when she saw the family's new home for the first time on Sunday, 4 November. She considered the apartment a slum even compared to their modest apartment in Fort Worth but especially compared to their beautiful, KGB-supplied apartment in Minsk overlooking the Svislach River.

The situation quickly turned ugly. After only 2-3 days, Marina fled, showing up on some friends' doorstep with their baby girl and a few diapers but no change of clothing for herself, no money, nothing. The friends tried to convince Marina to leave Oswald for good and offered to help her, but she spoke no English, had no job prospects, was scared, and was codependent. Inevitably, she returned to the Elsbeth slum on 17 November.

The situation only got worse. Oswald beat Marina regularly. She responded by taunting him as sexually inadequate. He retaliated by beating her even more savagely. Finally, on Saturday, 23 February, having just learned that she was once again pregnant, Marina tried to hang herself.[72]

On 3 March, complaints from the landlord and the other Elsbeth Street tenants caused Oswald to move to another apartment just a block away at 214 W. Neely Street. The new apartment was the second floor of a two-unit building. Marina liked it better than the Elsbeth apartment. The Neely apartment had a balcony where she could sit in the sun and a small back yard where she could dry clothes and play with

---

[72] *Reclaiming History* by Bugliosi, p. 679

the baby.

On Friday 29 March, Oswald was given one week's notice that he would be laid off from the job he had gotten at the graphics firm in Dallas, though he didn't tell Marina he had lost his job until 10 April. On Saturday 30 March, only five months after the Cuban Missile Crisis, Oswald stood at the corner of Main and Evray in downtown Dallas with a "Viva Castro" placard around his neck and passed out the pro-Castro pamphlet, "The Crime Against Cuba."

On Sunday, 31 March, Marina was in the backyard hanging out diapers to dry when Oswald came down the stairs dressed all in black with a revolver tucked in his belt, carrying a sniper rifle in one hand and copies of two leftist newspapers in the other. One newspaper was *The Militant,* the Trotskyite publication of the Socialist Workers Party of America; the other was *The Worker,* the Stalinist publication of the Communist Party of the United States. Oswald was either unaware of the bitter ideological rift between the Trotskyites and the Stalinists or dismissive of it.

Marina told Oswald that he looked silly, but he demanded that she take a photo of him posed in this costume. Oswald covertly developed the photo during his last week on the job at the graphics firm and made at least three, probably four copies. He gave one copy to Marina on the back of which he wrote, "For Junie, from Papa." We know he sent a second copy to *The Militant* and presumably sent a third to *The Worker.* Finally, he gave the last copy to the only person he respected and trusted, Baron George de Mohrenschildt. On the back of this copy, he wrote in Russian, "To my friend George from Lee Oswald, hunter of fascists, ha, ha, ha. 5 April, 1963."[73]

Oswald had not given up the life of Riley that he enjoyed in Minsk just to wear a "Viva Castro" placard around his neck and pass out pamphlets on a street corner. As noted by Vincent Bugliosi, "Oswald did not view himself as a mere foot soldier in the Marxist struggle but a potential leader."[74] He was frustrated that his plans were not moving forward, blaming the Soviets for backing down over Cuba and took out his frustrations on the nearest Soviet at hand, Marina. He began looking for a dramatic action that would change his luck. The dramatic action Oswald decided upon was to assassinate the virulently anti-Castro segregationist of recent Ole Miss notoriety, retired Army General Edwin Walker.

***

After the riots at Ole Miss, Walker returned home to Dallas to await trial. He remained frequently in the news and was a special focus of criticism by one of Oswald's favorite newspapers, *The Militant.* On 21 January 1963, an all-white federal grand jury in Mississippi dismissed all the charges against him. After the charges were dropped, Walker began beating the war drums, making repeated public statements that the US government should use its troops against Fidel Castro's communists in Cuba rather than against patriotic Americans like him. Intently following all this in *The Militant,*

---

[73] *Reclaiming History* by Bugliosi, p. 697

[74] Ibid, p. 683

Oswald concluded that if the federal courts were not prepared to enforce the laws and stop Walker from promoting fascism in America, then he, Lee Harvey Oswald, would.

On 27 January, Oswald used the alias "A.J. Hidell," a rhyme with Fidel, to buy a Smith-Wesson .38 revolver via a mail-order gun catalogue out of Los Angeles. After conducting a detailed surveillance of Walker's home in the upscale Turtle Creek section in Dallas on 10 March, Oswald modified his planning. On 12 March, he used the same alias to order a Mannlicher-Carcano 6.5mm carbine rifle with high-powered sniper scope via a separate mail-order gun catalogue out of Chicago. This rifle, which he used to kill President Kennedy eight months later, cost Oswald $21.45 including shipping. The pistol, which he used to kill Dallas police officer J.D. Tippit forty-five minutes after killing the President, cost Oswald $29.95 including shipping. Both weapons were shipped on 20 March to A.J. Hidell, care of Oswald's post office box #2915 at Dallas's main post office.[75]

As noted above, Oswald had Marina take the famous photo of him dressed all in black with the revolver tucked in his belt as he held the sniper rifle in his left hand on Sunday, 31 March. Ten days later, on the morning of Wednesday, 10 April, Oswald left a farewell note to Marina and baby June, then departed home before they got up. After dark, at 9:00 PM, Oswald quietly positioned himself in the alley behind Walker's house at 4011 Turtle Creek Boulevard, a 5-10 minute drive south of George de Mohrenschildt's apartment. The general was seated at his desk working on his 1962

[75] *Reclaiming History* by Bugliosi, p. 200

federal tax forms. Oswald had a clear shot at a sitting target just forty yards away. He fired one shot and saw the general's head slump towards the desk.

Oswald returned home around midnight. Marina confronted him with the farewell note and demanded to know what it was all about. Oswald confessed both that he had lost his job and that he had just assassinated General Walker. Marina was terrified for herself and for baby June. She expected the police to arrive at any minute.

Next morning, the radio news reported that a sniper had attempted to assassinate the controversial retired general but had missed. The only thing that had saved Walker was that he had his windows closed and the air conditioning on due to the unusually warm weather that spring evening. The sniper's bullet had smashed through the double-paned windows but glanced off the wooden frame that ran horizontally between the panes. This was just sufficient to deflect the bullet an inch to the left of the general's head. Witnesses reported to the police seeing two men flee the area in a car. Oswald was furious with himself for missing, and now, he was scared.

Three days after the attempt, on Saturday, 13 April, George de Mohrenschildt and his wife Jeanne showed up at the Oswald's Neely Street apartment unexpectedly. De Mohrenschldt said, "Hey Lee. How is it possible that you missed?" causing Lee to make an uncomfortable face. A few moments later, Jeanne saw the sniper rifle and called out, "Look, George, they have a gun here." Both couples became uncomfortable, so de Mohrenschildt and Jeanne left in short order. That evening and for the next few days, Oswald suffered from anxiety attacks and could not sleep.[76]

On 15 April, de Mohrenschildt and Jeanne abruptly departed Dallas. They moved to Haiti, a country that had no extradition treaty with the United States and where De Mohrenschildt had some vague business dealings. Years later, he admitted that he had feared being implicated in Oswald's attempted assassination of Walker. It is quite telling about the depth of his relationship with Oswald that de Mohrenschildt did not report what he knew about an attempted murder to the FBI or to the Dallas police. Had he done so, Lee Harvey Oswald would have been in jail on 22 November 1963 when President Kennedy visited Dallas.

Why did de Mohrenschildt fear being implicated in Oswald's action? From what we know, he was no more implicated in the act itself than Marina. Marina, at least, had some excuse for engaging in a cover-up; wives are not expected to testify against their own husbands. But, de Mohrenschildt's failure to report what he knew verges on criminal obstruction of justice. Why would he take such a monumental risk? What else was he trying to hide?

With no claim to certainty, an intelligence officer would say that odds were high that de Mohrenschildt feared that an investigation of Oswald would reveal de Mohrenschildt's own connections to Soviet intelligence. Any investigation of Oswald would focus some attention on his years living in Minsk. Did Oswald have any connection to Soviet intelligence? If so, was the assassination attempt against Walker sponsored by Soviet intelligence? Witnesses had seen two people flee from the scene of the crime. Who else was

---

[76] *Reclaiming History* by Bugliosi, p. 696

involved? Who was this other character from Minsk, that friend of the fascist hunter? Was he, too, involved in the Walker assassination attempt? Did he, too, have ties to Soviet intelligence? These were all questions that would be better left unasked from de Mohrenschildt's viewpoint and from the KGB's viewpoint as well.

On 29 March 1977, almost 14 years to the day after Marina took the photo of Oswald all dressed in black, George de Mohrenschildt put a shotgun in his mouth and pulled the trigger. He had just learned that investigators from the House Special Committee on Assassinations wanted to question him.

***

Oswald followed de Mohrenschildt's lead and fled Dallas as well on the evening of Wednesday, 24 April 1963. He arrived in New Orleans by bus the next morning and immediately telephoned his maternal aunt, Lillian Murret. Lillian had not seen nor heard from Oswald for years, but she was a kind woman. Until he got settled, she invited him to stay with her family at their home at 757 French Street in the pleasant Lakeview district in North New Orleans near Lake Pontchartrain. This home is a classic "shotgun" style New Orleans duplex, with #755 adjoining #757. The Lakeview area was devastated by Hurricane Katrina in 2005, but the house has been nicely refurbished since.

On 9 May, two weeks after arriving in New Orleans, Oswald found a job at the downtown end of Magazine Street and a duplex apartment to rent at the uptown end. He immediately called Marina and asked her and baby June to join him. They arrived by car on 11 May, the Saturday before Mother's Day. Their friend Ruth Paine had volunteered to drive them because she was concerned that the bus trip might prove too grueling for the pregnant Marina.

Circa 15 May and unbeknownst to Oswald, another FBI agent showed up at the Neely Street apartment back in Dallas hoping to interview Oswald. Special Agent James Hosty was the replacement for the now retired Special Agent John Fain. The interview was just a routine matter for Hosty to check up on the left wing returnee from the Soviet Union. Hosty could find no trace of the Oswald family, however. They had disappeared without leaving any forwarding address. So, Hosty wrote a short report for Oswald's file and then turned his efforts back to a more important investigation, the activities of the right wing retired Major General Edwin Walker who somebody had just tried to assassinate.

Oswald's apartment in New Orleans was at 4907 Magazine in Uptown between Robert and Upperline Streets. It was the same "shotgun" style as the Murret home in Lakeview but not nearly as nice. The location was very convenient, however. A bus line ran directly down Magazine to and from Oswald's work. The family did their normal grocery shopping at a Winn Dixie store five blocks north at 4901 Prytania Street (today a CVS Pharmacy). There was another, larger Winn Dixie at 4303 Magazine six blocks east, in the old Jefferson Market building, next door to the Napoleon Avenue Public Library. Oswald quickly became a regular at the library. Oswald's job was with the William B. Reily Coffee Company located at 640 Magazine in the Warehouse/Arts District, one block south of Lafayette

Square. The company still thrives at the location, selling the Luzianne brand of coffees, iced teas, and other foods.

According to Marina, Oswald's overriding interest in the spring and summer of 1963 was to use his time in New Orleans as a launch pad to a new life in Cuba. She testified to the Warren Commission, "I only know that his basic desire was to get to Cuba by any means, and that all the rest was window dressing for that purpose."[77]

On Sunday, 26 May, Oswald wrote a letter to the Fair Play for Cuba Committee (FPCC) headquarters in New York requesting membership, a picture of Fidel Castro suitable for framing, and a charter to open an FPCC chapter in New Orleans. On 29 May, the national FPCC mailed Oswald his membership card and the picture of Fidel but declined to issue a charter pending "several public experiences" to determine how well Oswald could operate in the New Orleans community. Moreover, the national FPCC warned Oswald that it might be dangerous to open a local FPCC office in New Orleans and, instead, suggested that he just use a post office box. Oswald received the FPCC response Saturday, 1 June.

Immediately the following Monday, 3 June, Oswald rented post office box #30061 at what was then New Orleans' main post office on Lafayette Square a block north of his job in downtown New Orleans. Today, this same building is the F. Edward Hebert Federal Building. There is still a post office branch office inside, but the main post office and all the PO Boxes are now located on Loyola Street further north. Oswald, Marina, and "A.J. Hidell, President of the FPCC New

---

[77] *Reclaiming History* by Bugliosi, p. 709

Orleans Chapter" were authorized to pick up mail from P.O. Box #30061. As we know, "A.J. Hidell" was the same alias that Oswald had used earlier in 1963 to order his sniper rifle and revolver.

***

On Sunday, 16 June, Oswald was threatened with arrest for passing out "HANDS OFF CUBA" leaflets on the old Dumaine Street Wharf behind Café du Monde in the French Quarter. He was protesting the visit of the aircraft carrier USS Wasp. As a result, Oswald was fired from his job at Reily's on 19 July and would remain unemployed for the remaining two months of his time in New Orleans.

Undeterred, Oswald passed out more "HANDS OFF CUBA" leaflets on Friday, 9 August, at Canal Street between Royal and Bourbon in downtown New Orleans. Oswald knew that the headquarters of anti-Castro Cuban exiles in New Orleans was just a few blocks away at 107 Decatur Street at the corner of Canal and Decatur Streets. Not unexpectedly, three anti-Castro Cuban exiles, Carlos Bringuier, Celso Hernandez, and Miguel Cruz, quickly mounted a counter-demonstration to Oswald. A scuffle ensued; all four were arrested and taken to the district police station on North Rampart Street. The three Cubans posted bail and were released. Oswald spent the night and most of the next day in jail, a fact that he seemed quite pleased about when he returned home to Marina Saturday evening.

On Monday, 12 August, Oswald and the three anti-Castro

Cubans appeared at the small courtroom inside the Ramparts Street precinct on charges of disturbing the peace. Oswald pleaded guilty and was fined $10. The charges against the three Cubans were dropped. Oswald got what he wanted, however. The incident was reported that evening on WDSU-TV News Channel 6 and the next day in New Orleans' main newspaper, *The Times-Picayune*. Oswald immediately wrote to the national FPCC and to the information director of the US Communist Party to advise them of his local success in bringing attention to the cause of Castro's Cuba.

The following Friday, 16 August, Oswald tried to bait the Cuban exiles again by passing out more "HANDS OFF CUBA" leaflets in front of the old International Trade Mart at the corner of Canal and Camp Streets, just one block away from the anti-Castro Cuban headquarters at Canal and Decatur. This time, two other men helped Oswald pass out the leaflets. One was an unemployed American named Charles Steele who Oswald paid $2. The other was a short, young Cuban who has never been identified.[78] About this same time, a "Latin-type" carrying pro-Castro leaflets came looking for Oswald one evening at the house on Magazine Street and spoke with his landlady.[79]

On Saturday, 17 August, Oswald was interviewed by WDSU Channel 6 and a four-minute thirty-second excerpt was played on the TV news that evening. WDSU also invited Oswald to appear on a live, 30-minute televised debate with

---

[78] According to Steele, the short young Cuban was accompanied by a taller, male companion (*Reclaiming History* by Bugliosi, p. 727). For the possible significance of this, see Chapter IX below.

[79] *Reclaiming History* by Bugliosi, p. 743

Carlos Bringuier the following Monday, 10 August. Once again, Oswald was quick to alert the national FPCC to his local, public relations success.

This spurt of pro-Cuba activity by Oswald did not escape notice by the FBI. The Bureau had learned in late June that Oswald was living in New Orleans but saw no urgency in trying to determine exactly where. On 5 August, the New Orleans office of the FBI got around to confirming Oswald's residence at 4907 Magazine Street. On 9 August, the New Orleans Police advised the FBI of Oswald's arrest. Then, on the morning of 12 August, prior to the televised debate with Bringuier, the FBI briefed WDSU on the facts of Oswald's defection to the USSR and his marriage to a Soviet woman. During the live broadcast, questions about his time in the Soviet Union and about financial support he received from the Soviet government took Oswald by surprise, making him look like a Soviet Communist stooge.

Despite the setback he suffered in the live, televised debate of 19 August, Oswald did achieve his objective of creating "several public experiences" in support of Castro's Cuba as requested by the national FPCC. He demonstrated his commitment to Castro's cause by serving jail time. He also generated a significant amount of positive publicity in New Orleans for the pro-Castro Cuban cause. This was a risky thing to do because in 1963, New Orleans was perhaps second only to Miami in terms of its strong and frequently violent anti-Castro sentiment.

That the DGI, Cuba's highly competent intelligence service, was clandestinely present in New Orleans is all but certain. Not only was the large anti-Castro Cuban exile community of concern to the DGI, but New Orleans was also the headquarters of Fidel and Che's long-time nemesis, the United Fruit Company. The ornate facade of the United Fruit headquarters building is still there at 321 St Charles Avenue, just a short walk from Lafayette Square.

That DGI operatives present in New Orleans would have noticed Oswald's pro-Castro Activities is equally certain. The historical question is whether or not these DGI operatives actually reached out and contacted Oswald. In that context, who was that short, young, pro-Castro Cuban who helped Oswald pass out the "HANDS OFF CUBA" pamphlets in front of the International Trade Mart on 16 August? Who was the "Latin-type" carrying pro-Castro leaflets that Oswald's landlady testified came looking for him one evening that summer? As a factual matter, we simply do not know the answers to these questions, but what is certain is that Oswald was seeking contact, and as we will see in the next section, the DGI had a compelling motive for clandestinely reaching out to him.

***

In establishing Cuba's new government, Fidel Castro first named his erstwhile revolutionary rival Rolando Cubela to the top rank in the new Cuban armed forces, a "commandante," and deputy minister of interior. Nominally, this made Cubela the second in command of Cuban intelligence after Ramiro Valdes. However, Cubela told his Mafia friend Santos Trafficante that in reality, he had been marginalized. Thinking Cubela disillusioned with Fidel, Trafficante brokered an introduction for him to the CIA.

During 5-8 September 1963, a CIA officer named Nestor Sanchez met with Cubela in Porto Alegre, Brazil. During those meetings, Cubela volunteered to assassinate Castro and establish a new Cuban government less hostile to the United States. Sanchez told Cubela that his proposal would be brought to the attention of the "highest levels" of the US government and promised a response at their next meetings, scheduled for October in Paris. The CIA gave Cubela the codename AM/LASH.

Coming less than a year after the Cuban Missile Crisis, during and after which Fidel Castro publicly lamented Nikita Khrushchev's decision to back away from a nuclear confrontation, Cubela's offer would have been understandably tempting to the US Government, including the President and his brother, the attorney general. Tragically, the strategic and political attractiveness of Cubela's offer caused the CIA to ignore clear warnings that Cubela was a blatant provocation. He was not an agent working secretly for the CIA; he was a double agent pretending to work for the CIA but really working secretly for Redbeard Pineiro, the head of Cuban counterintelligence. Everything Cubela raised with the CIA, including his "offer" to assassinate Castro, had been coordinated in advance with Redbeard. Everything the CIA asked Cubela to do was immediately reported back via Redbeard and Valdes to Fidel Castro.[80]

---

[80] In 1987, a senior Cuban intelligence officer named Florentino Azpillaga Lombard defected to the United States and stunned the CIA with evidence that all of the thirty-eight Cubans that the US thought it had recruited since 1961 had really been double agents working for Cuban counterintelligence.

On 7 September 1962, at the very same time that Nestor Sanchez was meeting with Cubela in Brazil, Fidel Castro made an impromptu appearance at a reception hosted by the Brazilian Embassy in Havana. Fidel took the initiative to approach an American reporter named Daniel Harker and offered him a quick, private interview. Fidel told Harker, "We are prepared to fight them and answer them in kind. United States leaders should think that if they are aiding terrorist plans to eliminate Cuban leaders, they themselves will not be safe. Let Kennedy and his brother Robert take care of themselves since they, too, can be the cause of an attempt which will cause their deaths."[81] When he gave this warning, Fidel knew that Cubela was meeting the CIA in Sao Paulo.

In addition, on 10 October, a Cuban-American living in Florida reported to the FBI that he had heard that Rolando Cubela had met with the CIA in Brazil on 7 September and had offered to assassinate Castro. When the FBI advised the CIA of this report, the CIA immediately concluded that the operational security surrounding the extremely sensitive AM/LASH operation had been compromised and, accordingly, terminated all further contact with Cubela. Tragically, the FBI did not advise the CIA of this October 1963 report until June 1965.[82]

Clearly, the DGI did, indeed, have a strong motive for making contact with somebody like Oswald. Did they, in fact, do so? Again, we do not know for certain, but the next chapter will demonstrate that the circumstantial evidence surrounding his departure from New Orleans and his brief

---

[81] *Reclaiming History* by Bugliosi, p. 941; *Wedge* by Riebling, p. 173

[82] *Wedge* by Riebling, p. 238

visit to Mexico City strongly suggests it did.

***

Suggestions for further reading:

1. *Wedge: From Pearl Harbor to 9/11, How the Secret War Between the FBI and the CIA Has Endangered National Security* by Mark Riebling, Simon and Schuster, 1994 & 2002.

Despite the melodramatic subtitle, this remains the single best history of US Counterintelligence through the end of the Cold War in 1989. The epilogue added in 2002 only superficially addresses events since 1990. Essential reading for American intelligence professionals.

2. *Thirteen Days: A Memoir of the Cuban Missile Crisis* by Robert F. Kennedy, W.W. Norton, 1969.

Released a year after Robert Kennedy's own assassination, this book focuses on JFK's leadership style during the crisis. It does not touch on the intelligence background to the crisis.

3. *The Kennedy Tapes: Inside the White House During the Cuban Missile Crisis* by Ernst May and Phillip Zelikow, Belknap Press, 1997.

A more historically accurate book than Bobby's memoir. This book was the basis of the excellent 2000 film *Thirteen Days* starring Kevin Costner as JFK's Chief of Staff Kenny O'Donnell.

A Spy's Walking Tour of New Orleans

This walking tour is divided into two distinct sections: one Downtown in the Business District and the French Quarter, and one Uptown mainly on Magazine. The Downtown section takes an hour at a normal walking pace and leaves you in the French Quarter next to the famous Café du Monde. The Uptown section takes thirty minutes and leaves you in between the popular restaurant Crepe Nanou for a meal and the equally popular Creole Creamery for some ice cream. The best mode of transportation between the two walking tours is the wonderful streetcar that runs the length of St Charles Avenue. See Chapter 8 for details related to all of the sites below. Also, see the PBS documentary "The Ghost of Oswald" for film clips of Oswald while he operated in New Orleans.

***

Downtown

1. 640 Magazine Street, the William B. Reily Coffee Company where Oswald worked during April-June 1963 before being

fired for demonstrating on the Dumaine Street Wharf against the USS Wasp. Walk north one block to Layfayette Street, turn right, and proceed one block to Lafayette Square.

2. Lafayette Square, south side, the F. Edward Hebert Federal Building, formerly the New Orleans main post office where Oswald rented his "Fair Play for Cuba" post office box. Walk north along Camp Street, and turn left on Poydras Street.

3. 610 Poydras, the Whitney Hotel, where the Mexican Consulate was located in 1963 and where Oswald received the travel document necessary for his trip to Mexico City to meet with Cuban officials. Proceed to the corner and turn right onto St Charles Avenue.

4. 321 St Charles Avenue, the beautiful façade of the old headquarters of United Fruit Company, the nemesis of Fidel Castro and Che Guevara. Proceed along St Charles Avenue to Canal Street and turn right.

5. The southeast location of the intersection of Canal and Camp Streets, the former location of the New Orleans Trade Mart, where Oswald handed out the "Hands off Cuba!" pamphlets inviting people to join the New Orleans chapter of the Fair Play for Cuba Committee. Proceed to the end of the block, turn left, and cross Canal Street to Decatur Street.

6. 107 Decatur Street, the New Orleans headquarters of anti-Castro Cuban exiles during 1963. Continue down Decatur Street through the heart of the French Quarter to Jackson Square, turn right on Dumaine Street, and proceed to the top of the levee.

7. The Dumaine Street Wharf, where Oswald staged a pro-Cuba demonstration to protest the visit of the USS Wasp, the

aircraft carrier that patrolled the waters around Cuba.

***

Uptown

1. 4303 Magazine Street, the old Jefferson Market, which in 1963 was the Winn Dixie at which Oswald cashed his last unemployment check before departing for Mexico City. Proceed one block west to Napoleon Avenue.

2. Napoleon Avenue Public Library at the northeast corner of the intersection of Napoleon Avenue and Magazine Street, where Oswald checked out books almost daily. Proceed six blocks west along Magazine Street.

3. 4907 Magazine Street where the Oswald family lived during May-August 1963 and where Lee probably met first with Cuban intelligence. It was on the back porch of this house that Lee began "dry fire" practice with his sniper rifle in late August 1963. Proceed five blocks north along Upperline Street to Prytania Street.

4. 4901 Prytania Street, currently a CVS drugstore, in 1963 it was the Winn Dixie grocery where Marina and Lee normally shopped.

This ends the tour.

14. The house at 4907 Magazine where Oswald probably first met Cuban intelligence

15. The old Jefferson Market at 4303 Magazine where Oswald cashed his last unemployment check

16. The William B. Reily Coffee Company at 640 Magazine where Oswald was employed

17. Facade of the old United Fruit Company headquarters at 321 St Charles Avenue

Chapter 9
Implicated in Mexico City

It would have been quite normal for the DGI, Cuba's intelligence service, to seek clandestine contact with Oswald in late August 1963, after newspaper, radio, and TV reports of his pro-Cuba activity in New Orleans had been relayed to the Fair Play for Cuba Committee. Indeed, it would have been odd if the DGI did not do so. Reaching out to people who might be helpful is what intelligence services do.

A standard DGI recruitment pitch during this period was that Fidel Castro needed help from like-minded people to defend the young Cuban revolution against American aggression. It is not known for certain that the DGI used this same recruitment approach with Oswald, but the circumstantial evidence would suggest that they did. Specifically, we know that in late August, Oswald began "dry fire" practice with his sniper rifle from the back porch of his apartment at 4907 Magazine Street. Oswald explained to a horrified Marina that he needed to practice because he had decided to volunteer as a revolutionary and help defend Fidel

Castro. [83]

On 9 September, Oswald would certainly have noted the headline in his regular New Orleans newspaper that reported Castro's threat to retaliate "in kind" against the Kennedy brothers for persistent American plotting to assassinate Cuban leaders. Having already tried on his own initiative to assassinate a prominent anti-Castro American, the retired General Walker, this threat by Fidel would have resonated deeply with Oswald. It was in this context that on 17 September, Oswald obtained a tourist card from the Mexican Consulate in New Orleans so that he could travel to Mexico City and meet with officials of the Cuban Embassy there. Both the Cuban DGI as well as the Soviet KGB regularly used Mexico City during the Cold War as a secure venue to meet with their American clandestine contacts.

Oswald departed New Orleans sometime on Wednesday morning, 25 September, and crossed the border at Laredo, Texas, into Mexico on the early afternoon of Thursday, 26 September. There is uncertainty about the route he took between New Orleans and Laredo, but according to scholar Vincent Bugliosi, the weight of the evidence indicates that he detoured via Dallas in a car with two Cubans who used the aliases Leopoldo and Angelo. After crossing the border, Oswald took a bus to Mexico City, arriving circa 10:00 AM on Friday, 27 September. Wasting no time, he visited the Cuban Embassy circa 11:15-12:15 that same morning and then the Soviet Embassy circa 12:30-13:30.[84]

---

[83] *Reclaiming History* by Bugliosi, p. 743

[84] *Reclaiming History* by Bugliosi, p. 752-759. Also see *Passport to Assassination* by Nechiporenko.

Thanks to CIA monitoring of a telephone call initiated by the Cuban Embassy to the Soviet Embassy, the US government knew at the time that inside the Soviet Embassy, Oswald had met with Valery Vladimirovich Kostikov, an officer of Department 13 of the KGB First Chief Directorate, the department responsible for sabotage and assassination operations, who was serving undercover as a Soviet consular official. Importantly, both the Cubans and the Soviets understood perfectly well that the CIA systematically monitored all telephone calls between the two embassies.[85] *Since the end of the Cold War, the KGB has additionally conceded that Oswald also met with two other KGB officers serving under consular cover, Oleg Maximovich Nechiporenko and Pavel Antonovich Yatskov. As noted in Chapter V, prior to his assignment in Mexico City, Nechiporenko had served as deputy to Nikolai Leonov in the KGB office responsible for Cuba.*

Publicly, the Cuban government has persistently denied that Oswald met with any Cuban intelligence officers when he visited the Cuban Embassy in Mexico City and that Oswald made threats against President Kennedy to Cuban officials. Prima facie, the public denial of contact with Cuban intelligence is simply not plausible to any professional intelligence officer. Indeed, DGI standard operating would have been for Oswald to be interviewed by Rogelio Rodriguez Lopez and/or Manuel Vega Perez, two DGI officers serving

---

[85] The fact that CIA had monitored the call from the Cuban Embassy to the Soviet Embassy which implicated Kostikov was made public in 1964 by the Warren Commission. Oswald's contact with Nechiporenko and Yatskov was made public in 1994 after the end of the Cold War in Nechiporenko's KGB approved book, *Passport to Assassination.*

under consular cover and responsible for targeting Americans. Moreover, in 1964, Fidel Castro privately told a trusted American Communist Party representative Jack Childs that during the discussions with the Cuban Embassy officials in Mexico City, Oswald had, indeed, threatened to assassinate President Kennedy. Castro did not realize that Childs was clandestinely cooperating with the FBI and would report to the Bureau everything that Castro said.[86]

***

On 20 September, Marina's friend Ruth Paine arrived in New Orleans to drive Marina and baby June back to Dallas. Marina was in the last month of her pregnancy, and Ruth was taking her back to Dallas where she could use Parkland Hospital free of charge for the upcoming delivery. On Monday morning, 23 September, Ruth, Marina, and baby June departed New Orleans. Oswald's landlord was suspicious when he noticed the departure preparations because Oswald was two weeks late on his rent. When the landlord confronted him, Oswald lied that Marina, baby June, and the new baby would return to New Orleans after the delivery.

On the evening of Tuesday, 24 September, a neighbor saw Oswald sneaking away from the house at 4907 Magazine carrying two suitcases. The FBI could find no trace of Oswald checking in to a hotel or motel, so it is unknown where he spent the night.

---

[86] *Reclaiming History* by Bugliosi, p. 204

Sometime between 5:00 and 10:30 AM on Wednesday, 25 September, Oswald picked up his unemployment check from his post office box #30061 at the Lafayette Square post office. He also filed a request for his mail to be forwarded to Ruth Paine's address in Dallas. Oswald traveled over three miles back to his neighborhood to cash the check at the Winn Dixie store located at 4303 Magazine, just as he usually did, and then slipped out of New Orleans without paying his overdue rent.

It is historically certain thanks to Mexican immigration records that Oswald crossed the border into Mexico from Laredo, Texas, sometime before 2:00 PM on 26 September. It is also historically certain that Oswald was on the Red Arrow bus #516 that departed from Nuevo Laredo on the Mexican side of the border at 2:15 PM, destination Mexico City. Oswald's true name appears on the passenger manifest, and numerous witnesses saw and spoke with him on that bus. It is not known for certain how Oswald traveled between New Orleans and Laredo, who he traveled with, or what route he took, but there are two hypotheses.

***

The hypothesis supported by the 1964 Warren Commission is that Oswald traveled on buses by himself directly from New Orleans to the US-Mexican border at Laredo and then on to Mexico City. The alternative hypothesis supported tentatively by Vincent Bugliosi in his exhaustively researched book, *Reclaiming History*, is that Oswald departed New Orleans by car with two Cubans and detoured to Dallas for an encounter with an anti-Castro Cuban exile named Sylvia Odio. Then, Oswald made his way from Dallas to the US-Mexican border at Laredo and on to Mexico City.

According to the Warren Commission hypothesis, Oswald departed from the bus station in downtown New Orleans at mid-day on the 25th, arriving in Houston circa 10:20 PM that evening. This scenario raises several questions. Why would Oswald pick up his unemployment check downtown, travel three miles to cash the check at the Winn Dixie near his apartment, and then travel back downtown to catch the bus? Why not just cash the check downtown as he could have easily done? Why doesn't Oswald's name or any of his normal aliases appear on any Houston-bound bus? Why is there no eye witness claiming to have seen him on any Houston-bound bus?

The Warren Commission hypothesis is that Oswald then departed Houston, again by bus, at 2:35 AM on the 26th, arriving in Laredo, Texas, circa 1:20 PM. Eight months later, well after the assassination, a British couple who were also on their way to Mexico City that September day gave an affidavit that they recalled seeing Oswald on the bus somewhere between Houston and Laredo. They believe they first noticed him circa 6:00 AM, but they did not actually talk to him until much later that afternoon while on the Red Arrow bus in northern Mexico. However, neither Oswald's name nor any of his normal aliases appear on the passenger manifest of the bus between Houston and Laredo.

The Warren Commission did not dispute the eyewitness testimony of Sylvia Odio and her sister Annie that three men, two Cubans and one American, visited their home in Dallas on the evening of either 25 or 26 September. However, the Commission dismissed the possibility that the American amongst the three men could have been Lee Harvey Oswald as Miss Odio claimed.

In contrast, Vincent Bugliosi, one of America's most experienced prosecutors, believes that the American amongst the three men who visited the Odio sisters in Dallas most likely was Oswald. As claimed in his book, Bugliosi says, "I feel the slight preponderance of evidence is that Oswald was, in fact, the American among the three men who visited Odio...there is that unmistakable 'ring of truth' to Odio's testimony." If Bugliosi is correct, then the visit to the Odios must have occurred on the evening of 25 September because it is historically certain that Oswald was on the bus somewhere in northern Mexico bound for Mexico City on the evening of 26 September.

Furthermore, if Bugliosi is correct, three important questions arise. Who were the two Cuban men that Oswald was with? Were they the short, young Cuban with a taller companion that Charles Steele saw Oswald with in New Orleans on 16 August? Why did Oswald agree to a detour to Dallas with these two Cuban men when it is historically certain that he was anxious to get to Mexico City?

The simple, most common sense answers to those questions would be (1) yes, these two Cuban men were the two men Steele saw Oswald with on 16 August, (2) they were traveling together to Mexico City, and (3) some errand involving Ms. Odio caused them to make a quick detour to Dallas. Anybody can postulate other, more convoluted scenarios, but respecting Ockham's Razor, it is hard to dismiss this simple, common sense explanation. At this point then, what Sylvia Odio said happened that late September night in Dallas requires further examination.

***

Sylvia Odio has testified, and her sister Annie has corroborated, that one evening in late September 1963 circa 9:00 PM, three men, two Cubans and one American, arrived by car to their apartment at 1084 Magellan Circle in Dallas. The two Cubans claimed to be friends of the Odios' imprisoned father and knew incredible details about their father, including where he was imprisoned in Cuba. The two Cuban men refused to provide Ms. Odio their true names. The driver was the taller of the two and used the alias Leopoldo. The shorter of the two used the alias Angelo. Leopoldo introduced the accompanying American as Leon Oswald, a former Marine. According to Ms. Odio, he mentioned the name Leon Oswald on at least two occasions.

Ms. Odio testified that the two Cubans claimed they were members of an anti-Castro organization called JURE and requested her help in translating into English a fund-raising petition written in Spanish for the JURE chapter in Dallas. Ms. Odio, however, was herself a member of the Dallas chapter of JURE and knew the head of the chapter, Antonio Alentado. She asked Leopoldo and Angelo if they had been sent by Alentado. They said no, they were trying to organize a separate JURE group in Dallas independent of Alentado. According to Ms. Odio, the two Cubans said that they had just arrived from New Orleans and that they would be traveling on to Mexico. Ms. Odio had never seen them before and never saw them again.

The next day, Leopoldo spoke again with Ms. Odio by telephone. He said that his American friend was "kind of crazy" and had volunteered to assassinate President Kennedy because of the President's failure to provide direct US military support to the Bay of Pigs invasion. Leopoldo asked if Ms. Odio could introduce the American to somebody in the Cuban underground who could smuggle him into Cuba so that he could assassinate Castro. Clearly suspicious of the entire incident and concerned about the safety of her imprisoned father, Ms. Odio told Leopoldo that she knew of no such people in the Cuban underground. In a letter just a few weeks later, Odio's father wrote that he had no idea who these men might be and warned his daughter to avoid further contact with them unless they provided her their true names.

Regardless of whether the avidly pro-Castro Oswald was the American amongst the three or not, professional intelligence officers, especially those from the KGB and the Cuban DGI, would conclude reasonably and with high confidence that Leopoldo and Angelo were provocations sent by the Cuban DGI to test Ms. Odio. She and her father apparently thought so as well. Moreover, it is noteworthy that Odio's father had been arrested and was in a Cuban prison because he had been involved the previous year in anti-Castro plotting with Rolando Cubela.[87]

If the avidly pro-Castro Oswald was the American with these two Cubans, then it would make even more common sense that Leopoldo and Angelo were likewise pro-Fidel.

---

[87] *Legend* by Epstein, p. 233

Otherwise, why would Oswald, who was clearly in a hurry to get from New Orleans to Mexico City, have taken the detour to Dallas with them? If Mr. Bugliosi is correct that Oswald was the American amongst the three men, then he was there almost certainly because all three of them were on their way to Mexico City together for some pre-arranged business. What is known with certainty about Oswald's visit to Mexico City is suspicious enough by itself. If we add that Oswald was in conspiratorial league with Leopoldo and Angelo, then the events in Mexico City become very suspicious indeed.

***

As noted above, Oswald arrived in Mexico City on Red Arrow Bus #516 circa 10:00 AM on Friday, 27 September. Oswald proceeded directly to a hotel rarely used by Americans, the Hotel Del Comercio on Calle Bernardino, four blocks from the bus station, circa 11:00 AM. After check-in, Oswald went straight to the Consular Section of the Cuban Embassy on Calle Francisco Marquez, eight blocks away, where he applied for a visa so that he could fly on to Cuba the next day. Reportedly, the first person he spoke to was a Mexican woman temporarily employed by the Cuban Embassy named Silvia Duran. Ms. Duran advised Oswald that the only visa that could be issued to him on such short notice was a transit visa for a person stopping in Cuba on the way to the Soviet Union. To obtain such a transit visa, however, the person needed an entry visa to the Soviet Union, which Oswald did not have. Reportedly, Ms. Duran's supervisor, Cuban Consul General Eusebio Azcue, came out of his office and confirmed what Ms. Duran had told Oswald.

Oswald departed the Cuban Embassy circa 12:15.

Oswald made his way two blocks from the Cuban Embassy to the Soviet Embassy, arriving there at 12:30, just thirty minutes before it closed for the weekend. Normally, the Consular Section of the Soviet Embassy would not receive visitors without an appointment, but an exception was made for this Russian-speaking American. Oswald was permitted entrance and introduced to the consular duty official, the undercover KGB officer, Valery Kostikov. Before stating his business, Oswald took special precaution to look at Kostikov's diplomatic identity card to insure that he was speaking with a Soviet official, not a Mexican employee. Kostikov spoke with Oswald for some period of time and then introduced him to his KGB colleague Oleg Nechiporenko. Oswald departed the Soviet Embassy circa 1:30 PM without being photographed by the surveillance cameras positioned outside the Embassy.[88]

Sometime after 2:00 PM, Oswald returned to the Cuban Embassy. Although the Consular Section had already closed for the weekend, Oswald was somehow permitted to enter and speak again with Ms. Duran. Oswald claimed that he had been promised an entry visa by the Soviet Embassy but had not yet received it. He tried to convince Ms. Duran to issue the transit visa so that he could catch the flight to Havana the next day. Ms. Duran made a telephone call to Kostikov to verify if Oswald's claim was true. This telephone line was monitored by the CIA, and Kostikov understood it to be so monitored.

Circa 9:30 AM on Saturday 28 September, Oswald

---

[88] *Passport to Assassination* by Nechiporenko

returned to the Soviet Embassy and was again permitted to enter even though the Embassy was closed. Oswald was inside until at least 11:00 AM speaking with Kostikov, Nechiporenko, and a more senior KGB officer, Pavel Antonovich Yatskov. As a result of this unusual after-hours meeting with Oswald, all three of these KGB officers missed the weekly volleyball game between the KGB team and the GRU military intelligence team. Oswald departed the Soviet Embassy sometime after 11:00 AM, again without being photographed by the surveillance cameras positioned outside the Embassy.

Oswald remained in Mexico City four more days until Wednesday, 2 October, engaged in unknown activities. The Cuban DGI intelligence service denies having met with Oswald at any time during his visit to Mexico City. To any professional intelligence officer, however, it is simply not plausible that the DGI did not meet Oswald at least once during his visit. Intelligence services place officers undercover in the consular sections of their embassies because that is the publicly accessible venue where foreigners come to volunteer secret information. It is standard operating procedure for intelligence officers to screen visitors to consular sections on the off-chance that they may be such volunteers. That is why Kostikov agreed to meet with the Russian-speaking American who arrived without an appointment just before closing time on Friday, 27 September. Cuban DGI officers were trained to do exactly the same thing that Kostikov did.

In 1964, Fidel Castro privately told a trusted American Communist Party representative, Jack Childs, that during the discussions with Cuban Embassy officials in Mexico City, Oswald had, indeed, threatened to assassinate President

Kennedy. In 1978, Fidel seemed to tell US Congressional investigators the exact opposite. Fidel told them that he would have felt a "moral responsibility" to warn the US government had Oswald threatened to harm America's President during his discussions with Cuban Embassy officials in Mexico City.

***

Oswald's visit to Mexico City raises a number of questions that remain unanswered even today:

1. When he visited the Soviet Embassy, Oswald took special care to verify that the first person he talked to, Kostikov, was a Soviet official not a Mexican national employed at the consulate. Why, then, would Oswald work with a newly hired Mexican national employee at the Cuban Consulate? Conversely, why would Cuban intelligence allow an American walk-in to their consulate to be directed to a newly hired Mexican national employee? Anything is possible, but to a professional intelligence officer, none of this is plausible.

2. Who else did Oswald meet with from the Cuban Embassy in Mexico City? For example, did Oswald meet with DGI officers Rogelio Rodriguez Lopez or Manuel Vega Perez?

3. If Oswald did talk to these two Cuban intelligence officers in Mexico City, what did he talk with them about? Did he tell them about his attempt to assassinate the anti-Castro American general, Edwin Walker? Did he offer to help Fidel retaliate in kind against Americans who were persistently trying to assassinate Fidel? Oswald wanted to go to Cuba, but

what was in it for the Cubans? For months, Oswald had been establishing a record of pro-Castro activity in order to earn an entry visa to Cuba. Why wouldn't Oswald tell Rodriguez Lopez and Vega Perez these things?

4. If Oswald did offer to assassinate President Kennedy for the Cubans, is it plausible that the young revolutionary firebrand Fidel Castro would have felt a "moral obligation" to warn the American government? Alternatively, did the 10 October report from the Cuban-American to the FBI regarding Rolando Cubela constitute a second such warning on Fidel's part?

5. What role did the Soviets play in all of this, if any? Three KGB officers would not miss the weekly Saturday morning volley ball game against their GRU military intelligence rivals just to spend time with a psychologically unstable American kid. It is also highly unlikely that the surveillance cameras outside the Soviet Embassy would have missed Oswald twice in a row unless the KGB helped him depart unnoticed, as they were well trained to do.

6. Most importantly, the telephone call from Ms. Duran to Kositkov implicated the KGB and the nuclear-armed Soviets in whatever the Cubans were plotting with Oswald. Was this intentional on the Cuban's part?

***

Without making any claim to certainty, I would offer the following scenario to connect the above dots in a fashion that would be realistic and plausible to any professional intelligence officer:

1. Leopoldo and Angelo were Cuban intelligence operatives who made clandestine contact with Oswald in New Orleans during August following Oswald's pro-Cuba radio and TV appearances.

2. After Fidel threatened to retaliate "in kind" for continued American assassination plots against Cuban leaders, Oswald, having already tried on his own initiative to assassinate one anti-Castro American political figure, volunteered to Leopoldo and Angelo that he would be willing to help defend Fidel in any way the DGI considered useful.

3. The DGI arranged for Oswald to travel to Mexico City for further assessment and evaluation in a more secure operational environment outside of the United States. The DGI understood that Oswald's chances of success were slim, but nonetheless, the operation was responsive to their leader's publicly stated desire.

4. The DGI understood the high risk of even discussing an operation to assassinate the American president and, hence, took precautions to maintain plausible deniability.

5. To deter American retaliatory action, the DGI created an appearance that the nuclear-armed Soviets were somehow implicated in whatever the Cubans were plotting with Oswald.

6. Cuba's senior-most political leaders felt justified in considering retaliation "in kind" but still, given the high risks, insisted on providing another warning before giving any final concurrence.

***

Suggestions for further reading:

1. *Passport to Assassination: The Never-Before-Told Story of Lee Harvey Oswald by the KGB Colonel who Knew Him* by Oleg Maximovich Nechiporenko, Carol Publishing, 1993.

The KGB spin as of 1993, when Russian intelligence officers were facing hard times. Nechiporenko reveals perhaps more than he and the KGB intended.

2. *Castro's Secrets: The CIA and Cuba's Intelligence Machine* by Brian Latell, Palgrave/McMillan, 2012.

This book contains golden nuggets of well-researched historical fact, particularly in Chapters 8, 9, and 10. To find them, however, requires digging through much anti-Fidel political diatribe. Retired after three decades of distinguished service analyzing Cuban politics for the CIA and now affiliated with the University of Miami, Latell appears to have forsaken the goal of cool and balanced objectivity.

Chapter 10
The Perfect Tragedy

On 22 November 1963, Lee Harvey Oswald, an avowed friend of Cuba and former resident of the Soviet Union who was known by the US government to have been in direct contact with KGB sabotage and assassination specialists in Mexico City just seven weeks previously, assassinated the President of the United States, John F. Kennedy.

On 24 November, Attorney General Robert Kennedy and CIA Director John McCone briefed our new president, Lyndon Johnson, on the very real possibility that CIA assassination plotting against Castro might have backfired and resulted in the assassination of America's own president, just as Fidel Castro had publicly warned might happen in early September.

If only the Cubans were involved, then President Johnson would have had little compunction in "bombing Cuba back into the stone age." But, if the nuclear-armed Soviets were also implicated, then the stakes were considerably higher. A strike against Cuba could result in the nuclear confrontation with the Soviets that had just been successfully avoided thirteen months previously during the Cuban Missile Crisis. That would be the worst "intelligence failure" imaginable.

Accordingly, on 25 November, President Johnson directed that "speculation about Oswald's motivation should be cut off and we should have some basis for rebutting the thought that this was a communist conspiracy."[89] *Thus was born the Warren Commission.*

Assessing the stark facts of the situation, President Johnson took the steps that he sincerely judged were necessary to fulfill his duty to protect the broader interests of the country as well as the lives of the American people. Nonetheless, until his own death nine years later, Johnson would tell his closest confidants, "Kennedy tried to kill Castro, but Castro got Kennedy first."

***

The nine months that followed the Cuban Missile Crisis were the most successful of the Kennedy presidency on both the personal and professional levels. In December 1962, the First Lady learned that she was again pregnant. Overjoyed but worried about the possibility of another miscarriage, Jackie signaled her intent to step back from center stage during 1963. She had been the most influential image-maker in the White House since the fall of 1961, creating a perception amongst the American public of JFK as a decisive and successful president during a period when the reality had been quite different. Now, with her husband truly emerging as the leader and statesman that she knew he could

[89] *Wedge* by Riebling, p. 200

be, Jackie could afford to focus more on the health of her family.

At the First Lady's insistence, JFK broke off his long-standing affair with Mary Meyer. The affair had become a public embarrassment on 12 January 1963 when, in the midst of a nervous breakdown, the publisher of the *Washington Post,* Phil Graham, told an audience of newspaper publishers from across the nation the truth about the President's relationship with Meyer. As unbelievable as it may seem for Americans today, not a word of Graham's comments on a presidential sex scandal appeared in print at the time. Even in his book twelve years later, Ben Bradlee said nothing, glossing over the scandal with the notes, "Phil Graham was seriously ill...a natural friend for Kennedy, as JFK was a natural friend for Graham...the strain that Graham was putting on their friendship, and Kennedy's loyalty to him and his wife, were sad and moving."[90]

Jackie brought the Meyer issue to a head in early March when JFK included Mary as a guest to a White House dinner and dance. On 6 March, Jackie struck Mary's name from the list of dinner invitees but left her on the list of those invited to the after dinner dance. That same day, Jackie embarrassed JFK in front of their personal friends the Bradlees by recalling that she "couldn't get hold of Jack" in 1956 when their baby was stillborn and that it had been brother Bobby who consoled her grief. Getting the message clearly, JFK pulled Mary aside during the 8 March dance and told her that the Graham scandal left him no choice but to terminate their relationship. Mary caused a bit of scene, wandering in a daze

---

90 *Conversations with Kennedy* by Bradlee, p. 139

around the snow-covered White House grounds without a wrap to her evening gown; some feared she might commit suicide.

Fidel Castro, under pressure from Moscow, gave JFK a Christmas present by exchanging the Cuban exiles taken prisoner at the Bay of Pigs twenty months earlier for $53 million in medicine and food provided by the US government. The President and First Lady received the freed exile leaders at the Kennedy family mansion at 1095 North Ocean Boulevard in Palm Beach on 27 December 1962. Two days later, on 29 December, JFK addressed a rally of 50,000 Cuban Americans at the Orange Bowl in Miami to welcome the prisoners home. Perhaps carried away by the emotion of the moment, JFK seemed to flout his secret commitment to Premier Khrushchev by vowing to the exiles that one day soon they would return to a free Havana. For her part, the First Lady thrilled the crowd by delivering warm welcoming remarks in well-spoken Spanish. This success called a quit to the worst leadership failure of the administration's first months in office.

On 10 June 1963, JFK delivered one of the great speeches in our nation's history at the commencement ceremonies of American University in northwest Washington DC, a wise speech well worth re-reading even today. Sometimes referred to as Kennedy's "Peace Speech," it was, like his inaugural address, written by Ted Sorenson, who had been a conscientious objector during World War II. The President underscored the need to "reexamine our own attitudes, as individuals and as a nation" in order to avoid driving unhelpful actions by our adversaries.[91]

Stressing the rational imperative of peace in a world armed with thermonuclear weapons, while also expressing deep respect for the Russian people and their sacrifices during World War II, the President declared a unilateral moratorium on US nuclear weapon tests in the open atmosphere. He called upon Premier Khrushchev to join him in a formal treaty banning such tests for the mutual benefit of their two countries as well as the common benefit of mankind.

Profoundly moved by the speech, Khrushchev overruled longstanding opposition from the Soviet military and, in late July, signaled his willingness to reach a Limited Test Ban Treaty (LTBT) that would permit nuclear tests to be conducted only underground. In August, less than three weeks later, the treaty was initialed in Moscow, and in October, it was ratified by the US Senate and signed by the President.

On 11 June, the morning after the American University commencement speech, JFK received a polite challenge from Martin Luther King to give an equally moving speech on America's most grievous domestic issue, civil rights. Over the objections of political advisers worried about whether JFK could carry Texas in the 1964 presidential election, but with endorsement from his brother Bobby, the President agreed to make an impromptu televised address to the nation that very same evening. Controversial civil rights legislation had become stalled in the interagency coordination process.

---

[91] The full text of the speech is available on the web at americanrhetoric.com.

Kennedy compelled that process forward by announcing to the nation that the administration would introduce comprehensive civil rights legislation to Congress the very next week. Despite the political risks, President Kennedy stressed the moral imperative for Americans to face up to racial discrimination.

Then, on 26 June, the President gave his famous speech in Berlin. Two years earlier, in August 1961, Premier Khrushchev thought he had successfully trumped Kennedy by constructing the Wall and cutting off the escape of talented East Germans to the West. Kennedy's 1963 speech turned the tables on Khrushchev and turned the Berlin Wall into a symbol of failure for communist ideology. To the roars of tens of thousands of West Berliners, JFK declared, "There are some who say that communism is the wave of the future. Let them come to Berlin. There are a few who say that communism...permits us to make economic progress. Let them come to Berlin.... Freedom has many difficulties and democracy is not perfect, but we have never had to build a wall to keep our people in."

Finally, JFK wrapped up his speech with the famous phrase that he had practiced for hours in the White House with his undercover CIA friend Frederick "Frecky" Vreeland:[92] "All free men, wherever they may live, are citizens of Berlin. And therefore, as a free man, I take pride in

---

[92] *Conversations with Kennedy* by Bradlee, p. 96. Vreeland was the son of Jackie's friend from Vogue magazine Diana Vreeland. After a career as a CIA clandestine operations officer, he went on to serve as President George H.W. Bush's Ambassador to Morocco during 1991-1994.

the words, Ich bin ein Berliner!"[93]

This nine-month period of happiness for the Kennedy presidency and family ended in early August. On Saturday, 3 August, JFK was spending the weekend on Cape Cod with the First Lady, seven and a half months pregnant, when they learned that *Washington Post* publisher Phil Graham had shot himself. The news was especially upsetting to Jackie because she was aware that JFK had taken back up with Mary Meyer in Washington during the summer vacation months. Indeed, upon his return to the White House on Monday, 5 August, JFK arranged to spend the evening with Mary. The President attended Graham's funeral service at the National Cathedral on Tuesday, 6 August Then, on Wednesday, 7 August, upon learning that Jackie had been rushed to the hospital in severe pain, he immediately flew back to the Cape. Their baby boy, Patrick Bouvier Kennedy, was born six weeks premature while the President was still in the air. The baby died from heart failure in the early morning hours of 9 August with the President at his side. The President and First Lady were emotionally devastated.

***

[93] In an effort to undercut the impact of the speech, some people, including perhaps some KGB disinformation specialists, have falsely asserted that JFK made a German language grammatical error which caused embarrassed laughter in the crowd. One look on the internet to see and hear the crowds' reaction to Kennedy's words will convince you otherwise.

In Moscow, the conclusion of the Cuban Missile Crisis had left Premier Khrushchev in deep political trouble. His authority as the supreme leader of the Soviet Communist Party was in jeopardy in the eyes of his Politburo colleagues, and the authority of the Soviet Communist Party vis-à-vis the Chinese Communist Party was in jeopardy in the eyes of other world communists. Khrushchev had convinced his Politburo colleagues in early 1962 that deployment of Soviet nuclear missiles to Cuba would tilt the strategic balance between the US and the USSR to Moscow's advantage and secure Cuba as the Soviets' operational bridgehead to Central America in its strategic effort to "bring imperialism to its knees" via sabotage and subversion operations in the Third World. Moreover, Khrushchev had assured the Politburo that it was his personal judgment that President Kennedy, face to face with a *fait accompli*, would not have the personal courage to confront the Kremlin and, thereby, risk nuclear war. During 13 days of October 1962, Khrushchev's personal judgment had been proven profoundly wrong.

The premier could not admit to such poor judgment and expect to survive in the brutal world of Kremlin politics. Khrushchev found one face-saving out in JFK's secret concession to withdraw outdated American intermediate-range nuclear missiles deployed in Turkey against targets inside the USSR. Thus, Khrushchev could and did argue that Kennedy had, indeed, blinked and that the whole adventure had, in fact, improved the Soviets' strategic position vis-à-vis the Americans. Likewise, JFK's commitment not to invade Cuba allowed Khrushchev to argue that the missile deployment had, in fact, achieved the objective of securing Cuba as an outpost of world communism. Khrushchev could and did claim that the missile deployment, having achieved both objectives, served no further purpose. Hence, withdrawing the missiles had been a demonstration of prudent and wise policymaking.[94]

In Havana, the 35-year-old Fidel Castro did not feel more secure despite Khrushchev's logic. Castro did not trust JFK's good faith. He did not trust the President's ability to control aggressive, anti-Castro elements of the CIA and the US military. Now, he had lost trust in the support of his most important ally. Castro lived only 90 miles from a life or death adversary that the entire world now recognized as the most powerful nation on earth, bar none. Castro considered his Christmas 1962 return of the Bay of Pigs prisoners as a signal of his own good faith but days later interpreted JFK's Orange Bowl vow that the Cuban exiles would soon return to a free Havana as confirmation of continued American hostility. Personally as well as politically, Castro felt in clear and present danger.

In Washington, JFK was respecting his specific commitment to not invade Cuba because he had bigger strategic fish to fry, most importantly the nuclear test ban treaty. In early November 1962, the President ordered the suspension of CIA sabotage and other covert action activities against Cuba. As a result, Edward Lansdale, the White House anointed coordinator of Cuban operations, departed into an early retirement. In late November, the President pulled back the US military forces encircling the island, including the USS Wasp, and released military reservists who had been called up to serve during the crisis. At the same time, JFK and his brother Bobby still considered Fidel an adversary and a political irritant. Hence, in March 1963, the newly appointed

---

94 *One Hell of a Gamble* by Fursenko and Naftali, p. 323-327

chief for Cuba operations at the CIA, Des Fitzgerald, was directed to seek out elements within Cuban leadership circles who, in the post-Missile Crisis atmosphere, might be interested in switching sides and, one way or another, getting rid of Fidel.

To repair the damage to Soviet-Cuban relations, Khrushchev invited Castro to visit the Soviet Union in the spring of 1963. Fidel traveled from Havana to Moscow in April at almost exactly the same time that Lee Oswald was fleeing from Dallas to New Orleans. Still miffed over the missile crisis, Fidel agreed to a visit of only four days, but Khrushchev turned on the charm and rolled out the red carpet. As a result, Fidel extended his visit to over forty days.

Both Moscow and Havana had strong political motivations for Fidel's visit to the Soviet Union to be seen as a great success. Any sign of tension between the two would only have encouraged anti-Castro elements in Washington and Miami. Khrushchev made Fidel a Hero of the Soviet Union. Fidel publicly exaggerated that the Cuban revolution would have been impossible without the military might of the Soviet Union standing behind it. Khrushchev and Fidel stood side by side atop the Kremlin Wall to review the 1963 May Day parade of that Soviet military might.

Although Fidel no longer trusted the Soviets to come to his support if push came to shove, he recognized that he needed them nonetheless. Castro and Khrushchev also seemed to like each other sincerely on a personal level. They spent scores of hours in direct personal conversation over the long visit. The old veteran of the Bolshevik Revolution enjoyed mentoring the young Cuban revolutionary hero and stressed one lesson in particular: "The defense of Cuba will not come only with building up Cuban military power but in effective intelligence activity abroad." Khrushchev encouraged Castro to emulate the success of the Bolsheviks by penetrating counter-revolutionary elements in exile with double agents in order to disrupt their planning and turn their malicious efforts back against them.[95]

***

On Thursday, 3 October, Lee Oswald arrived back in Dallas from his five-day visit to Mexico City. He was neither angry nor frustrated with the Cuban government as he had earlier been with the Soviet government; to the contrary, Oswald showed all the signs of a determined, pro-Castro man with a purpose.

Oswald didn't bother to call his pregnant wife until the next day, Friday, 4 October. Marina was living at Ruth Paine's home at 2515 W. Fifth Street in Irving, a suburb between Dallas and Fort Worth. Ruth did not care for Lee. She agreed to allow him to visit Marina on the weekends, but she was not willing to welcome Oswald into her home as a full-time resident. That arrangement suited Oswald just fine. On weekdays during October and the first three weeks of November, he lived in Dallas at a rooming house located at 1026 N. Beckley Avenue in Oak Cliff, not far from where he and the family had lived before fleeing to New Orleans. At the rooming house, Oswald used the simple alias "O.H. Lee."

---

[95] *One Hell of a Gamble* by Fursenko and Naftali, p. 334

On Tuesday, 8 October, the CIA station in Mexico City advised CIA headquarters that Oswald had conducted unknown business with Vice Consul Valery Kostikov, an undercover officer from the KGB First Chief Directorate, Department 13 (Sabotage and Assassinations). On Friday, 18 October, CIA headquarters advised FBI headquarters of Oswald's meeting with Kostikov but neglected to identify Kostikov specifically as a member of Department 13.

On Wednesday, 16 October, Oswald started work at the Texas Book Depository in Dallas overlooking Dealey Plaza. This was twenty-two days before the visit of President Kennedy to Dallas was even scheduled and a full thirty-three days before the final motorcade was decided. Hence, it was sheer coincidence that Oswald was employed in this building overlooking the presidential motorcade route.

On Sunday, 20 October, Marina gave birth to their second child, another baby girl they named Rachel. The baby was born at Parkland Hospital in Dallas, the same hospital where President Kennedy would be pronounced dead just thirty-three days later and Oswald himself would die just two days after the President. After work on Wednesday, 23 October, the proud father placed more importance on attending a right wing political rally than on visiting his wife and newborn baby in the hospital. Oswald was interested in the keynote speaker at the rally more than in the rally itself. The keynote speaker was the anti-Castro retired General Edwin Walker whom Oswald had tried to assassinate just six months previously.

On Friday, 25 October, FBI headquarters advised FBI /New Orleans of Oswald's meeting in Mexico City with KGB officer Kostikov. FBI /New Orleans promptly sent an agent over to 4907 Magazine Street in hopes of interviewing Oswald. On Tuesday, 29 October, FBI /New Orleans advised FBI/Dallas that Oswald had departed New Orleans without paying his last month's rent. The FBI determined via the main post office on Lafayette Square that Oswald was forwarding his mail to the address of a friend in Irving, Texas, Ruth Paine. Lead action for the Oswald case was, therefore, transferred back to FBI/Dallas and to Special Agent James Hosty. That same day, Hosty promptly went out to Irving and conducted a pretext interview with Ruth Paine's next door neighbor and learned that Marina and the two girls were, indeed, staying with Ruth. Oswald himself, however, only appeared from time to time.

Also on 29 October but thousands of miles away in Paris, Castro's man, Rolando Cubela, met with his regular CIA contact Nestor Sanchez and with the senior CIA officer responsible for all Cuban operations, Des Fitzgerald. Fitzgerald told Cubela that he had come to Paris as the personal representative of Attorney General Bobby Kennedy. Moreover, Fitzgerald offered assurances that once Cubela had killed Fidel and seized the presidential palace in Havana, the US would promptly respond to any request for political and military support from the new Cuban government. The next meeting with Cubela was set for Friday, 22 November, again in Paris.[96]

On Friday, 1 November, three weeks before the assassination of the President, FBI Special Agent Hosty returned to Irving and interviewed Ruth Paine directly. Ruth noted that Oswald would be arriving shortly from Dallas to

---

[96] *Wedge* by Riebling, p. 169.

spend the weekend with them. She suggested that Special Agent Hosty stay to meet him. Hosty claimed that he had other business elsewhere, but in fact, FBI regulations prohibited him from conducting what might become an adversarial interview without another FBI Agent present as a witness.

The new mother, Marina, was bathing. After drying her hair, Marina heard the ongoing conversation and joined Ruth with Special Agent Hosty. With Ruth acting as interpreter, Hosty asked Marina if Oswald was doing anything in support of Cuba as he had been doing in New Orleans. Marina nervously dismissed the idea saying, "He's just young. He doesn't know what he is doing. He won't do anything like that here." Earlier that same day, however, Oswald had opened post office box #6225 at the Terminal Annex Post Office just across Dealey Plaza from the Texas Book Depository. On the application form, Oswald stated that the purpose of the post office box was to receive mail on behalf of the newly created Fair Play for Cuba Committee, Dallas Chapter. Oswald used his true name in opening this post office box but provided a false address as his residence.[97]

On Monday, 4 November, Special Agent Hosty called the personnel department of the Texas Book Depository, where Oswald had been working since 16 October. The personnel department confirmed that Oswald was working there and vouched that he appeared to be a punctual and reliable worker, albeit very quiet and withdrawn. The next day, Tuesday, 5 November, Hosty and another FBI agent returned to Ruth Paine's home, evidently hoping to find Oswald. Not

---

[97] *Reclaiming History* by Bugliosi, p. 773-775

finding him there, they spoke briefly with Ruth on her front porch and then departed.

Oswald was miffed when Marina told him on 1 November about the first visit from the FBI. He was angry when he heard about the telephone call to his employer. He became furious when Marina told him on Friday, 8 November, about the second visit to Ruth's house earlier in the week.[98] He felt the FBI was harassing him and his family.

Also on Friday, 8 November, all the Dallas newspapers announced that President Kennedy, accompanied by the First Lady, would visit the city in two weeks. It was to be the first official trip by the First Lady since the death of their premature baby boy, Patrick, on 9 August.

The thought of trying to assassinate the President during the upcoming visit seems to have initially occurred to Oswald over that Veterans Day weekend of 9-10-11 November 1963. As the 11th was a national holiday, Oswald did not have to work on Monday. He returned to Dallas on the morning of Tuesday, 12 November. He would not see Marina and the girls again until Thursday, 21 November, the night before the assassination.

During his lunch break on Tuesday, 12 November, Oswald walked over to the FBI/Dallas office which was located just a few blocks away from the Texas Book Depository in the Santa Fe Building at 1114 Commerce Street. Oswald identified himself to the FBI receptionist and asked to meet with Special Agent Hosty. When the receptionist advised that Hosty was out of the office, Oswald

---

[98] Ibid, p. 778

gave her a hand written note to pass to him. The note threatened that if Hosty did not cease harassing him and his wife, Oswald would blow up either the Dallas Police Department or the FBI office. This written threat was never reported to the Secret Service Advance Team that had arrived in Dallas to prepare for the just announced visit of President Kennedy on Friday, 22 November 1963.[99]

During the same lunch break, Oswald mailed a letter to the Soviet Embassy in Washington, DC enquiring about the status of his application for an entry visa to the Soviet Union. This letter named Valery Kostikov and gave the impression that Kostikov and Oswald had close and friendly relations. As a matter of standard procedure, this letter was intercepted and read by the FBI in Washington before it was delivered to the Soviet Embassy.

On Tuesday, 19 November, all the Dallas newspapers announced the motorcade route that the President and Mrs. Kennedy would take through the city. The route was designed to give the President the maximum political exposure because Texas would be a key to the 1964 presidential elections. As all the newspapers reported, the motorcade would come down Main Street to Dealey Plaza, turn right onto Houston Street, and then a left onto Elm Street, before merging back on to the previous path down Main. This slight, crowd-pleasing maneuver would slow the President's motorcade and bring it directly in front of the

---

[99] *Reclaiming History* by Bugliosi, p. 124-125, 134, 778. There is some uncertainty whether Oswald left the note on 12 November or the previous week. Since Marina did not tell him about Hosty's second visit until Friday, 8 November, the 12 November date seems the more likely.

Texas Book Depository. Lee Oswald, of course, had been working at the Texas Book Depository since Wednesday 16 October. It was pure coincidence that the White House Advance Team had placed the President's motorcade right in the crosshairs. But, for Oswald, that coincidence must have seemed like an invitation from fate.

The other headline in the Dallas newspapers on 19 November read, "Kennedy Virtually Invites Cuban Coup." The article, reporting on the President's 18 November speech in Miami, said, "President Kennedy all but invited the Cuban people today to overthrow Fidel Castro's communist regime and promised prompt US aid if they do...The President said it would be a happy day if the Castro government is ousted."[100] Oswald did not know that senior CIA officer Des Fitzgerald had convinced Attorney General Bobby Kennedy to have those words put into the President's Miami speech as the reassuring signal of Presidential support for Rolando Cubela.[101] The Cuban DGI knew it, however. So did the American CIA. What the CIA did not know was that the DGI knew.

On Thursday evening, 21 November, Oswald unexpectedly arrived at Ruth Paine's house to spend the night. Oswald's secret purpose for this unusual, weekday visit was to pick up his sniper rifle and pistol. The next morning, he departed early before Marina got out of bed. On the table, he left his wedding ring and $170, a lot of money in

---

[100] *Reclaiming History* by Bugliosi, p. 783-784

[101] *Legend* by Epstein, page 240. The CIA officer who delivered the wording to the White House was Seymour Bolton, the father of senior George W. Bush administration official Josh Bolton.

1963, especially to the Oswald family.

***

Fidel Castro and the Cuban DGI had a motive for trying to kill President Kennedy before President Kennedy and his CIA killed Castro. Castro appears to have warned the US government on at least two occasions, 7 September and 10 October, that he knew about American plotting to assassinate him. Yet, as of 29 October, Castro knew that the plotting continued, and as of 18 November, he knew that President Kennedy was aware of and personally supported it.

According to Fidel's comments to Jack Childs in 1964, Oswald had offered during his late September - early October discussions with Cuban Embassy officials in Mexico City to attempt the assassination of President Kennedy. On 8 November, Oswald learned that an opportunity to assassinate the President might present itself in two weeks' time. On 19 November, Oswald knew that the President would pass right into his crosshairs.

The key historical question is whether there was any communication between Oswald and the Cubans after 8 November when Oswald learned about the President's visit to Dallas. More importantly, was there any communication after 19 November when Oswald learned that the President's motorcade would pass through Dealey Plaza right below Oswald's sniper's nest on the sixth floor of the Texas Book Depository? Did the Cuban DGI give Oswald a green light?

Chapter 11
Angleton Unhinged

The news that President Kennedy had been assassinated by Lee Harvey Oswald caused panic in the White House, the CIA, and the FBI over the weekend of 22-24 November. At least seven facts were known beyond a shadow of a doubt by the senior-most counterintelligence officials of the US government:

1. Oswald had resided in the Soviet Union for almost three years, during which time he would have been in contact with the KGB.

2. After returning from the Soviet Union to the United States, Oswald had publicly advocated on behalf of Fidel Castro's Cuba, even in the months immediately after the Cuban Missile Crisis.

3. Less than two months before the assassination, Oswald had met in Mexico City with Cuban officials and with Valery Vladimirovich Kostikov, an officer of Department 13 of the KGB First Chief Directorate, the department responsible for sabotage and assassinations.

4. Fidel Castro had threatened on 7 September to retaliate "in kind" against American leaders who tried to assassinate Cuban leaders.

5. Bobby Kennedy and the CIA had inserted language into President Kennedy's 18 November speech giving the green light to Rolando Cubela to assassinate Fidel.

6. Four days later, on 22 November, Oswald, an avowed friend of Cuba, had assassinated President Kennedy instead.

7. Two days after that, on 24 November, the assassin Oswald was himself eliminated just as the government had been warned he would be.

Looking at these facts with cool objectivity, James Jesus Angleton, the CIA counterintelligence chief as well as the designated CIA liaison to the Warren Commission, had full reason to conclude that the possibility of an international communist conspiracy behind the assassination of President Kennedy could not honestly be dismissed. Indeed, to his dying day, Angleton believed that Castro may have been true to his word and had retaliated "in kind" against President Kennedy for the persistent CIA planning to assassinate Castro.

Angleton knew that America could not respond to this possible act of war in American eyes or possible act of self-defense in Cuban eyes without risking a nuclear confrontation with the Soviets who also seemed to be implicated. Angleton knew that President Johnson would not risk a nuclear holocaust given the numerous skeletons in the various closets of the American government. Johnson had already directed that "speculation about Oswald's motivation should be cut off and we should have some basis for rebutting the thought that this was a communist conspiracy."

The resulting ethical conflict between his duty to honestly assess the facts and his duty to help the President protect the well-being of the American people caused Jim Angleton to lose his balance, both professionally and personally, and drove him first to alcoholism and then to paranoia. Angleton, the liberals' J. Edgar Hoover during the 1950s and early 1960s, turned to the dark side during the late 1960s and early 1970s. The mysterious murder of family friend and presidential mistress Mary Meyer on the Georgetown towpath in October 1964 could only have added to Angleton's anguish.[102]

***

Contrary to wild conspiracy theories, there seems little doubt that Oswald was the lone gunman involved in the Kennedy assassination. He fired three 6.5 millimeter bullets from his Mannlicher-Caracano rifle from the sixth-floor window in the southeast corner of the Texas Book Depository where he worked. His first shot missed the President, ricocheting off the street pavement and possibly grazing an innocent bystander named James Tague. The second bullet hit the President in the back of his upper right shoulder, exited the front, lower right part of his throat and went on to hit Texas Governor John Connally in the back of the chest. The third, fatal shot hit the President in the back, right side of his head, shattering his skull and irreparably damaging his brain. To all intents and purposes, this third shot killed the President instantly, a fact that poor Mrs. Kennedy was the first to recognize.

---

[102] Unless otherwise noted, the factual details included in this chapter are drawn from the authoritatively researched book *Reclaiming History* by Vincent Bugliosi, p. 3-319.

Despite all the adrenalin that must have been pumping inside him just after murdering the most powerful man in the world, Oswald remained incredibly calm. Indeed, Oswald behaved like a man who had a well-prepared escape plan. To delay the inevitable pursuit, Oswald crossed to the opposite, northwest corner of the sixth floor and skillfully hid his sniper rifle among some boxes. Then, he walked down to the second floor as if nothing had happened and bought a Coke from the vending machine. He was momentarily detained by a Dallas police officer but did not panic and was quickly released after a co-worker identified him as an employee of the Book Depository. Oswald was equally calm moments later as he slipped out of the building's main entrance, where a frantic young reporter named Robert MacNeil, lately of the PBS MacNeil/Lehrer News Hour fame, asked him for directions to the nearest phone.

In all the confusion, Oswald calmly walked a few blocks east along Elm Street to the bus stop he regularly used and boarded a bus to return to his rooming house at 1026 Beckley Street. When the bus got stalled in the traffic jam created by the attack on the President, Oswald calmly got out, walked a few blocks south to get around the traffic jam, and then grabbed a cab. Oswald had the cab driver pass by the front of the rooming house so that he could discreetly check for any unusual activity there. Seeing none, he got out of the cab at the intersection of Beckley and Neely and walked back, allowing him to check for any possible mobile surveillance behind him. Seeing none of that either, Oswald went to his room, altered his appearance by changing clothes, grabbed his .38 revolver, and then departed, never to return. It was 1:00 PM, the same moment that the President was formally pronounced dead at Parkland Hospital.

At this stage, Oswald was running a surveillance detection route or SDR. This is a basic clandestine tradecraft skill.

***

After exiting the rooming house, Oswald walked several blocks south and then turned east along 10th Street, a back street into a suburban neighborhood of modest family homes. There, for some unknown reason, he was stopped by a Dallas Police patrol car driven by Officer J.D. Tippit. After a momentary conversation with Officer Tippit, Oswald drew his revolver and shot Tippit three times in the chest in full view of several eyewitnesses. He started to walk away, thought better of it, and returned to fire one final shot at point blank range into Officer Tippit's right temple. Oswald then calmly walked away, reloading his revolver as he walked. It was 1:16 PM.

Like Michael Corleone in *The Godfather*, Oswald knew that none of the suburban homeowners would dare follow him too closely. So, he doubled back to the southwest in an attempt to lose himself on the more crowded business area of Jefferson Boulevard. He changed his appearance again by disposing of his jacket. Then, at 1:40 he tried to disappear into a movie house, the Texas Theatre at 231 West Jefferson Boulevard.

At this stage, Oswald was running a basic "escape and evasion route." KGB officers are trained to change their appearances and duck into movie theaters as escape and evasion techniques.

***

The movie theater tactic didn't work for Oswald that day, however. Some of the witnesses to the murder of Officer Tippit had bravely followed Oswald at a distance, spotted him ducking into the Texas Theatre, and flagged down another Dallas Police patrol car. After a short scuffle, the police apprehended Oswald inside the theater at 1:50. When they arrested Oswald, the police were certain that they had apprehended the killer of Officer Tippit. When they learned that Oswald was employed at the Texas Book Depository, they suspected that they had also apprehended the assassin of President Kennedy.

The police were certain that Oswald was the assassin several hours later when the FBI reported that the Mannlicher-Caracano rifle found hidden in the northwest corner of the sixth floor of the Texas Book Depository was purchased by a man using the name A.J. Hidell and mailed to P.O. Box 2915 at the Dallas main post office. At the time the rifle was purchased, P.O. Box 2915 at the Dallas main post office was registered to Lee Harvey Oswald. At the time of his arrest, Oswald was carrying in his wallet a false ID with his picture on it but in the alias of Alek James Hidell.

Oswald himself had created the alias ID, and the quality was quite good. Creation of alias documents is another basic clandestine tradecraft skill the KGB teaches.

***

Under professional interrogation for the next forty-five hours, Oswald struck all the officers involved, from the Dallas Police, the Secret Service, and the FBI, as intelligent and cool, disciplined and controlled. He was even a bit self-satisfied. He knew to offer details on things that did not matter, be vague on things that did matter, and simply deny evidence that contradicted his story. He denied he had killed the President. He denied he had killed Officer Tippit. He denied that he owned a rifle even when confronted with the famous picture of himself dressed all in black and holding that rifle.

When asked about his trip to Mexico City in September, Oswald simply denied that he had ever even been there. There was a CIA tape recording of the 27 September call from Silvia Duran at the Cuban Consulate to Valery Kostikov at the Russian Consulate in which Duran names Oswald. There was also a tape recording of a call to the Soviet Consulate on 1 October from somebody who identified himself as Oswald. But for some highly unusual reason, there were no CIA surveillance photos of Oswald coming out of either the Soviet or Cuban Embassies in Mexico City to prove definitively that he was there.

For a high school dropout, Oswald demonstrated considerable skill in counter-interrogation techniques. All appearances indicated that he had been trained.

***

On Saturday evening, 23 November, the Dallas FBI office as well as the Dallas Sheriff's Office received identical telephone calls warning that Oswald himself would be assassinated the following day. The caller stated, "I represent a committee that is neither right wing nor left wing. Tonight, tomorrow morning, or tomorrow night, we are going to kill the man who killed the President. We want to warn the FBI, the Police and the Sheriff's department so that none of them are hurt. In any case, however, we will kill him."

As threatened, at 11:21 AM, Sunday morning 24 November, inside what was supposed to be a heavily guarded area in the basement garage of Dallas Police Headquarters, Jack Ruby, an informant who had cooperated with both the Dallas police and the Dallas FBI, simply walked down the garage ramp, saw Oswald coming into view and shot him. The shooting was even broadcast live on national television. Oswald died 1 hour and 46 minutes later at Parkland Hospital in Emergency Room #2, the same room that had been used two days previously to treat Governor Connally. The attending doctors decided it would have been sacrilegious to treat Oswald in the adjacent Emergency Room #1 where President Kennedy had died exactly 48 hours earlier.

Upon witnessing Ruby murder Oswald on live TV, senior CIA official Des Fitzgerald broke down in tears and told his wife, "Now, we will never know."[103]

***

[103] *The Very Best Men* by Thomas, p. 308

The FBI had been investigating Oswald as a potential counterintelligence risk for over a year, ever since his return from the Soviet Union in the summer of 1962. The FBI knew that Oswald had visited the Cuban and Soviet Embassies in Mexico City in late September 1963. The FBI knew that Oswald was in communication with the Soviet Embassy in Washington, DC as late as 12 November. The FBI knew that Oswald had made threats of violence against the US Government just ten days before the assassination because Oswald had personally visited the FBI Dallas office and left a written threat to bomb either the Dallas FBI or the Dallas Police Department. Most importantly, the FBI knew that Oswald worked in the Texas Book Depository, overlooking the route of the Presidential motorcade, but they had not alerted the Secret Service to this danger.

About 8:00 PM on the day of the assassination, Special Agent Hosty returned to the FBI Dallas office and was summoned to the front office to meet with his immediate supervisor, Ken Howe, and the Dallas Special Agent in Charge, Gordon Shanklin. "What the hell is this?" Shanklin demanded, showing the threat letter from Oswald.

"It's no big deal," Hosty replied.

"What do you mean? This note was written by Oswald, the probable assassin of the President, and Oswald brought this note into this office just ten days ago! What the hell do you think Hoover is going to do if he finds out about this note? If Hoover finds out about this note, he's going to lose it," Shanklin yelled.

On Shanklin's orders, Hosty went back to his office, wrote up a two-page memorandum explaining the circumstances surrounding the threatening note from

Oswald, and then submitted the memo in draft for Shanklin's approval. Two days later, about 6:00 PM on the evening that Ruby killed Oswald, Shanklin called Howe and Hosty to the front office again. Handing the memorandum and threat note back to Hosty, Shanklin said, "Now that Oswald is dead, there clearly isn't going to be a trial. Here, take these. I don't ever want to see them again." When Hosty began to tear up the memorandum and note in front of him, Shanklin screamed, "No! Not here! I told you, I don't want to see them again. Now get them out of here." Whereupon, Hosty went to a nearby men's room, tore the memo and Oswald's hand-written note up into tiny pieces, and then flushed this evidence related to the assassination of an American President down the toilet.

The CIA had its own reasons to panic. In October 1962, a year earlier, the CIA had played a heroic role in preventing a nuclear war between the United States and the Soviet Union over Cuba. Now, in November 1963, there was a real possibility that a CIA plot to assassinate Cuba's Fidel Castro had boomeranged, resulting in the assassination of our own President Kennedy. In turn, the assassination of President Kennedy had sparked immediate public speculation in the US about an international communist conspiracy. If allowed to get out of hand, that speculation could lead the US and the USSR right back to the brink of nuclear war. That would have been the worst of all possible intelligence failures.

On Saturday, 23 November, upon hearing that Mexican authorities had detained for questioning Silvia Duran, the Mexican employed at the Cuban Consulate in Mexico City, the CIA's Deputy Director for Clandestine Operations sent a "flash" message to the CIA station in Mexico City stating, "Arrest of Silvia Duran is extremely serious matter.... Request you insure that her arrest is kept absolutely secret, that no information from her is published or leaked, that all such information is cabled to us.... We could well create flap with Cubans which could have serious repercussions."

On Sunday, 24 November, CIA Director John McCone, along with Attorney General Bobby Kennedy, briefed the new President, Lyndon Johnson, on the details of the CIA's plots against Fidel. The next day, President Johnson directed that, "speculation about Oswald's motivation should be cut off and we should have some basis for rebutting the thought that this was a communist conspiracy."[104] Johnson was deeply worried that evidence of Cuban-Soviet complicity could lead to nuclear war.

President Johnson and Attorney General Kennedy instructed J. Edgar Hoover and the FBI to conduct a thorough yet expeditious investigation to determine whether there was any compelling evidence that would prove that Oswald was not the lone gunman in the assassination. The FBI formally opened its "exhaustive" investigation of the President's assassination on Tuesday, 26 November, and formally closed it thirteen calendar days later on Monday, 9 December. The FBI concluded that Oswald was a lone madman who acted without the assistance or encouragement of any other parties. Just as President Johnson had directed, on 25 November, the FBI concluded that there was no international communist conspiracy behind the Kennedy assassination.

However, Deputy Attorney General Nicholas Katzenbach doubted that anybody or any organization within the U.S. government had sufficient credibility to conduct an

---

[104] *Wedge* by Riebling, p. 200

investigation that would be seen by world opinion as honest, complete, and conclusive. So, Katzenbach recommended that President Johnson appoint a commission of wise men to look into the assassination. Johnson agreed fully and immediately concluded that the country needed Supreme Court Chief Justice Earl Warren to lead this commission of wise men.

Warren had no desire whatsoever to take responsibility for this political hot potato. He declined the offer two times, but the President refused to let Warren off the hook. Summoning the chief justice to the Oval Office on 29 November, Johnson explained the gravity of the situation, the risk of war, and the Defense Department estimate that the first nuclear exchange with the Soviet Union would cost the lives of millions of Americans. Reluctantly, Warren agreed to take on the responsibility.

The Warren Commission members, including former CIA Director Allen Dulles, were sworn in on Monday 16 December 1963, one week after the FBI submitted the report of its "exhaustive" investigation. The Commission presented its final report to President Johnson on Thursday 24 September 1964. After nine months of intense effort, the Commission reached the same conclusions as the FBI had reached in thirteen calendar days: that Oswald was the lone gunman and that there were no indications of a broader international conspiracy to assassinate the President. Many critics have suggested that the commission was a sham, that it was a foregone conclusion that the commission would have to agree with the FBI. Those criticisms are in some ways unfair. In concluding that there was no broader communist conspiracy, the Warren Commission was kept in the official dark about two key sets of facts.

***

First, the Warren Commission was never briefed on the plot between the CIA and Rolando Cubela to assassinate Fidel Castro. The FBI felt it could not tell the Warren Commission what it had learned about the Cubela plot in October 1963 because the FBI did not tell the CIA what it knew until 1965. The CIA felt it could not tell the Warren Commission a word about the Cubela plot because it remained in active operational contact with him until 1965, when the FBI advised the CIA what it knew. This all meant that the Warren Commission reached its conclusion that there was no international communist conspiracy without knowing that Fidel Castro had a clear and present motive for killing Kennedy before Kennedy killed him, just as President Johnson would tell his closest confidants.

***

Second, the Warren Commission submitted its final report having never interviewed Yuri Ivanovich Nosenko.

A KGB officer, Nosenko met clandestinely in Geneva during late January and early February 1964 with two CIA experts on the Soviet Union, Tennent "Pete" Bagley and George Kisevalter. Nosenko immediately dropped a bombshell. He claimed that he, Nosenko, had been personally responsible for overseeing the Lee Harvey Oswald case for the KGB during the time the President's assassin had lived in the Soviet Union and that he, Nosenko, could certify that the

KGB had never, ever had any operational relationship with Oswald and was not implicated in any way in Oswald's assassination of the President. Nosenko claimed that he could state "authoritatively" that Oswald was not part of an international communist conspiracy to assassinate President Kennedy.

Bagley and Kisevalter, as well as CIA Counterintelligence Chief Jim Angleton, were deeply concerned.The CIA had met clandestinely with Nosenko once before in 1962 and, after carefully assessing the information that he provided, had concluded that he was at best factually unreliable and at worst a KGB double agent whose job was to intentionally provide the CIA with false information that the KGB wanted the CIA to take as true. If, indeed, Nosenko was a double agent directed to mislead the CIA, then what were the sinister implications of Nosenko's "authoritative" comment that there was no international communist conspiracy to assassinate President Kennedy? On the other hand, why would the KGB go out of its way in the early months of 1964 to use a double agent to dupe the CIA into believing that there was no international communist conspiracy to assassinate the President when the FBI had already reached that conclusion publicly two months before on 9 December 1963?

Nosenko told the CIA that he wanted to defect permanently to the United States. Even at the height of the Cold War, entry into the United States was not a right for just any Soviet citizen seeking to escape the backward Soviet economy. No, entry into the United States, especially when that entry was sponsored by the CIA, was a privilege that had to be earned. Nosenko had done nothing to earn this privilege.He had told the CIA some tantalizing but highly dubious stories of no real value. Now, Nosenko wanted the CIA to believe that he had been the KGB officer responsible for Oswald and that Oswald was not part of any international communist conspiracy to assassinate the American President. Whatever their doubts, the CIA had no real choice but to welcome Nosenko to America as a defector. To turn away a KGB officer who two months after President Kennedy's assassination claimed authoritative access to information about the relationship between the assassin and the KGB would have been politically impossible, and Nosenko knew it.

Yuri Nosenko arrived secretly at Andrews Air Force base in Washington, DC on Tuesday, 11 February 1964. During the following interviews, Angleton and his counterintelligence officers caught Nosenko in falsehood after falsehood. Nosenko had initially claimed to be a KGB lieutenant colonel but eventually admitted that he was only a captain. Nosenko had claimed that the KGB had discovered his treachery and ordered him home to Moscow but eventually admitted that he had fabricated that entire story in order to pressure the CIA into accepting him as a defector. Nosenko could not accurately describe common KGB procedures, facilities where he claimed to have worked, or people he claimed to have known. When he did not know something he should, Nosenko would improvise an answer. When one improvisation conflicted with an earlier improvisation, he would come up with a third.

Comparing the two, Oswald was much better trained than Nosenko to withstand a professional interrogation. Incredibly, Nosenko claimed that the KGB did not know that Oswald had been assigned to Atsugi Naval Air Station alongside the U-2s because they had never even bothered to ask him where he had served as a US Marine.

The FBI, nonetheless, welcomed Nosenko's testimony. The FBI conclusions that Oswald had acted as the lone gunman and that there was no international communist conspiracy behind the assassination had already been leaked to the public the previous December. Nosenko's testimony supported the FBI conclusion. Any doubts about Nosenko would raise doubts about the FBI investigation as well. Any doubts about the FBI investigation after the assassination would inevitably raise questions about the FBI's handling of the Oswald investigation before the assassination.

On Friday, 6 March, FBI Director Hoover sent a memo to the Warren Commission suggesting that the commissioners might find Nosenko to be an interesting witness. Hoover wrote to Commission Chief Counsel Lee Rankin, "In the event you desire to have Nosenko appear, it is suggested that you try to make arrangements with the Central Intelligence Agency, which Agency has custody of Nosenko."[105] Rankin immediately contacted Richard Helms, who was then the CIA deputy director in charge of clandestine operations, and asked for access to Nosenko.

Irritated with the FBI, Helms met with Rankin on Thursday, 12 March, to explain the controversy regarding Nosenko's credibility. Rankin was very frustrated with both the FBI and the CIA. The question of an international communist conspiracy was the central concern facing the Commission, the principal reason the Commission had been established in the first place. Neither the CIA nor the FBI seemed to be helping the Commission clarify that central

---

105 *Wedge* by Riebling, p. 215

point. To Rankin, it seemed the two agencies were more consumed by their internecine bickering than helping Americans understand the death of their President. Helms expressed his understanding to Rankin but simply could not deny the facts: the CIA had serious reservations about Nosenko's credibility. Helms assured Rankin that the Agency was working the issue as fast as it could and recommended that the commissioners patiently "await further developments."

By late July, the commissioners' patience was running thin. Further delays were becoming more and more untenable politically with each passing day. Rankin was inclined to go with the FBI view of Nosenko because that view coincided with everything else the commission knew. Then, Pete Bagley, the CIA officer directly involved with Nosenko, brought it all to an abrupt halt. On Friday 24 July, Bagley told the full commission, "Nosenko is a KGB plant. He may be exposed as such sometime after the appearance of the commission report. Once Nosenko is exposed as a KGB plant, there will arise the danger that his information will be mirror-read by the press and by the public, leading to the conclusion that the USSR did direct the assassination." That was enough for the commissioners. They directed that it would be "undesirable to include any Nosenko information" in the final Warren Commission report.[106]

***

---

[106] *Wedge* by Riebling, p. 217

CIA counterintelligence led by James Jesus Angleton feared that Nosenko was a "disinformation agent" whose mission was to dupe the Warren Commission into believing that the Soviet KGB was not implicated in the assassination of the President of the United States. FBI counterintelligence led by J. Edgar Hoover trusted Nosenko as a reliable witness who could authoritatively confirm the FBI conclusion that there was no international communist conspiracy behind the President's assassination. Unbeknownst to the American public, a bitter war between the CIA and the FBI over Nosenko's credibility lasted for eleven years.

The Warren Report completed, Jim Angleton still insisted on the need for an answer one way or the other: was Nosenko a KGB plant or was he a bona fide defector? In an attempt to find the answer, the CIA locked Nosenko up in a 12 by 12 solitary confinement cell with no windows, nothing to read, and nothing to do for over three years. He was not even allowed to brush his teeth. Nosenko nearly went crazy, but he never broke down and never confessed to being a KGB plant.

In 1968, with still no confession in sight, Richard Helms, who had by then become CIA Director, tried to bring an end to the debate with a compromise. He declared Nosenko a genuine defector but declined to validate Nosenko's information regarding Oswald as reliable. Realistically, Helms had no other choice. Personally, however, Helms told an interviewer in 1989, "I still haven't the faintest idea whether Nosenko is bona fide."[107]

Angleton could not accept the Helms compromise.

---

[107] *Cold Warrior* by Mangold, p. 160

Angleton was a complex and powerful man, feared by many, and frequently caricaturized as a monster. But, he and his wife Cicely had been social acquaintances of Jack and Jackie Kennedy prior to Kennedy's election as President. Angleton was consumed by the fear that the Cuban DGI, possibly with the support of the Soviet KGB, had used Oswald as a pawn to assassinate America's President and that intimidated America's security services had let them get away with it scot-free. This drove Angleton first to alcoholism and then to paranoia. Late in life, he even compared the Kennedy assassination to the famous scene in *The Godfather* movie when the mafia used the decapitated head of a horse to intimidate a movie producer into cooperation.[108]

Sam Papich, the FBI's liaison to the CIA since 1952, was caught between his friend Angleton and his boss Hoover. Papich did not believe Nosenko to be a KGB-controlled double agent but neither did Papich fully trust Nosenko. Papich simply thought Nosenko exaggerated what he knew and fabricated some information out of whole cloth in order to make himself appear more important than he truly was. In 1970, Hoover forced Papich into retirement for daring to disagree with the official FBI line. After a distinguished thirty-year career, Papich went off into internal exile in New Mexico without even the perfunctory retirement letter from the FBI Director.

At CIA as well, Helm's successor, William Colby, decided in 1974 that enough was enough; it was time for the agency to move on from the Kennedy assassination. Officers like Angleton who could not move on were likewise forced into

[108] *Wedge* by Riebling, p. 208

retirement, thus cutting off any further internal debate. Retired, still convinced of his views, and now angry, Angleton leaked considerable amounts of information to author Edward Jay Epstein as background for the book, *Legend: The Secret Life of Lee Harvey Oswald.*

***

Suggestions for further reading:

1. *Cold Warrior: James Jesus Angleton, The CIA's Master Spy Hunter* by Tom Mangold, Simon and Schuster, 1991.

The quintessential book on Angleton as monster. A must read for counterintelligence professionals, but it is too one-sided. A more balanced biography that more fully considers Angleton's early years remains to be written.

2. *Spy Wars: Moles, Mysteries, and Deadly Games* by Tennent "Pete" Bagely, Yale University Press 2007.

Pete Bagley's most recent response to Oleg Nechiporenko. A clear indication of how hot some internal CIA controversies remain even forty-five years later.

A Spy's Walking Tour of Dallas

This walking tour includes two interrelated sections, one downtown and one in the Oak Cliff section of just south of downtown. The downtown section takes forty-five minutes at a normal walking pace and leaves you at Dealey Plaza in front of the Sixth Floor Museum of the old Texas Book Depository Building. After visiting the museum, take a cab to Beckley Street in Oak Cliff. The Oak Cliff section takes another hour and, with only a slight detour, retraces the escape and evasion route that Oswald took after assassinating the President.

***

Downtown

1. Harwood Street between Main and Commerce Streets, Dallas Police Headquarters where Oswald was jailed after his arrest on 22 November. In the basement garage of this building, Oswald was shot by Jack Ruby on the morning of 24 November (see Chapter 11). Ruby just walked down the

garage ramp that is located on Main Street just east of Harwood. Proceed west down Commerce Street.

2. 1114 Commerce Street, the Santa Fe Building where FBI/Dallas was located in 1963 and where the bomb threat letter from Oswald was flushed down the toilet on 24 November (see Chapter 11). Proceed down Commerce Street to Dealey Plaza.

3. Dealey Plaza at Commerce Street, the Terminal Annex Building, the former post office where Oswald opened a post office box in October 1963 for his Fair Play for Cuba Dallas Chapter. As you face north across Dealey Plaza to the Texas Book Depository, the Grassy Knoll is to the left of the depository. Proceed north on Houston Street across Dealey Plaza.

4. Dealey Plaza at Elm Street, the Texas Book Depository from which Oswald shot the President and which today houses the Sixth Floor Museum. After visiting the museum, walk east along Elm Street to Lamar Street and proceed south to the intersection with Commerce Street. Catch a cab and have it take you across the Houston Street viaduct to the intersection of Beckley and Neely Streets in Oak Cliff. Walk one block west on Neely and turn left onto Elsbeth.

***

Oak Cliff

5. 604 Elsbeth. This derelict building is where the Oswalds lived from November 1962 until March 1963. It was here

that Marina tried to hang herself. Return to Neely Street and turn left.

6. 214 W. Neely. The Oswald family lived in the second-floor apartment of this building during March-April 1963. The famous photo of Oswald dressed all in black and carrying his sniper rifle was taken in the backyard of this house on 31 March, ten days before Oswald tried to assassinate General Walker. Walk back east along Neely Street to Beckley Street and turn left.

Oswald's Escape and Evasion Route

7. Oswald got out of the cab at the northwest corner of the intersection of Beckley and Neely Streets. He then walked north along the west side of Beckley checking to determine whether he had any surveillance behind him.

8. 1026 N. Beckley Street, where Oswald resided using the alias O.H. Lee after returning from Mexico City. After assassinating the President at 12:30 PM, Oswald arrived back at this house at 1:00 PM, quickly altered his appearance by changing clothes and armed himself with his .38 revolver.

9. Oswald departed the house at 1:03 PM and walked back down the east side of Beckley to Davis Street. He turned east onto Davis Street and then angled off southeast on Crawford Street, checking for surveillance as he made these maneuvers. At 10th Street, he angled back to the northeast.

10. Just after Oswald crossed over Patton Street, he was stopped on the south side of 10th by Dallas Police Officer JD Tippit. At 1:16 PM and in front of several eyewitnesses, Oswald shot Tippit three times in the chest and then made

sure he was dead with one additional shot to the temple.

11. Oswald then moved quickly back southeast along Patton Street to the more heavily trafficked Jefferson Boulevard, where he again altered his appearance by discarding his jacket. He then continued southwest down Jefferson.

12. 231 W. Jefferson Boulevard. Oswald entered the Texas Theatre at 1:40 PM in an effort to lose himself for a time and thus evade arrest. However, witnesses to the Tippit murder saw him enter the theater and alerted police. They arrested Oswald inside the theater at 1:50 PM after a short scuffle.

This ends the tour.

18. The slum apartment at 604 Elsbeth in Oak Cliff where Marina tried to hang herself

19. The house at 214 West Neely in Oak Cliff. The Oswald's lived on the second floor. Marina took the famous picture of Oswald with his sniper rifle in the back yard.

20. The house at 1026 North Beckley in Oak Ridge where Oswald lived in alias at the time of the assassination

21. The Texas Book Depository from near the spot where the fatal shot hit the President. Oswald fired from the window on the far right, second from the top.

22. The spot on 10th St in Oak Cliff where Oswald murdered Officer Tippitt

23. The Texas Theater at 231 West Jefferson Boulevard where Oswald was arrested

24. Dallas Police Headquarters on Harwood St where Oswald was shot

25. The garage ramp on Main St that Jack Ruby walked down on his way to shoot Oswald

Chapter 12
Who Murdered Mary?

The clubby, genteel atmosphere of the Washington elite in the 1950s and early 1960s died with President Kennedy. The naïve belief that America could get away with anything gave way to divorces, nervous breakdowns, suicides, and internecine squabbling. The murder of Mary Meyer was left unresolved because to investigate vigorously would have turned over stones that America's political elite just could not bring itself to turn over. Home addresses and personal telephone numbers were quietly withdrawn from the public telephone listings.

***

Jackie Kennedy, the widowed former First Lady, insisted on wearing her blood-stained pink suit until she and the assassinated President's body arrived back in Washington. Tony and Ben Bradlee awaited her at the White House along with other friends and family. Upon seeing them, Jackie hugged Ben and sobbed, "Oh Benny, do you want to hear what happened?" but then had the presence of mind to add, "Not as a reporter for *Newsweek,* ok?"[109] A remorse-stricken Bobby Kennedy busied himself arranging for his older brother to be laid to rest in Arlington Cemetery at a beautiful site looking across Memorial Bridge to the Lincoln Memorial.[110]

After the funeral, Jackie had to address the mundane problem of where she and the children would live. The new President and First Lady, Lyndon and Lady Bird Johnson, graciously offered to remain at their personal residence at 4921 30th Place NW near the National Zoo so that Jackie and the children could remain in the White House until after Christmas.[111] Jackie accepted the Johnsons' kindness through 6 December, at which time she moved from the White House into the vacant Georgetown home of Under Secretary of State Averill Harriman at 3038 N Street. In late January 1964, the family moved across the street into a hurriedly purchased mansion at 3017 N Street.[112]

Given Jackie's love for Paris, President Johnson kindly

---

[109] *Conversations with Kennedy* by Bradlee, p. 243

[110] The site lies directly below the former mansion of Civil War General Robert E. Lee in honor for whom Robert E. Lee Oswald and his son Lee Harvey Oswald were named.

[111] Johnson's neighbor was FBI Director J. Edgar Hoover at 4936 30th Place NW.

[112] In 1983, after divorcing Tony and marrying the young Washington Post reporter Sally Quinn, Ben Bradlee purchased the Todd Lincoln mansion at 3014 N Street across the street from Jackie's former home.

offered to make her his ambassador to France. Joe Alsop and other Kennedy family acolytes who had never been comfortable with Johnson discouraged Jackie from indebting the family legacy to a political rival by accepting the ambassadorship. Over the course of a few months, she came to conclude that Washington was just too full of politics and painful memories. So, for the well-being of her children, she escaped permanently and moved to Manhattan in September.

***

The news that President Kennedy had been assassinated by a former resident of the Soviet Union caused panic in the Kremlin and in the KGB as well. The Soviets reacted quickly with a multi-pronged strategy: (1) publicly demonstrate grief over the President's death, (2) deny any Soviet government involvement whatsoever with Oswald, and (3) make counter-accusations about an American right wing or US government conspiracy to eliminate the liberal young President so beloved by the Soviet people.

Premier and Mrs. Khrushchev sent a personal letter of condolence to Mrs. Kennedy. Khrushchev and Foreign Minister Gromyko were among the first visitors to the US Embassy in Moscow on Saturday 23 November to pay their tributes and sign the condolence book. In a letter to President Johnson, dated 25 November, Premier Khrushchev called Kennedy's death, "a grievous blow to all people for whom the cause of peace and Soviet-American cooperation is dear." The Soviet Ambassador to the United Nations said that "Kennedy's death was very much regretted by the Soviet

Union and had caused considerable shock in Soviet government circles." Church bells tolled for the fallen President throughout the atheistic Soviet Union.

At the same time, the official Soviet press agency, TASS, asserted on 23 November that Kennedy had been killed by "extreme right wing elements" in the United States. Radio Moscow called the assassination, "a provocation by the Fascist forces and the reactionary circles who are madly resisting all steps leading to international relaxation. These are the elements who not only killed the US President but strike at the interests of the US people." "Ordinary" Soviet citizens who were allowed to socialize with western reporters questioned how it could be that the President was not better protected by the American security services.[113]

Less publicly, KGB headquarters sent a message to its offices around the world stating, "President Kennedy's assassination poses a problem for the KGB... It is imperative that all KGB officers lend their efforts to solving this problem by ascertaining with the greatest possible speed the true story surrounding the President's assassination... The KGB is interested in knowing all the factors and all the possible groups which might have worked behind the scenes to organize and plan this assassination."[114]

Initially, the KGB had feared that the President's assassination would, indeed, be tied to an international communist conspiracy. Within a few years, however, KGB disinformation efforts had successfully exploited the

---

[113] *Reclaiming History* by Bugliosi, p. 1255-1259

[114] Ibid.

skeletons in American closets to convince the vast majority of the American public that there was, indeed, an intelligence conspiracy behind the Kennedy assassination but that it was masterminded not by the KGB or the Cuban DGI, but by America's own CIA and FBI.

***

In a public speech after Kennedy's assassination, Fidel Castro took pains to offer sympathy but without being insincere. He said, "As a Marxist-Leninist, we recognize that the role of a man is small and relative in society. The disappearance of a system would always cause us joy. But the death of a man, although this man is an enemy, does not have to cause us joy."[115]

In 1965, the FBI finally got around to telling the CIA what it had learned in 1963 about the Cubela plot. The CIA terminated its relationship with Cubela the very same day. The CIA justified this termination officially with the simple explanation that the operation had been compromised. What was apparent to all the officers involved, though, was that Rolando Cubela had been a double agent under DGI control all along, reporting to Red Beard Pineiro every detail of the CIA plot to have Castro assassinated.

By 1965, however, the war in Viet Nam was growing. American involvement that had focused on an advisory and support role during the Kennedy administration escalated in

---

[115] *Reclaiming History* by Bugliosi, p. 304

1965 to include American ground combat troops and heavy bombing of North Viet Nam. Rising American casualties increasingly diverted the attention of the White House and the American public away from Cuba.

***

Mary Meyer was invited along with the Bradlees to the President's funeral Mass at St. Matthew's Cathedral on Rhode Island Avenue, just north of the White House, and walked with them in the long funeral procession from the cathedral to Arlington Cemetery. At the First Lady's insistence, JFK had tried to break off his relationship with Mary in March 1963, but he had resumed it in June. In mourning for baby Patrick, JFK distanced himself again from Mary in August 1963 but had recalled her to a White House rendezvous in early November.[116] Being a favorite of the President had helped fulfill Mary's life-long dream to be consort to an international statesman and peacemaker in a way that her marriage to Cord had never done. Distraught when JFK's assassination shattered the remnants of that dream, she threw herself into her own work in an effort to become recognized as an artist of serious consequence.

Mary's own murder on the C&O towpath in Georgetown eleven months later re-ignited fears that the slain President's image and reputation might be damaged and in a fashion that might prove publicly hurtful to Jackie and the children. Not

---

[116] *Mrs. Kennedy* by Leaming, p. 323

only was there the sexual affair with the President and the acrimonious divorce from a senior clandestine officer of the CIA, there was also Mary's reputation as a convert of Timothy Leary in promoting the "therapeutic" use of hallucinogenic drugs like LSD. Questions in an open courtroom about aspects of Mary's personal life that might have motivated somebody to have her killed would have created tremendous political risk. As a result of these fears, the politically well-connected federal judge who presided over the murder trial, Howard Corcoran, ruled that any discussion in court of the victim's private life was prohibited.[117]

The Washington Police claimed in court that they had blocked off all northern exits from the towpath murder scene within four minutes of the shooting. They then searched through the cordoned area south between the towpath and the Potomac River. In so doing, the police found only one person, an unemployed black man named Ray Crump, who allegedly fit the description of a man claimed by a witness to have been seen standing over Mary's body moments after the shots rang out. The police accused Crump of killing Mary after she resisted a sexual assault. The case did not stand up in court, however.

The witness was himself black, a former military policeman who was working as a mechanic at the Canal Road Exxon station just west of Key Bridge. He was on Canal Road

[117] Judge Howard Corcoran was the brother of influential Democratic lobbyist Tommy "The Cork" Corcoran and had been just appointed to the federal bench by President Johnson. The US Attorney overseeing prosecution of the case was David Acheson the son of former Secretary of State Dean Acheson and had been appointed by Attorney General Bobby Kennedy.

above the murder scene working on a stalled car when he heard the two shots. He walked over to see what had happened and saw another man he described as black, 5'8" and 185 pounds standing over Mary's body. The witness claimed to have watched the suspect standing over the victim looking at her for 30 seconds, then the witness ran back to his car, drove the half mile to the Exxon station, and made the telephone call that first alerted the police.

This account raised a number of questions at the trial of Ray Crump. First, that the witness could do all this and that the police could then block off the northern exits from the towpath in just four minutes was dubious. Second, Ray Crump was only 5'5" and 145 pounds, considerably smaller than the person described by the witness who was a trained military policeman. Third, the police could not find the murder weapon anywhere in the cordoned off area south from the towpath to the river despite a thorough search, including the dredging of the river line and the canal itself.

These questions left open the obvious possibility that the murder was committed by a person other than Crump who had quickly escaped from the crime scene and carried the murder weapon out of the area. As noted in Chapter 1, a professional who had pre-cased the crime scene could easily have escaped to the north side of the canal in 90 seconds. In July 1965, these unanswered questions led the jury to conclude that there was insufficient evidence to convict Ray Crump of murdering Mary Meyer. Further investigation of other possible motivations for somebody to murder Mary was, under the circumstances, considered unwise and quietly shelved.

***

In November 1964, a bare month after Mary's death, her estranged husband, Cord, moved from his rented room at 3615 Prospect Place into the house at 1523 34th Street that the couple still owned jointly. He remarried in 1966. In his 1975 memoirs, Cord states, "I was satisfied by the conclusions of the police investigation that Mary had been the victim of a sexually motivated assault...I never suspected the tragedy of having any other explanation than the one the metropolitan police reached after careful investigation of all the evidence."[118] However, when asked a month before he died of cancer in 2001 who had killed Mary, Cord said, "The same sons of bitches that killed John F. Kennedy."[119]

[118] *Facing Reality* by Meyer, p. 143-144

[119] *The Georgetown Ladies Social Club* by C. David Heymann

A Spy's Observations

Tragedy: A serious play having a disastrous ending brought about by the central characters impelled by fate or by their own moral weakness, psychological maladjustment, or their response to social pressures

-- Webster's Unabridged Dictionary, second edition

***

Americans by and large prefer melodrama over tragedy when it comes to their political narrative. Melodrama is peopled by simple, one-dimensional characters engaged in black and white struggles between good and evil. It offers a comforting clarity.

The story of the Kennedy assassination is, however, a tragedy in the true definition of that term. It is peopled, with one exception, by characters of great power and complexity, all of whom were trying to fulfill their individual responsibilities in the best way they knew how. The conflicts between their individual responsibilities created a potential for disaster. That potential, in turn, provided an opportunity for a psychologically unstable kid to become a big man.

Nobody comes out of a true tragedy looking particularly good. In this case, the KGB and the DGI don't look much better or much worse than the CIA or the FBI. Khrushchev and Castro can and should be criticized for their imprudent behavior during the Cuban Missile Crisis. In the aftermath of that existential crisis, it should not be surprising that some well-meaning Americans came to see the elimination of Castro as a way to eliminate any future threat of another nuclear confrontation over Cuba. Not surprising perhaps, but still not wise.

Before his own assassination five years later, Bobby Kennedy said, "I have...wondered at times if we did not pay a very great price for being more energetic than wise about a lot of things, especially Cuba."[120]

---

[120] *Reclaiming History* by Bugliosi, p. 1292

Historical Chronology

1939: October 18: Lee Harvey Oswald born.

1941: July 17: Marina Prusakova Oswald born.

1956: **July 4: The first of 24 U-2 flights directly over the Soviet Union, 22 by America's CIA and 2 by the British Royal Air Force.**

October 26: Oswald enlists in the US Marine Corps.

1957: September 12: Oswald arrives in Atsugi Naval Air Station.

September - October: Oswald frequents Blue Bird Café and the Queen Bee.

October 4: With Sputnik, the Soviets demonstrate an intercontinental missile that can deliver a nuclear weapon deep inside the US from the USSR.

November 20: Oswald and unit deploy to Southeast Asia.

1958: March 18: Oswald and unit return to Atsugi from deployment.

April 29: Oswald is court martialed.

March 18 - June 29: Oswald socializes with left wing Japanese.

June 29 - August 13: Oswald is confined to the Atsugi Brig.

August: Mao provokes Quemoy and Matsu Crisis.

September 14 - October 4: Oswald and unit deploy to Taiwan.

October 5: Oswald and unit return to Atsugi from deployment.

November 15: Oswald departs Atsugi and returns stateside.

1959: **January 1: Fidel Castro seizes political power in Cuba.**

January: Oswald has contact with the Cuban Consulate in Los Angeles.

January - September: Oswald plans defection to the USSR.

September 11: Oswald is released from active duty in the Marines.

September: CIA learns that its prize agent, GRU Lt. Colonel Pyotr Popov has been arrested by the KGB.

September 20: Oswald departs New Orleans for Europe by freighter.

September: U-2 #360 crashes outside of Atsugi Naval Air Station.

September: Khrushchev visits the United States.

October 16: Oswald arrives in Moscow; requests Soviet citizenship.

October 21: KGB officer "Shaknarazov" tells Oswald

to go home to the US; Oswald attempts suicide.

October 21 - 28: Oswald is confined in Botkin Hospital.

October 31: Oswald visits the US Embassy; threatens to provide Soviets with information.

November: Stand-down of American U-2 flights over the USSR.

November 4: KGB officer "Andrei Nikolayevich" meets with Oswald in room 214 of the Metropole Hotel to discuss possible KGB work abroad.

November 16: KGB advises Oswald that he can remain in the USSR for the time being.

November 27: Central Committee resolution authorizes Oswald to remain in the USSR as well as housing, employment, and stipend.

1960: January 7: Oswald arrives in Minsk.

March 16: Oswald moves into his Minsk apartment.

April 9: American U-2 flights resume.

May 1: Frances Gary Powers' U-2 is shot down.

November 2: John F. Kennedy is elected President.

1961: **January 3: US breaks diplomatic relations with Cuba.**

January 20: President Kennedy is inaugurated.

January 21: Ella German rejects Oswald's marriage proposal.

January 28: President Kennedy authorizes Bay of Pigs planning.

February 13: US Embassy in Moscow receives a letter from Oswald reconsidering his defection.

March 17: Oswald meets Marina.

April 15-19: The Bay of Pigs invasion of Cuba.

April 30: Oswald marries Marina.

May: Marina becomes pregnant.

May 25: US Embassy in Moscow receives another letter from Oswald advising that he is now married.

June: Vienna Summit, Khrushchev gives an ultimatum regarding West Berlin.

July 8: Oswald and Marina appear in person at the US Embassy in Moscow.

August 12-13: Construction of the Berlin Wall begins.

December 25: Oswald and Marina receive permission to depart the USSR.

1962: **February 10: Frances Gary Powers is exchanged for Soviet spy Rudolph Abel in Berlin.**

February 15: June Oswald is born.

March 15: Marina's US visa is approved.

May : Yuri Ivanovich Nosenko walks-in for the first time to the CIA in Geneva.

May: Oswald, Marina, and June depart Minsk for Moscow.

June 1: Oswald, Marina, and June depart Moscow.

June 13: Oswald, Marina, and June arrive in New York City.

June 14: Oswald, Marina, and June arrive in Dallas-Fort Worth.

June-September: Oswald befriends George De Morhenschldt.

October 8: Oswald moves to Dallas.

October 14-28: The Cuban Missile Crisis

December 29: President Kennedy gives speech to freed Bay of Pigs prisoners in Miami.

1963: **January 1: Fidel Castro publicly calls Kennedy a pirate.**

January 21: Sedition charges against Edwin Walker are dropped.

January 27: Oswald mail orders .38 revolver.

March 10: Oswald surveils Walker's home in Dallas.

March 12: Oswald mail orders Mannlicher-Caracano sniper rifle.

March 31: Marina takes famous photo of Oswald

carrying rifle.

April 10: Oswald attempts to assisinate Walker.

April 13: De Mohrenschildt asks Oswald how he missed Walker.

April 15: De Mohrenschildt abruptly departs Dallas for Haiti.

April 25: Oswald abruptly departs Dallas for New Orleans.

April-May: Fidel Castro visits the Soviet Union.

May 26: Oswald founds the Fair Play for Cuba, New Orleans branch.

August 9: Oswald is arrested as a result of altercation with Cuban exiles.

August 13: Article on Oswald in the New Orleans newspaper lists his address.

August 17: New Orleans radio interviews Oswald.

August 19: Televised debate between Oswald and Cuban exile Bringuier.

Late August: Oswald's landlady directs an unknown man with a Spanish accent and carrying pro-Castro pamphlets to Oswald's house.

September 5-8: CIA discusses Castro assassination with Cubela.

September 7: Castro threatens to retaliate for CIA assassination plots.

September 9: Article on Castro's threat appears in New Orleans newspaper.

September 17: Oswald receives tourist card to visit Mexico.

September 23: Marina departs New Orleans with Ruth Paine.

September 24: Last time Oswald is seen in New Orleans.

September 25 or 26: Three men visit Sylvia Odio in Dallas.

September 26: Oswald known for certain to cross border into Mexico.

September 27: Oswald arrives in Mexico City and visits the Soviet and Cuban Embassies. There are no surveillance photos of him leaving either embassy.

September 28: Oswald visits the Soviet Embassy a second time. No surveillance photo of him leaving the embassy.

September 29-October 1: Unknown activity by Oswald in Mexico City.

October 2: Oswald departs Mexico City by bus.

October 3: Oswald crosses border into the US, arrives back in Dallas.

October 16: Oswald starts work at the Texas Book Depository.

October 20: Rachel Oswald is born.

October 23: Oswald attends speech by Edwin Walker.

October 29: CIA again discusses Castro assassination with Cubela.

October 29: New Orleans FBI advises Dallas FBI that Oswald has moved back to Texas.

October 29: FBI Agent Hosty interviews Ruth Paine's neighbor.

November 1: FBI Agent Hosty interviews Ruth Paine and Marina.

November 4: FBI Agent Hosty inquires about Oswald at the Texas Book Depository.

November 5: Hosty and another FBI Agent briefly interview Paine again.

November 8: Dallas visit by President Kennedy is publicly announced.

November 12: Last time Oswald sees Marina until eve of assassination.

November 12: Oswald leaves threat at FBI Dallas and mails letter to the Soviet Embassy in Washington.

November 18: President Kennedy gives a speech in Miami inviting Cuban coup.

November 19: Kennedy speech reported in Dallas

newspapers.

November 19: The President's motorcade route published in Dallas newspapers.

November 21: Oswald spends his last evening with Marina, June, and Rachel at Ruth Paine's home; collects his rifle and pistol.

November 22: CIA meets again with Rolando Cubela.

November 22: Oswald assassinates President Kennedy and murders Officer Tippit.

November 22: FBI special agent in charge directs Agent Hosty to draft a memorandum explaining the circumstances of Oswald's threatening note.

November 23: CIA sends "flash" message to the CIA station in Mexico City regarding the arrest of Cuban Embassy employee Silvia Duran.

November 23: Dallas FBI and Dallas Sheriff's Office receive identical threats against Oswald's life.

November 24: Jack Ruby kills Lee Harvey Oswald.

November 24: FBI special agent in charge directs Agent Hosty to destroy Oswald's threatening note as well as the memorandum.

November 24: CIA Director McCone and Bobby Kennedy brief President Johnson on the details of CIA plotting against Castro.

November 25: President Johnson directs that

"speculation about Oswald's motivation should be cut off and we should have some basis for rebutting the thought that this was a communist conspiracy."

1964: February: Yuri Nosenko defects to the United States, claiming he was Oswald's KGB control officer.

List of Photographs

Washington D.C. Area

1. The home at 2237 48th Street where Charlie Bartlett matched Jack and Jackie.

2. Mary Meyer's home in Georgetown at 1523 34th Street in Georgetown.

3. Mary's art studio in the alley garage behind the Bradlee residence.

4. Jack and Jackie Kennedy's home at 3307 N street in Georgetown.

5. Ben and Tony Bradlee's home at 3321 N Street in Georgetown.

6. The spot on the towpath where Mary was murdered.

7. The underpass through which the murdered may have escaped.

8. The home at 3017 N Street where the widowed First Lady lived.

9. Journalist Joe Alsop's home at 2720 Dumbarton Street.

10. The home of Allen and Clover Dulles at 2723 Q Street in Georgetown.

11. The home of CIA official Des Fitzgerald at 1511 30th Street in Georgetown.

12. Jim and Cicely Angleton's home at 4814 33rd Street in North Arlington.

13. View from the President's gravesite in Arlington cemetery across Memorial Bridge.

New Orleans

14. The house at 4907 Magazine Street in New Orleans where Oswald probably first met Cuban intelligence.

15. The old Jefferson Market at 4303 Magazine Street where Oswald cashed his last unemployment check.

16. The William B. Reily Coffee Company at 640 Magazine Street where Oswald was employed.

17. Façade of the old United Fruit Company headquarters at 321 St. Charles Avenue.

Dallas

18. The slum apartment at 604 Elsbeth in Oak Cliff where Marina tried to hang herself.

19. The house at 214 West Neely in Oak Cliff. The Oswald's lived on the second floor. Marina took the famous picture of Oswald with his sniper rifle in the back yard.

20. The house at 1026 North Beckley in Oak Cliff where Oswald lived in alias at the time of the assassination.

21. The Texas Book Depository from near the spot where the fatal shot hit the President. Oswald fired from the window on the far right, second from the top.

22. The spot on 10th Street in Oak Cliff where Oswald murdered Officer Tippitt.

23. The Texas Theater at 231 West Jefferson Boulevard where Oswald was arrested.

24. Dallas Police Headquarters on Harwood Street where Oswald was jailed.

25. The garage ramp on Main Street that Jack Ruby walked down on his way to shoot Oswald.

Front Cover: President Kennedy prepares to address the nation on the Cuban Missile Crisis, October 22, 1962. Courtesy of the JFK Presidential Library.

Back Cover: Lee Harvey Oswald's self-made alias identification card. Courtesy of the U.S. National Archives (Warren Commission exhibit).

Index

Made in the USA
Middletown, DE
02 August 2019